Strategic Responsiveness

LEGISLATIVE POLITICS & POLICY MAKING

Series Editors

Jamie L. Carson, University of Georgia

James M. Curry, University of Utah

RECENT TITLES IN THE SERIES:

For a complete list of titles in this series, please see www.press.umich.edu.

STRATEGIC RESPONSIVENESS

How Congress Confronts Presidential Power

Scott H. Ainsworth, Brian M. Harward,
and Kenneth W. Moffett

University of Michigan Press
Ann Arbor

For questions or permissions, please contact um.press.perms@umich.edu
Published in the United States of America by the
University of Michigan Press
First published May 2025

A CIP catalog record for this book is available from the British Library.

Library of Congress Cataloging-in-Publication data has been applied for.

ISBN: 978-0-472-07741-0 (hardcover : alk. paper)
ISBN: 978-0-472-05741-2 (paper : alk. paper)
ISBN: 978-0-472-90501-0 (OA ebook)

DOI: https://doi.org/10.3998/mpub.12581176

The University of Michigan Press's open access publishing program is made possible thanks to additional funding from the University of Michigan Office of the Provost and the generous support of contributing libraries.

Authorized Representative: Easy Access System Europe, Mustamäe tee 50, 10621 Tallinn, Estonia, gpsr.requests@easproject.com

*Ainsworth dedicates this book to his 100-year-old father
and the memory of his mother for their lasting lessons.*

*Harward dedicates this book to his mother and father, Ann M.
and Donald W. Harward, for their commitment and contributions
to civic life, liberal education, and generations of students.*

*Moffett dedicates this book to his dad, Vern, who encouraged him to
question the status quo and to avoid doing anything halfheartedly.
He thanks his dad for fighting for him, believing in him, and leading
by example. For his unconditional support and encouragement,
Moffett is proud to dedicate this book to his dad.*

Contents

Digital materials related to this title can be found on the Fulcrum platform via the following citable URL: https://doi.org/10.3998/mpub.12581176

Tables

Figures

Preface

On January 28, 2008, President George W. Bush signed the National Defense Authorization Act (NDAA). In part, the act authorized funding for the Department of Defense, military construction abroad, and the Department of Energy's national security efforts. As he signed the measure, President Bush also issued a signing statement that identified constitutional objections to specific provisions of the bill. He wrote:

> Provisions of the Act, including sections 841, 846, 1079, and 1222, purport to impose requirements that could inhibit the President's ability to carry out his constitutional obligations to take care that the laws be faithfully executed, to protect national security, to supervise the executive branch, and to execute his authority as Commander in Chief. The executive branch shall construe such provisions in a manner consistent with the constitutional authority of the President. (American Presidency Project 2013)

The constitutional objections that Bush identified implicated key discrete elements of the massive, multidimensional bill. In light of the signing statement, the likelihood of implementing sections 841, 846, 1079, and 1222 consistent with congressional intent was diminished. Attentive legislators, including the House Armed Services Subcommittee on Oversight and Investigations and Representatives John Tierney (D-MA) and Thomas Allen (D-ME), were alerted to the possibility that the Department of Defense would construe those provisions as advisory rather than compulsory.

Hearings were held just over one month later, on March 11, 2008. The chair of the subcommittee convened the proceedings with the following statement:

> Because of the statements contained in the signing statement, Chairman Skelton requested that this subcommittee hold a hearing to ask a simple question of the Department of Defense: Are you implementing or planning to implement the law, this fiscal year defense bill, as Congress wrote it? (House of Representatives 2008, 2)

The vague, boilerplate character of the signing statement and its broad constitutional objection to specific provisions particularly concerned the chair. Without a specific rationale for the president's concerns, it was unclear how the Department of Defense would implement those provisions. Indeed, the department did not send a representative to the hearing to testify, furthering congressional uncertainty about implementation.

Representatives Tierney and Allen submitted testimony reflecting their concerns with respect to the president's objection to a specific provision, section 841, which established "the Commission on Wartime Contracting to study and investigate federal agency contracting for: (1) the reconstruction of Iraq and Afghanistan; (2) the logistical support of coalition forces operating in Iraq and Afghanistan; and (3) the performance of security functions in such operations. [Further, it] requires interim reports and a final report from the Commission to Congress." They wrote,

> This testimony was prompted by the troubling and extremely vague constitutional assertions contained in the signing statement issued by the President in connection with the National Defense Authorization Act for Fiscal Year 2008. Specifically, we noted with great dismay and confusion the President's assertion that the establishment of a Wartime Contracting Commission "purport[s] to impose requirements that could inhibit the President's ability to carry out his constitutional obligations." . . . It is our sincere hope that the President's signing statement is merely boilerplate rather than an indication that the Administration will not fully support the establishment and work of the Wartime Contracting Commission. On behalf of U.S. taxpayers, we will closely monitor the Administration's actions in the coming days and weeks, and, with like-minded colleagues, will use all Congressional rights and powers at our disposal to both ensure that the American people receive a full accounting

of the President's intentions and, at the end of the day, ensure that this Commission is quickly constituted and able to fully conduct its important work. (House of Representatives 2008, 108–111)

The uncertainty regarding the fate of those provisions alarmed other members of Congress, including Representative Todd Akin (R-MO) the ranking member of the Subcommittee on Oversight and Investigations, and the president's co-partisan. He stated,

> In my view, when the Congress and President do disagree about the constitutionality of a specific provision of the law, the most important equity to be preserved is transparency and communication. If the President believes his independent duties under the Constitution preclude him from implementing the law in the matter Congress prescribed, then I want to know. What I do not want is an executive that does not communicate with the Congress. Therefore, it seems to me that the Presidential signing statements . . . are important tools of communication so that the legislative branch knows which provisions of law will require increased oversight over executive implementation. With respect to fiscal year 2008 National Defense Authorization Act (NDAA), the President highlighted four provisions in his signing statement. I think the prudent course for this committee is to oversee the implementation of those provisions to ensure that they are carried out consistent with our legislative intent. (House of Representatives 2008, 3)

The story of the NDAA of 2008 illustrates the struggle over policy control in our system of separated powers. Specifically, it highlights the degree to which Congress is sensitive to anticipated policy loss as a result of presidential unilateralism. Of course, this exchange occurred during a period of heightened public and congressional attention to presidential signing statements. But as we show throughout this book, this same dynamic persists over time and exists independently of which party controls Congress. All presidents, not just Bush, have incentives to consolidate power and exert constitutional authority, but members of Congress are not always quiescent in the face of presidential actions.

Members' concerns may be broad (reflecting a principled objection to an accretion of presidential power) or narrow (reflecting unease tied to anticipated losses). There is little reason to expect individual members to resolve to overcome significant collective action problems posed by such obstacles as supermajoritarian requirements, bicameralism, and polarization to challenge general presidential aggrandizement. But legislators can, and do, take action to constrain executives' unilateral actions on specific dimensions of policies, as they did in the case of the NDAA of 2008.

This dynamic is not limited to signing statements, as the evidence indicates that similar patterns occur in the context of executive orders and policy memoranda. The interactions between the White House and members of Congress related to the NDAA of 2008 are not unique. This dynamic—which we call strategic responsiveness—underpins the analyses in this book. We find similar patterns of strategic responsiveness across presidents, congresses, and policy areas and for different types of unilateral tools.

Unilateralism has become a defining feature of the American presidency and American national politics (Reeves and Rogowski 2022), making the degree of congressional sensitivity to those actions relevant for the separation of powers. Those who prefer "guardrails" on unilateral executive power may not find the robust, broad, and decisive congressional action that they seek. Yet there is power in the seemingly small ordinariness of particular policy struggles. As presidents take unilateral actions on specific dimensions of multidimensional legislation, members of Congress might anticipate individualized policy loss and choose to respond. In that exchange, the politics of the particular shapes the constitutional order, as surely as broad, statutory constraints might.

Acknowledgments

We consider presidential unilateralism in relation to long-standing claims about our system of separated powers. Scholars and laypeople have connected policy gridlock, general frustration, and obstruction to the powers that are separated across the legislative, executive, and judicial branches of government. In practice, our constitutional checks and balances do not operate to allow one branch to "proofread" or refine work in the other branches. Checks and balances do not necessarily lead to moments of "coming together" or untroubled group efforts. Instead, "the constitutional separation of powers operate, *as they were designed*, to delay or obstruct action rather than to facilitate it" (Truman 1951, 354, emphasis added). Sundquist makes an even more forceful statement: the overall impact of our separation of powers is "not just to delay action in the interest of full and free debate, but *to forbid action*" (1968, 510–511, emphasis added).

Against this backdrop of delay and inaction, presidents increasingly take unilateral actions to move policy. Indeed, the most powerful single actor able to affect policy in the United States is the president. In the face of presidential unilateralism, what checks and balances are left to Congress? Can Congress counter presidential unilateralism? Under what conditions is it likely to do so? These are some of the questions explored in this book.

Rigorous explorations of critically important questions about our system of separated powers require both careful reasoning and empirical analysis. Much of the data that we use in this book are original to this project. We thank graduate and undergraduate research assistants at Allegheny College, Southern Illinois University Edwardsville, and the University of

Georgia for providing us with crucial research support. These students include Emma Bibina, Triniece Cummins, Annie Fulgenzi, Chelsea Harris, Claudia Huber, Jackson Kendrick, Destanee Liston, Olivia Lute, Ryan Mayo, Sydney McNece, Daniel Mead, Emily Pfeffer, Jorgia Pitzer, Brandon Rahn, Alex Robinson, Emma Siebert, Ramsay Smith, and Emily Warshal.

The data that we use in this book are derived from archives at the American Presidency Project, Comparative Agendas Project, Library of Congress, Office of Management and Budget, Bureau of Labor Statistics, Federal Bureau of Investigation, and the *Federal Register*. Other data were generously shared with us by Lowande (2014) and Bailey (2020). We appreciate the research funding and support received from programs at our home institutions, Allegheny College, Southern Illinois University–Edwardsville, and the University of Georgia.

We presented preliminary versions of some of this work at professional conferences. Comments from Julia Azari, Michael Bailey, Dan Butler, R. Steven Daniels, David Foster, Gary Hollibaugh, Jason MacDonald, Tony Madonna, Daniel Magleby, Yu Ouyang, Jesse Richman, Jason Roberts, Larry Rothenberg, Andy Rudalevige, Thomas Sedelius, John Wilkerson, and Don Wolfensberger improved our work immeasurably.

Colleagues near and far kindly reviewed rough drafts of key chapters and provided comments that made our work significantly better than it otherwise would have been. They include Jamie Carson, Keith Dougherty, Grete Graf, Nic Guehlstorf, Michael Lynch, Ashley Moraguez, Laurie Rice, and Joel Sievert. We are particularly indebted to Chris Weber, who kindly assisted with our empirical analysis in Chapter 4, as well as to Bill Bianco, Gyung-Ho Jeon, Matt Lebo, Terry Moe, Ian Ostrander, and Dan Ponder for their careful guidance. Comments from anonymous reviewers and editorial assistance from the University of Michigan Press were also exceptionally helpful. We also thank seminar participants at the University of Notre Dame for encouraging us to think more carefully about causal inference in our work. As always, any errors or omissions are our responsibility.

ONE

Unilateral Actions in a Separated System

Comprehensive and undefined presidential powers hold both
practical advantages and grave dangers.

—Robert H. Jackson, concurring in
Youngstown Sheet & Tube Co. v. Sawyer, 343 U.S. 579 (1952)

Presidents from Bill Clinton to Joe Biden have been criticized for taking actions that unilaterally altered policy without congressional input. President Clinton acted unilaterally on climate policy when he did not have the votes on Capitol Hill to support his legislative agenda. President George W. Bush acted alone in multiple contexts after the September 11 attacks, and President Barack Obama took unilateral steps when Congress would not act on issues ranging from immigration to gun control (Major 2016). Not to be outdone, President Trump acted unilaterally on issues like immigration, health care, environmental policy, and the federal unemployment supplement during the COVID-19 pandemic (Thiessen 2020). President Biden has followed a similar pattern.

Presidents' unilateral actions are at the center of a growing area of scholarly inquiry and public concern, which intensified during the Trump administration (see, e.g., Potter et al. 2019, 2022; Harriger 2020). We approach presidential unilateralism by focusing on our system of separated powers. Whittington (2009) and others have long noted that the constitutional order can only be understood in a political context. Challenges to constitutionalism posed by emergency powers of executives, for example, and the means by which constitutional questions are resolved are both found within politics itself (see, e.g., Belco and Rottinghaus 2014; Bolton and Thrower 2016; Lowande and Potter 2021; MacDonald and McGrath 2016; Ouyang and Waterman 2015; Turner 2020). If constitutionalism is understood as constrained by and maintained within politics, then the character of our politics has implications for the constitutional order as actors in each branch anticipate the reactions from the other branches (e.g., Cameron 2000; Howell 2003; de Figueiredo, Jacobi, and Weingast 2008; Kriner and Schickler 2016; McGrath 2013). In short, despite its strong, forceful labeling, unilateralism cannot be studied in isolation. Rather, congressional response to presidential unilateralism underlies the competition between opposing partisans and different branches of government for control over policy (Lowande and Potter 2021; Moraguez 2020a, 2020b).

Our primary objective is to explain when members of Congress are more likely to respond to presidential unilateralism. Broader concerns about institutional authority and the scope of executive power generally do not create specific, individualized losses and therefore rarely generate coordinated action among members of Congress. However, unilateral efforts on *specific* policy dimensions are more likely to prompt a congressional response. Congressional responses can limit presidential power through, among other mechanisms, limitation riders (MacDonald 2010), restrictions on statutory discretion (Huber and Shipan 2002), and *ex post* policy oversight.

Two premises inform this book. First, policymaking is a multidimensional process. This premise has a strong and long-standing empirical foundation (e.g., Krutz 2001). Indeed, multidimensionality plays a key role in legislative success (e.g., Casas, Denny, and Wilkerson 2020) and is a defining characteristic of contemporary lawmaking. Many models of American political institutions are simplified to be one-dimensional (e.g., Cameron 2000; Howell 2003; and Chiou and Rothenberg 2017, related to the presidency, and Krehbiel 1998, related to Congress). Although simpler, one-dimensional models cannot address a critical political concept that multidimensional models can. Specifically, multidimensional spatial models can reveal how proposals from separate dimensions can be aggregated or disaggregated as actors compete over policy development. Proposals that had been doomed to fail can sometimes be folded into other legislation and passed. In this way, a multidimensional model allows us to construct a more complete picture of politics than is possible in a single dimensional model.

Our second premise is that members of Congress seek to avoid blame and claim credit (see, e.g., Mayhew 1974; Fiorina 1982a; Arnold 1990). As they develop legislation, members of Congress recognize that the executive branch might take unilateral actions to refine the implementation of statutes. Those same members might be able to shift blame and claim credit as they respond to the policy implications of unilateral actions. On those measures where members anticipate policy loss, congressional oversight provides a means by which they can respond to presidential unilateralism without incurring the significant collective action difficulties that new legislation faces.[1]

What Congress aggregates into a multidimensional bill the president can disaggregate via unilateral actions. By taking unilateral actions, the president creates (potential) policy losses for legislators on *specific dimensions* of a multidimensional bill. As legislators foresee the increased likelihood of policy loss on discrete issue dimensions, we predict heightened oversight activity on those same dimensions, as we observed in the NDAA of 2008 example. McCubbins and Schwartz (1984) note that oversight can allow for credit claiming. Of course, legislators lack the incentive to respond to every unilateral action, especially as some unilateral actions allow legislators to avoid blame. For instance, members of Congress have not addressed immigration policies in a comprehensive manner from 1996 to 2023. Instead, presidents have driven immigration policy with executive actions, especially from 2011 to 2023. For many years, immigration has been a hard issue for members of Congress to derive electoral gains, making blame avoidance more likely. In 2023, Democratic and Republican members and senators appeared ready to tackle the issue, only to have former President Trump urge Republicans to kill it. For other issues, members of Congress may be motivated to respond when an executive action appears to reshape or gut a statute, as when President Trump's unilateral actions undercut the Affordable Care Act or stayed the payroll tax deferment which could erode the Social Security Act. Strong responses would allow some legislators to claim credit.

Executive orders and the certainty of the subsequent bureaucratic implementation create clear winners and losers on discrete policy dimensions. Signing statements also create winners and losers, but the statements are not typically binding policy directives for agencies. Signing statements often articulate positions, whereas executive orders and policy memoranda obligate agencies. While signing statements, executive orders, and memoranda are elements of unilateralism, they convey different information to Congress and generate different responses. Our book explores these distinctions.

When considering the role of legislators developing proposals in the shadow of unilateral actions, we adopt the long-held notion that legislators must explain their votes. In particular, legislators must explain their support for a multidimensional policy package to separate audiences that are themselves focused on specific issue dimensions of the new, multidimensional legislation. Elected officials seldom need to explain an entire statute, let alone the policy trade-offs in a statute. Indeed, it would be hard for a legislator to master all of the intricacies of all legislation (Madonna, Ostrander, and Williamson 2021). Whether they have mastered the legislation at hand or not, legislators cannot afford to explain all the policy trade-offs inherent in a complex piece of legislation.[2] Instead, legislators must explain any narrow aspect of a statute that a particular audience finds troublesome. Altogether, the key behavioral postulate that we introduce in our model is that legislators must be able to explain their support for *discrete* elements of a multidimensional bill to select audiences, often called "attentive publics" in the congressional literature. Attentive publics embrace traceability, linking legislators' actions to legislative policies (Arnold 1990; Converse 1964), which in turn prompts vote explanation and blame avoidance. The need to explain votes and the tendency to avoid blame underpin a status quo bias in members of Congress. What if scholars seriously considered these behavioral tendencies and incorporated them into spatial models of legislative decision-making? How might the canonical model change, and could there be a rational basis for a status quo bias?

Consider illustrations drawn from the Affordable Care Act (ACA, or Obamacare). For some Democrats, explaining their ACA support in 2009 meant explaining how the ACA affected access to abortion-related services (e.g., Good 2011). Republicans urging repeal of the ACA often had to explain how preexisting conditions would be handled by health insurance companies in the absence of the ACA (e.g., Kapur 2020). For key attentive publics, the entirety of the ACA was less important than one issue dimension or another. Interestingly, the repeal of the individual mandate under the ACA during the Trump administration was also multidimensional. The same omnibus bill that repealed the individual mandate also provided for tax cuts of varying sizes for Americans. Thus, those who supported the individual mandate and favored tax cuts faced trade-offs across these dimensions.

A simple illustration portrays the importance of explaining narrow elements of a bill and highlights the fact that politics, fundamentally, involves the aggregation and disaggregation of issues. As issues are aggregated or disaggregated, revealed preferences for policies often appear to change, and paradoxes can emerge. Ultimately, the fate of legislative efforts often

TABLE 1.1. Utility from Aggregated and Disaggregated Proposals for Factions D, R, and F

Proposal	Legislative Factions		
	D	R	F
A	3	–1	–1
B	–1	–1	3
C	–1	3	–1
Omnibus Package ABC	1	1	1
Status Quo	0	0	0

depends on the aggregation of various proposals into single bills. Consider the three legislative proposals: A, B, and C in Table 1.1. Given the utilities indicated for the equally sized legislative factions D, R, and F, none of the proposals pass the House when considered separately. Only the D faction supports proposal A, only the F faction supports B, and only the R faction supports C. Any proposal alone loses to the status quo, yielding zero utility. However, if the three proposals were aggregated, each faction would prefer passing the omnibus package to maintaining the status quo.[3]

Suppose a president evaluated the ABC omnibus package depicted in Table 1.1. The president could use a signing statement to tweak proposal A without legislative retribution as long as two of the three legislative factions were made no worse off. Given that the R and F factions suffer a utility loss (–1) from proposal A and faction D secures a gain (+3), the president has considerable wiggle room to consider unilateral actions that affect the implementation of proposal A. The president could similarly tweak proposal B or C. Within this framework, signing statements with specific objections disaggregate the policy proposals that the legislative body had earlier aggregated. Executive orders and policy memoranda can have a similar effect. Omnibus bills aggregate disparate policy and can garner supermajorities sufficient to permit legislation to overcome filibuster and veto pivots (Krutz 2000, 546). Unilateral tools can disaggregate some of those same policies. Even when statutes do not rise to the level of being an omnibus measure, there are multidimensional elements to legislation, offering circumstances for a president to change the policy unilaterally. Factions D, R, and F in Table 1.1 are better off with the omnibus package (ABC) than the status quo, even knowing that the president might unilaterally alter the legislation's impact. As long as the president ensures that no two legislative factions are worse off with the unilateral action, there is no pushback with new legislation.

The illustration in Table 1.1 is generalized in the spatial model developed in Chapter 3, in which the multidimensionality of legislation can even provide opportunities for presidents to make Pareto improvements by taking unilateral action on specific policy dimensions, especially when Congress remains largely silent on those dimensions. Pareto improvements are policy changes that make at least one actor better off and no actor worse off. If a unilateral action can secure a Pareto improvement in policy for legislators and the president, then such unilateralism creates an advantage unforeseen by prominent advocates of a strong executive. For instance, energy and dispatch in the executive, important to Hamilton and other founders, cannot speak to the composition of policies themselves. Pareto improvements trade policy gains on some dimensions with losses on others. Of course, legislators might have engaged in legislative bargaining to be a partner in those policy trade-offs, but uncertainty and the incentive to avoid blame impel legislators to remain silent on some issue dimensions. Importantly, silence at one time does not ensure subsequent acceptance. Thus, legislators resist some unilateral actions through *ex post* oversight activity. Legislators can claim credit for some policy gains during legislative bargaining, avoid blame when difficult policy trade-offs are made through unilateral efforts, and reassert themselves in the politics of separated powers, fighting perceived executive overreach—not because of diffuse institutional concerns—but because of particularized policy losses.

Electoral concerns lead legislators to justify their support of specific policies that have been rolled into a larger legislative package. To the extent that legislators speak to more homogeneous audiences and have more parochial concerns, these behavioral tendencies are reinforced (see, e.g., Boatright 2013). Anderson, Butler, and Harbridge-Yong (2020) highlight the rejection of compromise in Congress due to electoral concerns. When trade-offs are complicated, legislators' status quo biases facilitate vote explanation; and when legislation is passed, explaining a vote often means explaining one's support for a narrow slice of a larger piece of legislation. Trade-offs generally imply compromise, and Anderson, Butler, and Harbridge-Yong (2020) highlight how difficult compromise is when electoral concerns are prominent.[4] We argue that explaining a vote on a multidimensional proposal is more challenging than on more narrow legislation. In short, due to electoral concerns, policy movement on some dimensions will be attenuated. If presidents use unilateral tools to capture policy gains that were not secured during legislative bargaining, members of Congress have the incentives and means to respond. In Chapters 4 and 5, we find that Congress responds through increased oversight when unilateral actions trade gains in one dimension for losses in another.

In exploring interbranch competition over policy control, we examine the consequences of policy multidimensionality and congressional sensitivity to presidential unilateral action on specific policy dimensions. Multidimensional policies create opportunities for distinct unilateral actions, which can subsequently generate focused responses from Congress. When the president issues a signing statement with specific objections (or an executive order), Congress is alerted to areas of possible noncompliance or policy drift. Congress can respond by exercising *ex post* oversight to counter movement away from its preferred policies. The difficulties posed by bicameralism, polarization, and collective action problems mean that new statutes are unlikely to be common reactions to presidential unilateralism. However, congressional decentralization may serve Congress well in terms of responding to unilateralism on specific dimensions of multidimensional bills with heightened oversight activity. Indeed, oversight remains a key expression of congressional control in a highly polarized context (see, e.g., McGrath 2013; Lewallen 2020). Fiorina (1982a, 340) notes, for example:

> Members of Congress are given the opportunity to exercise disproportionate influence over segments of the federal bureaucracy that are of special concern to them. If an agency is causing problems for a members' constituents, the member need not organize a coalition of 51 or 218 members to discipline that agency. All that's needed is agreement from a couple of subcommittee colleagues.

Congressional oversight does not automatically negate presidential influence over policy (MacDonald and McGrath 2016), but we suggest that signing statements, executive orders, and memoranda, along with congressional oversight, typify the ongoing interbranch struggle to assert control over policy implementation.

Conventional Views of Unilateralism

For some observers, recent incidents suggest that the conventional wisdom regarding unilateral presidential actions, like signing statements or executive orders, is accurate. To wit: presidents utilize their powers in an imperial fashion and at the expense of members of Congress (Schlesinger 1973). Members of Congress are irked, yet they do not meaningfully respond beyond condemnation through the media and failed attempts to pass laws to counter presidential actions. If this conventional wisdom holds, then the instruments of unilateral policymaking are effective means for outmaneuvering anyone who might question presidential authority. If the conventional assessment were accurate, the imperial presidency would have arrived. The list of scholars and journalists writing of the (purportedly) unconstitutional usurpation of power by the president grew steadily during Bush's, Obama's, and Trump's presidencies.

Presidential signing statements, such as those just introduced, are highly suspect to Fisher (2007–2008), Pfiffner (2009), the American Bar Association (2006), and numerous others. Fisher (2007–2008, 210) contends that signing statements that object to varying provisions of law "encourage the belief that the law is not what Congress puts in public law but what the administration decides to do later on." Pfiffner (2009) writes that the use of signing statements effectively nullify provisions of law and undermine the checks that the Framers of the Constitution placed on the executive. More pointedly, Fisher (2007–2008) elaborates that no single branch has the power to single-handedly determine the contents of public policy or what the Constitution says. Thus, only the most innocuous or rhetorical statements are harmless.

Executive orders and memoranda, which presidents use to direct agency actions, are more generally accepted. Nonetheless, the scope or the particular policy targeted by an executive order can provoke congressional backlash (e.g., Howell 2003; Mayer 2001; Rudalevige 2021). To accomplish many of the same ends with less congressional reaction, Lowande (2014, 725) finds that presidents use policy memoranda alongside executive orders. He defines policy memoranda as "a class of presidential actions that contains orders to administrators [and that] is not subject to the statutory reporting requirements of executive orders and proclamations" (Lowande 2014, 725). Policy memoranda need not be recorded in the *Federal Register*, and the president can bypass Office of Management and Budget review. Since presidents use memoranda as policy documents to convey important policy directives, they can provide additional opportunities for presidents to act unilaterally, beyond executive orders (Lowande 2014, 725).

Public awareness of unilateral actions is increasing as presidents deploy them with varying degrees of success over a wide array of issues. Perhaps that is part of the larger goal of presidents—to create the impression of the inevitability, ubiquity, and appropriateness of unilateralism. In fact, as current justice Elana Kagan noted when she served in the Clinton administration, the goal of using unilateral mechanisms like executive orders, signing statements, and policy memoranda is to "make presidential intervention in regulatory matters ever more routine and agency acceptance of this intervention ever more ready" (Kagan 2001, 2299). In effect, prolific use of unilateral tools "softens the system" to accept the propriety of presidential dominance in the implementation of policy, independent of—or at least not overly conditioned by—congressional preferences. It is noteworthy that Kagan echoed some of the same sentiments earlier presented by current justice Samuel A. Alito Jr. when prior he worked for the Reagan administration. The public expectations of presidential unilateralism reflect the degree to which the regularization of those actions has taken hold.[5]

The Practical Advantages and Grave Dangers of Presidential Powers

The quotation at the start of this chapter comes from Supreme Court justice Robert H. Jackson's concurrence to *Youngstown Sheet & Tube Co. v. Sawyer* (343 U.S. 579 (1952)) in which he noted "both practical advantages and grave dangers" of comprehensive and ill-defined presidential powers. As noted in the preceding section, over the last four presidencies, the "grave dangers" of unilateral presidential actions received more attention than the "practical advantages."

For a robust discussion of the "practical advantages," one could return to debates during the founding era. In *Federalist #70*, Alexander Hamilton promoted the establishment of a "vigorous Executive" to advance "the steady administration of the laws." Hamilton feared legislative encroachment on executive authority. He argued that a weakened executive creates a dangerous imbalance in a system of separated powers, stating that a weakened executive undermined policy implementation and sound governance. In *Federalist #70*, Hamilton wrote:

> A feeble Executive implies a feeble execution of the government. A feeble execution is but another phrase for a bad execution; and a government ill executed, whatever it may be in theory, must be, in practice, a bad government.

Hamilton's emphasis on the "practical advantages" was designed to counter the widely held fears at the time of all-powerful executives.

A common concern during the founding era was that a single individual embodied the presidency. Debates at the Constitutional Convention regarding dual executives gained little traction, and attempts to attach a council of advisers composed of legislators or judges to the presidency failed. Although checked by other branches, the president remained an individual figure.[6] In *Federalist #69*, Hamilton wrote that "executive authority, with few exceptions, is . . . vested in a single magistrate," suggesting that the presidency was following long-established practices. Executive authorities are typically singular, so singularity by itself cannot be a distinctive feature of the U.S. presidency. Aspects of this reasoning resonate in recent debates about unitary executive theory. Many scholars have explored the origins and applications of unitary executive theory of presidential power (Calabresi and Yoo 1997, 2003; Crouch, Rozell, and Sollenberger 2020; Fitts 1996; Waterman 2009). Understanding the scope of executive power as based on reading Article II, Section 1 with an *exclusive* grant of broad unilateral powers to the president underpins the unitary executive theory. Under this broader reading, the president has complete and exclusive executive authority with few limitations.[7]

As former president Trump's attorney general William Barr (2019) argued, the president has unitary executive powers independent of the circumstances or situation. The president wields plenary authority to execute law without regard for congressional or judicial concerns. In Barr's view, a president solely decides to exercise that latent authority in any particular situation. Of course, friction can occur when Congress seeks to delegate authority with *ex ante* procedural or substantive controls to federal agencies, some of which are themselves independent. Friction also occurs when members of Congress seek *ex post* control of a bureaucracy or seek information from the executive branch to conduct oversight. On November 15, 2019, Barr (2019) stated, "If Congress attempts to vest the power to execute the law in someone beyond the control of the President, it contravenes the Framers' clear intent to vest that power in a single person, the President." In Barr's view, Congress cannot bypass the president as it tries to guide implementation or engage in oversight.

Unitary executive theory, with its ties back to Hamilton, implies unilateral tools. That said, many presidents have employed unilateral tools without adhering to any sort of all-powerful, unitary executive theory. The ubiquity of unilateralism is thus distinct from the rather exceptional claims of unitary authority.

What Is a Unilateral Action?

It is unsurprising that scholars have different ideas about what constitutes a unilateral presidential action. For Howell (2003), first-mover status is key, arguing that a president working in concert with others or reacting to others does not operate unilaterally. Ostrander and Sievert (2013a, 2013b) consider whether a presidential action carries the weight of law. By this view, executive orders are unilateral, but signing statements are not. Contrasting with Ostrander and Sievert (2013a, 2013b), Cooper (2002, 2005) includes signing statements among a president's unilateral tools. Increasingly, scholars include presidential recess appointments among unilateral presidential actions (e.g., Black et al. 2007; Kinane 2021). There are other conceptions of presidents' unilateral tools, but these provide a reasonable overview.

We see no reason to adjudicate between different understandings of what efforts constitute unilateral action. Instead, we note that ambiguities exist across the separate definitions. For instance, when issuing an executive order, a president must do so pursuant to statutory or constitutional authority. The statutes can be from earlier congresses or very recent ones, but every executive order must have a link to a congressional statute or the U.S. Constitution. Policy memoranda, which can be used instead of an executive order, are also powerful tools. Consequently, many scholars, including us, view memoranda as unilateral tools. However, even the simplest of claims about any of the unilateral tools quickly become complicated when applied to our governing system with its separation of powers. For instance:

- Do presidents move first when they issue an executive order that relies on recent statutory authority, or does Congress?
- Suppose an executive order is enabled by a long-ignored congressional statute. Does the statute's enacting coalition of legislators need to be present to consider an executive order based on that statute as unilateral?
- Consider recess appointments made by a president when the Senate is not in session. Do presidents respond to the failures of a Congress to move nominees from committee? Or do presidents sneak appointees past the Senate? Perhaps both are in play. By making a recess appointment, the president could be acting first or second.[8]

In sum, it is sometimes unclear who moved first in the most meaningful and demonstrable fashion.

Ostrander and Sievert (2013a, 2013b) emphasize that signing statements are not statutory because they cannot *make* law. We agree that signing statements are not statutory, but we also note that the Reagan administration began archiving signing statements with their associated statutes. Signing statements do not establish law but exist adjacent to law and may affect the interpretation of law. Working in President Reagan's Office of Legal Counsel, then-deputy attorney general Samuel A. Alito Jr. wrote that signing statements "would increase the power of the Executive to *shape the law*" (1986, 2, emphasis added). In that same memo, Alito argued that bills should be identified for short, deliberately crafted signing statements to encourage the courts to rely favorably on the statements. That is, Alito wanted to introduce signing statements in a manner that would maximize their impact on legal interpretation, even recognizing that "our new type of signing statement will not be warmly welcomed by Congress" (1986, 2). As it happened, members of Congress have seldom if ever welcomed signing statements, and there is reason to believe that presidents continue to be savvy about the Supreme Court's interpretations of their signing statements (Thrower 2019).

Black et al. (2007, 646) use three attributes to characterize a unilateral action. First, the president must "manipulate ambiguities in the Constitution." Second, presidents must have first-mover status, forcing Congress and the courts to determine how to respond. Finally, the "president's action must affect policy."

How do we characterize unilateral efforts? In contrast to Howell (2003) and Black et al. (2007), we are agnostic as to first- or second-mover status. After all, it is not always clear who moves first (see, e.g., Belco and Rottinghaus 2017). In addition, there can be either first-mover advantages or disadvantages in strategic interactions, and sometimes there are late-mover advantages, as often happens when one has the last word in a debate. In Chapters 2 and 3, we consider last-mover advantages that a president with residual rights might have. If presidents possess residual rights, as we and Moe and Wilson (1994) contend, then there are potential last-mover opportunities. Residual decision-making rights allow one "to take unilateral action at his own discretion when the formal agreement is ambiguous or silent about precisely what behaviors are required" (Moe and Wilson 1994, 14). Residual rights do not oblige one to move last or prevent one from moving first. Rather, they ensure an opportunity to make important decisions even after an agreement has been reached. The remaining residual rights in this setting include a president's ability to finely tune the execution and implementation of law, thereby affecting policy.

We summarize our sense of the president's unilateral actions with three key points. First, we assume that presidents possess residual policymaking powers. Second, we assume that unilateral tools reveal presidential policy preferences. When using a unilateral tool to affect policy, presidents cannot hide their policy motives from agencies without undermining implementation nor from the courts without possibly skewing judicial interpretations.[9] Third, for our analyses, unilateral tools need not create new law, but they do *perfect* law. Executive orders and memoranda often perfect law by indicating what to implement or how to implement existing statutes. Executive orders and memoranda have the force of law. In contrast, signing statements do not have the force of law, but they do signal the president's policy preferences regarding the execution and implementation of law and can therefore perfect the law. For instance, signing statements offer an interpretation of the relevant statute and the president's authorities vis-à-vis that statute. Unilateral tools perfect law through interpretation, execution, and implementation, even when the tools themselves might not create law.[10]

In this book, we focus on key instruments of unilateralism (memoranda, executive orders, and signing statements) and consider how members of Congress react to the president's deployment of these tools.[11]

Earlier Work on Unilateralism

Our focus on congressional responses to unilateral actions contributes to the growing literature on congressional oversight and interbranch relations. Mayer (2001) analyzes the institutional interplay between the president and Congress by focusing on executive orders as a unilateral policy instrument. He argues that presidents' executive orders provide a decisive advantage over Congress that cannot be easily overcome. Mayer discovers that prior to 2000, Democratic presidents used executive orders more frequently than Republican presidents, that presidents used them more in the latter half of their terms, and they were used most frequently in reelection years. Howell (2003) presented a more expansive view of presidential unilateralism and argued that the presidency is far more unilateral than commonly assumed. For instance, Howell argues that presidents use unilateral actions to enhance their already considerable proposal powers. Mayer's and Howell's works provide motivation for our research in this area, but Howell's work (2003) presumes a unidimensional policy space, which limits the consideration of policy trade-offs across issue dimensions.[12]

Kriner and Schickler (2016) argue that the president is only unilateral to the extent that Congress does not respond. They find substantial evidence that Congress regularly investigates executive branch wrongdoing as a constitutional check on its powers. Kriner and Schickler (2016) highlight the most public congressional investigations and find that those investigations erode presidential approval ratings. Of course, major events are likely to move presidential approval for an array of reasons well separated from congressional investigation. The congressional oversight hearings in our work are more inclusive and not restricted to major investigations of malfeasance, wrongdoing, or gross mismanagement.

Lewallen (2020) finds that committees have devoted more attention to oversight in response to their decline in control over the legislative agenda. We identify a second mechanism prompting the increase in oversight activity by congressional committees: unilateral presidential action. We build upon these works while departing from them in important ways, as we provide a formal, theoretically based rationale to demonstrate that Congress selectively holds the president accountable for unilateral action through higher levels of oversight activity. In this way, our book contributes to an important literature that examines congressional influence on public policy apart from its power to legislate (see, e.g., Crouch, Rozell, and Sollenberger 2020; Chafetz 2020).

Summary and Plan for This Book

In the next chapter, we explore unitary executive theory, unilateralism, and unilateral actions in light of the role that Congress plays. The nature of congressional responsiveness is key to the distinction between a unitary executive and unilateralism. The second chapter explores the legal and historical foundations for presidents' use of unilateral tools and examines the role of Congress in overseeing executive branch actions.

In Chapter 3, we develop a multidimensional spatial model of presidential-congressional interactions over policy development, explicitly allowing the president to take unilateral actions. Increasingly, congressional proposals are long and complicated. As the executive and legislative branches compete to articulate policy, they aggregate and disaggregate issues. Sometimes issues are folded into proposals and sometimes they are peeled away. We view politics as inherently multidimensional, wherein political actors strategically aggregate and disaggregate issues.

Unilateral actions taken by a president trade policy gains on some dimensions for losses on others. As a result of these trade-offs, which create losses in some policy areas, legislators selectively resist unilateral actions through *ex post* oversight activity and new bill introductions. With signing statements and executive orders, the president creates winners and losers for specific dimensions of a multidimensional bill. As legislators foresee implementation loss as a result of unilateralism, we predict that losses on specific dimensions of legislation due to unilateralism spur heightened oversight activity.

In Chapters 4 and 5, we empirically evaluate the strategic responsiveness of Congress. In Chapter 4, we investigate whether Congress responds to signing statements and executive orders with increased oversight activity. We built a dataset including every nonclassified oversight hearing that the House and Senate conducted between 1997 and 2018. These hearings cover four presidencies, including Bill Clinton's second term, all of George W. Bush's and Barack Obama's presidencies, and nearly half of Donald Trump's term. We also include data on the number of executive orders and policy memoranda that each of these presidents issued during this period. We examine the 437 signing statements that were placed on bills during that time to query the number of times that presidents objected to *specific* provisions in the bills. The signing statements in our data contain on average four unique objections. We expect that increases in unilateral efforts (through policy memoranda, executive orders, and objections in signing statements) lead to enhanced congressional oversight activity.

In Chapter 5, we refine our empirical exploration by examining a single policy domain, defense, in which presidents have traditionally dominated (e.g., Canes-Wrone, Howell, and Lewis 2008; Wildavsky 1966). Defense policy differs from other policy areas in two key ways. First, it is a policy area in which the federal government has more authority relative to states. Second, it is a policy area where even though constitutional prerogatives are outlined for both the president and Congress, the president seems to have gained greater authority as Congress has either lost or ceded authority (e.g., Fowler 2015; Wildavsky 1966). Domestic policy might be a free-for-all, but many scholars have argued that foreign and defense policy are the president's domain. Indeed, by some accounts, defense policy is an area in which Congress has struggled to oversee the executive branch (Auerswald and Campbell 2012; Chiou and Rothenberg 2017; Fowler 2015).

On two grounds, defense policy represents a perfect opportunity to test our theoretical expectations that members of Congress respond to policy losses tied to unilateral actions. First, defense policy represents a "hard case" for our theory precisely because it is an area in which Congress has purportedly deferred to presidents. Thus, if we find evidence that favors our theoretical expectations, we have a stronger argument. Second, unilateral efforts occur most frequently in the defense policy area. For instance, the highest number of objections to varying provisions of law have occurred on bills related to defense policy, with 747 such objections occurring between 1997 and 2018. By comparison, the policy area with the next highest number of unique objections, government operations, had only 277. Additionally, defense policy is one of the top three policy areas in which presidents have issued nonclassified executive orders. Further, defense policy is the top area in which policy memoranda have been promulgated, with 123 having been advanced between 1997 and 2018. Given these data, any examination of unilateralism demands a careful look at defense policy.

Chapter 6 concludes the book. We review our theoretical argument along with the empirical evidence related to it. We compare Trump and Biden, both to one another and to predecessors—Clinton, Bush, and Obama. We visit some of the normative implications of this study and consider ways that other researchers can build upon our work, aiming toward a better better understanding of the interplay between unilateral presidential action and the responsiveness of other branches. As presidents push the boundaries of the vague provisions of Article II, they do so in full view of multiple audiences. Those audiences, including Congress, may have neither the capacity nor the incentive to respond to institutional, regime-level threats to the balance of power, but they can and do respond on specific issue dimensions where policy loss is anticipated. In doing so, Congress is able to respond strategically to particular exercises of presidential power and shape the contours of the constitutional order.

We began this chapter with a selection from Supreme Court justice Jackson's concurrence in *Youngstown*: "[U]ndefined presidential powers hold both practical advantages and grave dangers." Jackson, however, offered no advice as to how to manage this tension between advantages and dangers. Indeed, Jackson stated, "[One] may be surprised at the poverty of really useful and unambiguous authority applicable to concrete problems of executive power." This puzzle of ambiguous authority begets the central question of this book: Does Congress respond in a meaningful fashion when presidents employ unilateral policy instruments? If so, what is the nature and timing of this response?

TWO

Presidential Unilateralism
and Congressional Control

> It is relevant to note the gap that exists between the President's
> paper powers and his real powers. The Constitution does not
> disclose the measure of the actual controls wielded by the modern
> presidential office. . . . Subtle shifts take place in the centers of
> real power that do not show on the face of the Constitution.
>
> —Robert H. Jackson, concurring in
> *Youngstown Sheet & Tube Co. v. Sawyer* (1952)

The passage from Justice Robert H. Jackson highlights a distinct theme
in this book. There are clear limitations to relying on the plain text of the
Constitution to delineate the powers available to presidents because these
"paper powers," derived solely from the Constitution or from statutory
law, fail to portray the full array of "actual controls" at a president's dis-
posal. Akin to congressional implied or inherent powers, the ambiguities
of Article II invite presidents to expand the scope of their authority. Limitations on presidential authority are largely defined by the other branches
of government on a case-by-case basis. That is, congressional pushback or
judicial findings occur in response to one or more particular presidential
actions, not to general presidential authority. In this way, the authorities
enjoyed by the president are implicated in the policymaking process.

Congressional efforts to restrain presidential power are historically
infrequent and often ineffective (see, e.g., Schlesinger 1973; Moe and Howell 1999).[1] That Congress generally does not exercise that latent power is

a key theme from which we derive our core argument: specific exercises of presidential unilateralism generate congressional reaction on key issue dimensions due to anticipated *policy loss*. The policy focus of presidential power, not broad, collective constitutional objections to that power, motivate congressional responses. Constitutional handwringing by stewards of congressional power seldom motivates collective action among members to constrain executive action that challenges the constitutional order. But at the policy level, individualized incentives may lead to key moments of strategic responsiveness by Congress.

Although all presidents have acted unilaterally, the frequency with which recent presidents do so is a defining feature of the contemporary presidency (Moe and Howell 1999; Howell 2003). The conditions under which presidents pursue unilateral strategies are important to understand, especially for members of Congress competing with the executive over the placement of and control over policy. As tools of unilateralism, presidents can employ executive orders, as Obama did 276 times during his two terms and as Trump did 220 times during his single term (*Federal Register* 2021). In addition, policy memoranda, national security directives, executive agreements, policy directives, and proclamations are also among the instruments of unilateral power that presidents can deploy to make law and shift policy without the explicit consent of Congress (Moe and Howell 1999, 851).

As noted in Chapter 1, unilateralism cuts two ways and presents a paradox between two beliefs: a desire for efficacious, efficient, energetic executive leadership that features swiftness of action juxtaposed against a concomitant fear of unfettered executive power. Americans expect presidents to be agenda-setters, aggressively confronting the pressing public issues of the day (Kernell 2006; Rutledge and Larsen Price 2014). At the same time, the public is mindful of the dangers posed by a president unfettered by statutory or constitutional authority (Lowande and Rogowski 2021; Reeves and Rogowski 2015, 2016a, 2018).

In the next section, a brief review of executive power in different eras highlights features of the contemporary presidency as well as the vital distinction between policy-level disputes and constitutional contestation between branches of government.

Historical Perspectives on Presidential Authority

By itself, the brief text of Article II says little about the contemporary scope of presidential power. While considerable attention is given to presidential selection (Section 1) and impeachment (Section 4), Sections 2 and 3, which identify the powers of the office, appear both narrow and dated. Presidential powers noted in those sections address the roles for the president as commander in chief and as an agenda-setter for Congress. Presidential pardons, treaty-making, and appointment powers are also addressed. Beyond the list of carefully prescribed powers, Article II includes key provisions that grant vague levels of authority. For example, Section 1 states, "The executive power shall be vested in a President," and Section 3 requires that the president "shall take care that the laws are faithfully executed."

A Literalist View

Different interpretations of these provisions seem reasonable, given the ambiguous language. For instance, one interpretation of Section 1's vesting of executive power designates an official duty that identifies the president as the sole person who has the executive authority derived from subsequent, more explicit, language in Article II. And the Section 3 "take care" clause could be interpreted as limiting the president to enacting laws passed by Congress only in a manner that is consistent with congressional intent (Epstein and Walker 2020, 200). Moreover, given that the enumerated and implied powers are among the powers designated in Article I (the article of the Constitution focused on Congress), it might follow that Article II only grants the president the power to execute the laws passed by Congress, not to make law unilaterally. This is consistent with a literalist, or traditionalist, interpretation of the text.

As a principal adherent to this literalist approach, William Howard Taft (1916, 139–40) wrote that:

> the president can exercise no power which cannot be fairly and reasonably traced to some specific grant of power or justly implied and included within such express grant as proper and necessary to its exercise. Such specific grant must be either in the Federal Constitution or in an act of Congress passed in pursuance thereof. There is no undefined residuum of power which he can exercise [simply] because it seems to him to be in the public interest.

Taft suggests that the president has only expressed or enumerated powers, complemented by those powers that are necessary to execute the enumerated powers. For Taft, the implied powers of a president are those that are absolutely necessary to fulfill the limited constitutional duties of the office and are not independent sources of presidential power.

Prerogative Authorities

President Theodore Roosevelt offered an alternative perspective on presidential power, recognizing Article II as granting broad authority to the president. By this view, the president has enumerated, implied, and inherent powers that endow the presidency with independent authority to be an energetic "steward" of the public interest. Roosevelt (1913, 614–45) wrote:

> [M]y view was that every Executive officer in high position was a steward of the people bound actively to do all he could for the people and not to content himself with the negative merit of keeping his talents undamaged in a napkin. . . . My belief was that it was not only his right but his duty to do anything that the needs of the nation demanded.

The only restraint on executive power, he reasoned, would arise from constitutional or congressional prohibitions. This stewardship theory of executive power suggests that, like Congress in Article I, the president has all the enumerated powers identified in Article II *in addition to* those powers necessary and proper to protect the public interest. The power that the president can muster, then, can only be limited by explicit prohibitions found elsewhere in the Constitution or in statutory law. For Taft, there are implied powers only to the extent that they are directly tied to the execution of a constitutional duty. They are secondary and subservient. For Roosevelt, implied powers emanate from the office itself and from the needs of the nation.

Could dangerous circumstances affecting the national interest demand the swift efficiency of executive action beyond, or even in contravention of, the constitutional or statutory power of the president? Seventeenth-century philosopher John Locke reasoned that under certain circumstances, national emergencies can warrant expanded executive authority. Locke (1689, 11955, 136) wrote:

> [T]his power to act according to discretion for the public good, without the prescription of the law and sometimes even against it, is that which is called prerogative; for since in some governments the law-making power is not always in being and is usually too numerous, and so too slow for the dispatch requisite to execution, and because, also, it is impossible to foresee and so by laws to provide for all accidents and necessities that may concern the public, or make

such laws as will do no harm. . . . therefore there is a latitude left to the executive power to do many things of choice which the laws do not prescribe.

This approach is consistent with what scholars have called the prerogative, or emergency powers, view of executive power.

The emergency powers assumed by presidents have often been taken in the absence of or sometimes contrary to explicit congressional or constitutional authority. On many occasions, those actions were *retroactively* approved by Congress or the courts (e.g., *Prize Cases, Ex Parte Quirin*).[2] In that sense, the constitutional order accommodated executive emergency powers with *ex post* legitimization. Could congressional or judicial approvals after the fact encourage presidents to engage in ever more unilateral actions? Justice Jackson lamented the generative power that judicial approval of otherwise unconstitutional presidential actions would have for the political order in his dissent in *Korematsu v. U.S.* (1944), warning that such authority would lie "about like a loaded weapon" for future presidents to wield.[3]

Unitary Executive Theory versus Unilateralism

Although these historical eras are beyond the focus of our subsequent empirical analyses, the competing interpretations of executive authority and the circumstances that led to sweeping unilateral actions contextualize more recent events. The terrorist attacks of September 11, 2001 presented new challenges to national security that were distinct from previous challenges, and in that respect the attacks broadened presidential emergency powers once again. In response to those attacks, the Bush administration viewed the other branches as either lacking the authority to interfere with the administration's actions or having implicitly granted him the power to act unilaterally to address the crises associated with terrorism. This view of unfettered presidential power is based on a reading of Article II, Section 1, as an exclusive grant of broad unilateral powers to the president. Under this so-called *unitary executive theory*, the president has complete and exclusive executive authority. Section 1 explicitly vests "*the* executive power" in the president. If one accepts the unitary executive theory, whenever Congress demands reporting requirements from administrative agencies before promulgating rules, it encroaches upon the president's plenary authority to execute the law. Under this reading, Article II's "take care" clause obliges the president to execute laws in a manner consistent with the president's view of the laws' faithfulness to the Constitution, independent of congressional preferences or judicial interpretations.

The unitary executive theory received widespread attention during the George W. Bush presidency. Although Bush's tenure was marked by the 9/11 attack and prospect of ongoing global terrorism, adherence to unitary theory is not necessarily limited to emergencies. As we noted in Chapter 1, then-attorney general Barr (2019) held the view that the president has unitary executive powers at all times and under all circumstances. By this account, the presence of an emergency is unnecessary to justify the president's plenary authority to execute law. Unitary authority is not situational but is enduring and insulated from congressional or judicial encroachment. It is simply within the president's discretion to exercise that authority. In practice, this means that a president can ignore laws passed by Congress and disregard court decisions that limit executive power not just in dealing with national emergencies but in other policy areas as well.

Although a key feature of the unitary executive is presidential unilateralism, not all unilateral action is taken in pursuit of the unitary presidency. *Presidential unilateralism* remains distinct from the unitary executive theory in important respects. The unitary executive refers to a general approach to executive power with the president as the sole, exclusive authority with the power to implement policy. Unilateralism refers to the means of exercising executive power by acting alone to make policy, consistent with the statutory authority and discretion granted to the executive by Congress (Howell 2003; Moe and Howell 1999). All presidents act unilaterally, even if they do not adhere to the unitary executive theoretical approach.

Unitary executive theory presumes that presidents have unlimited means to deploy any tool associated with presidential unilateralism at any time. Unilateralism refers to presidents acting alone in the exercise of that power as they make and shape policy, consistent with the statutory authority and (often broad) discretion granted to the executive by Congress (e.g., Howell 2003; Moe and Howell 1999). The challenges facing constitutionalism and rule of law emerge from the unitary executive approach and not from a particular unilateral action or the tools of unilateralism. We argue that the tension between energy and dispatch in the presidency and democratic accountability is most keenly felt *not* when presidents issue executive orders, memoranda, or signing statements, but when they, for example, refuse lawful subpoenas or impound funds.

The president's ability to take particular actions is conditioned by the willingness and ability of Congress (and the courts) to constrain the president. If Congress lacks the incentive or capacity to restrain executives or if courts refuse to impose constraints (or cannot enforce their rulings), the unitary executive can pose dramatic challenges to a system of limited government under the rule of law. This is the difference between policy-level challenges (and particular expressions of policy preferences) and regime-level challenges (and challenges to the political order itself).

Whether or not presidents ground their approach to governing within the unitary executive theory, unilateral actions are here to stay (Howell and Moe 2020). As Elena Kagan wrote soon after her time in the Clinton White House as deputy assistant to the president for domestic policy, "[S]omething significant has occurred: an era of presidential administration has arrived" (2001, 2385). Indeed, given the regularity of unilateral actions, the increased party polarization over the last 40 years (McCarty, Poole, and Rosenthal 2016) is disconcerting for those concerned about heightened presidential power. In the face of extreme party polarization, the likelihood of major statutory inaction on any policy dimension is high, and the likelihood of congressional reaction to presidential unilateralism is low. This dynamic invites presidents to extend executive power through unilateral actions rather than to bargain with a gridlocked Congress over policy development and implementation. Thus, the polarized character of contemporary American politics expands the set of possible actions of presidents that resist constraint.

Today's Presidents, Today's Congresses

Recent presidents, from Clinton to Biden, have cited the vague provisions of Article II of the U.S. Constitution as bases for unilateral presidential action independent of Congress. Sometimes these unilateral actions remain unnoticed. The unnoticed unilateral actions might simply be expedient devices designed to promote efficiency or further a limited policy goal of the executive branch. Other unilateral actions establish bold initiatives that dramatically alter established policies. Whatever the nature of specific actions, unilateralism is now a cornerstone of the presidency (Howell and Moe 2020). We argue that unilateral actions are currently a defining feature of governance, not just the presidency. Unilateral actions play prominently in today's power struggles inherent in the separation of powers.

Presidents have successfully fought for greater institutional powers consistent with unitary executive theory. Congress has difficulty in challenging such actions, as members have little individualized incentive to assert collective, institutional prerogatives. Even those legislators in a political party opposed to the president face collective action problems whenever they try to enforce constitutional "guardrails" on executive power. Members also face supermajoritarian hurdles, bicameralism, and partisan divisions. However, in regard to the policy-level disputes that are rooted in unilateral actions, policy gains and losses can be acutely felt by members of Congress and congressional committees. Therefore, at the level of contestation over policy, members might be prompted to react to the president. We maintain that, regardless of the high dudgeon, challenges to the political order as rendered by unitary executive theory are usually less problematic for individual members of Congress than policy losses tied to particular deployments of the tools of unilateralism.

Members' and senators' concerns for blame avoidance can enhance presidential authority and increase the likely deployment of unilateral tools. The only way to maximize one's ability to avoid blame is to do nothing ever. Congressional silence or acquiescence during legislative struggles, as a practical matter, can enable, if not invite, independent presidential action. Recent presidents have understood their executive position as that of steward, meaning that they will not step away from the needs of the nation. Why do members of Congress express such lassitude or quiescence, especially if it enables presidential deployment of executive branch powers? The challenges of crafting legislation can be tremendous, and close involvement with legislative efforts undermines one's ability to avoid blame. Perhaps congressional inaction is less about lassitude than about holding cards "close to the chest." Members and senators can legislate (or not) recognizing the possibility of unilateral presidential action. Members of Congress can always revisit a policy to oversee or counter executive branch actions. Congressional oversight, which allows members of Congress to claim credit (McCubbins and Schwartz 1984), most clearly expresses this dynamic. Even when Congress initially remains silent and avoids blame, the struggle to develop and implement policy can still pit one branch against the other.

Presidential Unilateralism or Presidential Bargaining

Discussions of unilateralism, the unitary executive, departmentalism, and coordinate construction spread beyond academic circles as President Bush's popularity waned and the wars in Iraq and Afghanistan showed no signs of ebbing. Members of Congress from both parties, scholars, numerous groups, including the American Bar Association, and the public joined the debates regarding the appropriate powers of the president. Scholars rediscovered Rossiter's warnings of a "'constitutional dictatorship'" with a president invoking emergency powers (Tichenor 2013, 769). Unilateralism, whether through executive orders, policy memoranda, or signing statements, continues to be at the center of public and scholarly inquiry into the boundaries of executive authority. Actions by Presidents Bush, Obama, Trump, and Biden regularly refresh these debates (Potter et al. 2022).

For an example of a unilateral action, consider the swirl of activities related to the 2014 Defense Authorization Act signed into law in late December 2013 by President Obama. This act explicitly limited the president's authority to transfer detainees out of prisons in Afghanistan and Guantánamo Bay, Cuba. In particular, the act required the secretary of defense to notify Congress 30 days prior to transferring any detainee and provide evidence that those transferred would not pose a threat to U.S. national security. Within a few months of signing the act, the president released five Taliban commanders from Guantánamo Bay in exchange for army sergeant Bowe Bergdahl, a prisoner being held by the Taliban. However, in releasing the detainees, the administration did not consult with Congress pursuant to the act. In fact, Congress was not alerted to the transfer until several days *after* it occurred. For that, members and senators substantially criticized the president. This criticism included public rebukes from Senate Intelligence Committee chair Dianne Feinstein (D-CA) for not reporting the plans for the prisoner swap to her committee.

Senator Feinstein and others on Capitol Hill could have anticipated the president's actions because he had clearly articulated his objections to the reporting requirements when he signed the Defense Authorization Act of 2014. When signing the law, Obama (2013) attached a statement that rejected Congress's attempt to limit his power:

> The detention facility at Guantanamo continues to impose significant costs on the American people. I am encouraged that this Act provides the Executive greater flexibility to transfer Guantanamo detainees abroad, and look forward to working with the Congress to take the additional steps needed to close the facility. In the event that the restrictions on the transfer of Guantanamo detainees in sections 1034 and 1035 operate in a manner that violates constitutional separation of powers principles, my Administration will implement them in a manner that avoids the constitutional conflict.

Through this signing statement, President Obama acknowledged "separation of powers principles," admitted potential "constitutional conflict," and revealed his intent to disregard the provisions of the bill that obligated him to report to Congress.

Concerns about unilateral presidential actions were not always so prominent, partly because scholars viewed presidents as being tightly constrained by other political actors. Indeed, Neustadt (1990) presents a view of presidential power that is limited and contingent. Neustadt argued that presidential power is the power to persuade. Since the president is only one person, the president must *rely upon others* to achieve the policy objectives the president deems important. Yet these other actors (whether they are from another branch of government or within an executive branch agency) are not always incentivized to work with the president (Neustadt 1990). Neustadt reasons that the president can do little more than persuade the others that it is in their interest to support the president's agenda because presidents have a limited set of command tools. Thus, the president must induce cooperation from these other actors through political promises to be fulfilled later, employing varying gains from trade in crafting proposed initiatives (Kamlet and Mowery 1983; Neustadt 1990). Where Hamilton and others imagined energy and efficiency stemming from the sole occupancy of the presidency, Neustadt saw a "glorified clerkship," a lone agent enfeebled by solitude and barely able to ensure any sort of implementation.

The president's ability to persuade others comes from the prominence of the position as well as the person in it. When it comes to bargaining with the legislative branch, though, this advantage can wane. Edwards (1989) and Fett (1994) examine the degree to which the president successfully persuades Congress to cooperate with executive branch policy initiatives. Perhaps unsurprisingly, Edwards discovers that popular presidents from the same party as a majority of both houses of Congress are more likely to persuade Congress on legislative initiatives. Fett (1994) develops an original measure of the president's revealed policy priorities. The importance of a policy issue yielded a greater tendency for co-partisans in the Congress to support the president. Depending on the president being considered, cross-pressured legislators, regardless of party, could also be effectively swayed by a president's priorities.[4]

Bond and Fleisher (1990), Peterson (1990), and Ponder (2017) examine similar questions, as they, too, consider what factors affect presidential success in Congress. Bond and Fleisher (1990) and Peterson (1990) again find that the ideology of individual members of Congress predominantly explains presidential success rates. Other findings are less intuitive. For example, Bond and Fleisher (1990) discover that their measures of presidential skill do not affect overall legislative success rates and that presidential popularity is a weak predictor of presidential success with Congress. Peterson (1990) discovers that the president tends to work collaboratively with Congress on relatively minor measures, but not on major bills. On major legislation, presidents are often more assertive, and they secure policy wins most of the time (Peterson 1990). In two separate works, Edwards (1989, 2009) argues that the presidents are most effective working in the background to exploit existing opportunities and coalitions in Congress that provide a favorable environment to enact their preferred policies. Alternatively, Ponder (2017) finds that expressions of presidential unilateralism are contingent on the relative strength of presidential public leverage. Presidents with weaker leverage are more likely to centralize policymaking.

Light (1998) builds upon several themes introduced in this section. Most importantly, he suggests that the presidency is limited in several ways and that it depends on Congress for legislative and policy successes. We summarize Light's arguments, making four points. First, presidents become less effective over the course of their term. As presidents become less effective, they become more beholden to others they must work with. Second, Congress has become more competitive with the executive when it comes to agenda space. Third, Congress has become more internally complex over time, and, consequently, it has more devices available to it by which to surveil executive branch activities and initiatives. Finally, the shift in issue composition has constrained presidential effectiveness. Increasingly, issues lack readily identified constituencies, which has limited the president's ability to draw support for policy proposals from outside organized interests or groups of legislators. Consequently, Light (1998) argues that the president is in a "no win" situation when it comes to working with Congress.

Jones (1994) concurs with Light's (1998) general insight that the president operates in a competitive environment. In particular, this competitive environment is marked by a system of separated powers with the different branches regularly competing with one another for power and influence (Jones 1994). "Laws are made in a series of stages . . . and several institutions are legitimately involved" (Jones 1994, 185–186). The multiple stages and the several institutions, as described by Jones, both complicate and perpetuate the struggles over lawmaking. In sum, no formulas indicate how institutions should manage their roles in the lawmaking processes, which bolsters the competition and struggle over policymaking. Accordingly, Jones strongly cautions against analyzing the presidency as a unit by itself, instead commending the inclusion of other branches of government into analyses to capture the system of shared powers better (Jones 1994).

Congressional Delegation and Presidential Unilateralism

The congressional-delegation literature provides a bridge from the literature that emphasizes presidents' limitations and their constant bargaining and endless search for support from the more recent literature on presidential unilateralism. The congressional-delegation literature builds from the fact that no law is self-implementing. While Congress would prefer to set policy itself, the decision to delegate discretionary statutory authority to the executive branch is the result of a political transaction cost analysis undertaken by members who weigh the costs of crafting detailed legislation against the benefits of administrative expertise and reduced congressional workload (e.g., Epstein and O'Halloran 1999). Therefore, under most conditions, Congress must rely on the expertise and implementation capabilities of the executive branch. Knowing this, members and senators essentially decide two things whenever they legislate. First, what is to be delegated to the executive branch? Second, how much discretion should the enabling statute allow the executive branch as it implements policy? The delegation decision is analogous to a binary switch—authority is either delegated or it is not. Discretion is analogous to a dimmer switch. Congress can delegate and leave virtually no discretion, complete discretion, or any level of discretion between those two extremes. Whenever Congress chooses not to delegate, there is no discretion decision to make; but wherever Congress does decide to delegate, it also makes a decision regarding discretion. The degree of discretionary authority Congress chooses to delegate is shaped by a number of factors, including whether the government is divided or unified, issue salience, and policy complexity.[5]

Delegation decisions that confer broad discretion allow the president to act as a policy entrepreneur rather than just a clerk who implements law in the most prosaic, unadorned manner. Moe (1993) argues that the more energetic and entrepreneurial presidents have benefited greatly from the increasingly institutionalized office. Throughout the last eighty years of the 1900s, the office of the presidency was strengthened by an expanding set of independent capabilities. Many scholars mark the start of the emergence of greater presidential powers to the Budget and Accounting Act of 1921. With the passage of that act and the development of the

Bureau of the Budget, presidents for the first time could develop their own budget numbers rather than rely on those from Congress. Less than 20 years after the passage of the Budget and Accounting Act, the Bureau of the Budget was moved from the Department of the Treasury to the Executive Office of the President. The most prominent descendant of the bureau today is the Office of Management and Budget, which operates out of the White House.[6]

Moe (1993) and Moe and Howell (1999) use this historical backdrop to contextualize an alternative vision of the presidency, contra Neustadt (1990). They argue that the Constitution gives the president the power of chief executive and, with this position, certain formal powers (cf. Pious 1979). Moe and Howell (1999) note that the Constitution does not completely enumerate all of the powers available to the presidency. Taking advantage of those ambiguities, presidents are incentivized to push the boundaries of their Article II powers, expanding the set of presidential actions that have come to typify the modern executive branch. Thus, presidents can make many important decisions independently without having to go through Congress (Moe 1993; Moe and Howell 1999). Further, Moe (1993) and Moe and Wilson (1994) state that presidents have residual decision-making rights that give them the power to take unilateral action at their own discretion. Residual rights do not oblige a president to take unilateral actions during the policymaking process, but they do allow the president to finely tune the execution and implementation of law, thereby affecting policy.

Given this new interpretation of presidential power, perhaps a president's best strategy is *not* to bargain with other institutional actors or, at least, not to focus energy on legislative politics. Indeed, in the polarized politics marking the period of our study, members and senators might have little reason to invest too heavily in risky bargaining strategies. When facing shortcomings from a bargaining process, a president can act unilaterally to make policy and to shift the structure of politics (see, e.g., Moe 1993). By acting unilaterally, presidents shift the politics from an unfavorable defensive posture (as when bargaining or working with Congress) to one in which the president sets the agenda for others.

We accept that there are obvious limits to the effectiveness of bargaining; but presidential bargaining still occurs. Indeed, the bargaining might never fully resolve. The end of bargaining with one institutional actor, whenever and however it concludes, does not mark the end of presidential effort or presidential action. As Jones (1994) noted, lawmaking is continual. As Moe (1993) and Moe and Wilson (1994) argued, presidents have residual decision-making powers. There are unilateral actions that presidents can take to implement policy or develop new policy. Consequently, bargaining does not cease, but its form changes.

The greater attention given to the unilateral actions taken by presidents is entirely appropriate. That said, a president's deployment of one or another unilateral tool does not end the struggle over policymaking. Unilateral presidential actions whenever or however deployed are not a denouement. In the next section, we offer several examples to illustrate some of the ways in which presidents and members and senators have struggled over policymaking. We then consider ways in which members and senators anticipate certain kinds of executive branch actions and, subsequently, how they react to the actions actually taken.

Policymaking via Congressional Responsiveness to Presidential Unilateralism

In this section, we present vignettes illustrating how the ongoing struggle between the branches operates. Congressional responsiveness plays a key role in each. That is, neither the interbranch bargaining nor the president's actions concluded the struggle over policymaking. The examples highlight important debates surrounding unilateral actions and congressional responses to them.

Even in the 1800s, a time when Congress was typically deemed the most powerful branch of government, presidents acted unilaterally. President Andrew Jackson's unilateral actions illustrate key aspects of the separation of powers, particularly regarding issues of executive branch appointments and congressional delegation. After his reelection in 1832, Jackson worked to eliminate the Bank of the United States, an institution that he viewed as unconstitutional. Shortly after his reelection, the House of Representatives, with consideration of its role in controlling the "purse strings," voted to keep federal deposits in the federal bank. President Jackson disregarded the House vote and ordered the secretary of the treasury, Louis McLane, to begin removing the federal deposits and to redirect the monies into state banks (Wilentz 2007). McLane refused to transfer the deposits and was fired immediately. As a replacement for McLane, President Jackson appointed William Duane, a critic of the national bank. Shortly after his appointment as secretary of the treasury, Duane, too, was fired because he did not believe that President Jackson had the legal authority to order the removal of the deposits (Cheathem 2013).

Members of Congress argued that they delegated responsibility to the secretary of the treasury, not the president. This line of reasoning is entirely distinct from the unitary executive theory. Nonetheless, Congress believed that its delegation of authority implicated the Department of the Treasury, not the president as the embodiment and magistrate over the executive branch agencies. Therefore, members of Congress argued only the secretary could decide whether to deposit federal monies in the federal bank or in state banks (Fisher 1997, 55). The Senate responded to the president's removal of two treasury secretaries by formally censuring President Jackson. The resolution stated:

> *Resolved*, That the President, in the late Executive proceedings in relation to the public revenue, has assumed upon himself authority and power not conferred by the Constitution and laws, but in derogation of both.

As the only president to be censured by both chambers of Congress, President Jackson responded in two ways. First, he argued that he was "responsible for the entire action of the executive department" and therefore had the right to employ whomever he chose to assist him (Fisher 1997, 55). In keeping with that position, President Jackson also argued that he had the "exclusive power of removal from office" whenever he no longer wanted to assume responsibility for the actions of a particular department appointee (Fisher 1997, 55).

Second, President Jackson appointed Roger Taney as the new secretary of the treasury. Once appointed, Taney began the process of depositing government revenues from the national bank into state banks. Not to be outdone, the head of the national bank, Nicholas Biddle, acted in a manner consistent with the wishes of Congress to maintain the bank (Cheathem 2013). Biddle began restricting loans from the national bank to state banks in an effort to redirect the monies back toward the national bank. Biddle's ploy was to force the state banks to recall their own loans to remain financially solvent, hoping that the presence of a large number of weakened state banks would strengthen the rationale for the continued existence of the national bank. The struggles over the Bank of the United States illustrate how the president and Congress fought to influence and control a federal bureaucracy.

The 1800s are often considered the century of congressional government, which contrasts with the 1900s, when the presidency gained ascendancy. Our next example occurred during the transitional period between congressional dominance and presidential ascendance. Consider one of President Theodore Roosevelt's signature initiatives: environmental protection. Roosevelt worked with Congress on several laws, including the Antiquities Act of 1906.[7] This act authorized the president to:

> declare by public proclamation historic landmarks, historic and prehistoric structures, and other objects of historic or scientific interest that are situated upon the lands owned or controlled by the Government of the United States to be national monuments, and may reserve as a part thereof parcels of land, the limits of which in all cases shall be confined to the smallest area compatible with proper care and management of the objects to be protected.

But soon after the passage of the Antiquities Act, the Senate tried to limit the president's authority under this act by attaching an amendment to the agriculture appropriations bill in 1907. Senator Charles Fulton's (R-OR) amendment stipulated that the president could not create any forest reserves in six western states except through an act passed by Congress (Redekop 2012). Effectively, Senator Fulton was concerned about the amount of discretion that the Antiquities Act had given the president. Per the analogy we presented earlier in this chapter, Fulton wanted to adjust the dimmer switch. Fulton's amendment would not affect the delegation of authority inherent in the Antiquities Act, but it would limit the president's discretion under the act. After the agricultural appropriations bill passed both houses of Congress as amended by Fulton's language, Roosevelt faced the choice of vetoing or signing the bill. As amended, the 1907 Appropriations Act limited Roosevelt's discretionary authority just recently granted by the 1906 Antiquities Act.

Roosevelt delayed a formal signing decision and in the interim ordered his aides to complete the necessary paperwork to enlarge 11 forest preserves and create 21 additional forest preserves through an executive order (Redekop 2012; Skowronek 1997). To antagonize his political opponents further, all of these preserves were located in the six states covered by the Fulton amendment (Redekop 2012). Roosevelt argued that he had the authority to "do anything except what the law explicitly forbade" (Skowronek 1997, 250), and the law at the time of Roosevelt's expansion of the forest reserves did not include the 1907 Agricultural Appropriations Act because Roosevelt had not yet signed it. Roosevelt warned, "'[In]sofar as the Senate becomes a merely obstructionist body it will run the risk of seeing its power pass into other hands'" (Sollenberger and Rozell 2012, 44).

Roosevelt was formidable and decisive, but Congress responded. Members of Congress from western states joined Roosevelt's political opponents from eastern states. This new coalition scuttled the work that Roosevelt was trying to accomplish through three administrative commissions, including the Inland Waterways Commission (Skowronek 1997, 250). In addition, Congress passed a law that formally restricted the president's use of the Secret Service. Roosevelt denounced the Secret Service restrictions as "congressional protection for criminals" (Skowronek 1997, 250). Not to be outdone, the House of Representatives formally censured him for abusing the Secret Service through his remarks.

Franklin Delano Roosevelt's election to the White House occurred in 1932 during the depths of the Great Depression, and it marked another surge in presidential power. During his first several years in office, FDR worked with Congress to enact several New Deal programs, including the Works Progress Administration, Social Security, and the Federal Deposit Insurance Corporation (Neustadt 1990). However, Congress did not readily cooperate with the president when he wanted to help African Americans by acting on civil rights (Howell 2003). On July 1, 1941, the NAACP and the Urban League scheduled a mass demonstration that was expected to draw over 100,000 people to Washington, DC (Howell 2003, 131). In anticipation of this demonstration and in the face of likely congressional inaction on civil rights legislation, FDR (having consulted with the NAACP [Bracey and Meier 1991]) issued Executive Order 8802, which established the Federal Employment Practices Commission (FEPC) (Howell 2003; Morgan 1970). In part, this executive order stated that "there shall be no discrimination in the employment of workers in defense industries or government because of race, creed, color, or national origin."

In May 1943, FDR built upon his earlier order because of a crucial weakness in the original document: there was no definition of discrimination. With Executive Order 9346 FDR placed the FEPC under the control of the Office for Emergency Management (Howell 2003). This order also required that all government contracts, regardless of policy area, include a nondiscrimination clause. By placing this commission under the Office of Emergency Management, this executive order provided a viable route to resolve discrimination complaints.

Initially, FDR funded this commission with discretionary funds because of congressional opposition to civil rights initiatives at the time and, in doing so, bypassed the normal appropriations process (Howell 2003; Nathan 1969, 88). With the issuance of Executive Order 9346, Congress became much more involved in pushing back against the president. While

Congress could not pass legislation that dissolved the FEPC outright, Senator Richard B. Russell (D-GA) took another route: the appropriations process (Nathan 1969, 87–88). To counter the president's use of discretionary funds without congressional approval, Russell introduced an amendment to the Independent Offices Appropriation Act of 1940. Russell's amendment "required congressional approval for all funds for agencies established by executive order and operational for more than one year" (Howell 2003, 132). In June 1944, Congress passed this amendment as part of H.R. 4070, and the president signed it into law in July. Ultimately, this amendment led to the FEPC being disbanded in 1946 due to a lack of funds being appropriated by Congress (Howell 2003). FDR, one of the most powerful and popular presidents, suffered a key policy loss due to the continued pushback on his unilateral efforts from members of Congress.

The Delegation Dilemma and Congressional Controls

The illustrations in the preceding section highlight distinctions between the specific and the general. Members and senators opposed to unilateral actions were typically spurred to action because of the policy focus of the unilateral action rather than the action itself. That is, the focus of the concerns raised in opposition to a presidential unilateral action was on the national bank, states' forest reserves, or civil rights for African Americans, rather than the aggrandizement of presidential influence due to the deployment of a unilateral tool. No modern president has embraced a limited view of presidential powers, but when Congress takes offense at unilateral actions, it is because of the policy target of the unilateral tool rather than the tool itself.

Even the most assertive presidents might feel they are simply fulfilling constitutional mandates in partnership with Congress. After all, in addition to the president's expressed and implied powers, Article II confers on the president the authority to "take Care that the laws be faithfully executed." This suggests that by constitutional design, the president has the obligation to execute the laws passed by Congress, and by extension, Congress has an interest in providing the executive branch with the means by which to do so. This is the source of what is known as the delegated powers of the president—the powers that presidents have to fulfill congressional will with respect to specific statutes. For example, when Congress passes a law and the president signs it (or when Congress overrides a president's veto), the executive branch is tasked with "faithfully executing" that law—that is, implementing the policy.

Very often Congress cannot know with certainty how best to implement a particular measure or have the means by which to do so. Some policy areas are highly complex and require the technical expertise of policy experts. Consider, for instance, the complexities tied to regulating technology, food, drug, pesticide, vehicle, or even workplace safety. The lawyers in Congress probably know less about drug safety than the chemists, doctors, and pharmacists working in the executive branch agencies. Other legislation might be less complex, but the scale might be so large that Congress simply cannot write detailed legislation for every circumstance. Establishing rates and standards for the interstate shipment of goods is only limited in scope by the number of the types of goods being shipped. Whether due to scale or complexity, executive branch agencies are given the responsibility to write regulatory law that "fills in the details" and implements the general provisions of legislation.

The fact that Congress can delegate its legislative power to another branch of government is seemingly inconsistent with James Madison's argument in *Federalist #47*. Madison wrote, "The accumulation of powers, legislative, executive, or judiciary, in the same hands, whether of one, a few, or many, and whether hereditary, self-appointed, or elective, may justly be pronounced the very definition of tyranny." Madison continues, quoting Montesquieu, from whom the Framers borrowed in developing the separation of powers, "There can be no liberty where the legislative and executive powers are united in the same person, or body of magistrates." But Madison continued in the same essay, stating that Montesquieu:

> did not mean that these departments ought to have no *partial agency* in, or no *control* over, the acts of each other. His meaning . . . can amount to no more than this, that where the whole power of one department is exercised by the same hands which possess the whole power of another department, the fundamental principles of a free constitution are subverted.

The second quotation from *Federalist #47* is more nuanced than the first. The first quotation is often used when writers introduce rationales for the separation of powers in the United States. The second quotation admits the possibility of *partial agency*. That is, Congress could delegate *some* authority to the executive branch and the executive branch could fine-tune legislation *within limits*.

The delegation of power appears to run afoul of the ancient legal maxim, "A power once delegated cannot be redelegated." That legal principle, embodied in the so-called nondelegation doctrine, suggests that Congress may not cede to the executive branch its rightful legislative power to maintain democratic accountability. The idea is that legislators, as the people's representatives, have been given power to be held in trust. If they then redelegate their legislative power to another institution, the accountability for the actions taken pursuant to that power is unclear. Are the legislators responsible? Are the designees responsible? Even if those responsible for the policies are identifiable, it is not clear how the people can hold them to account for the actions they take. If sovereignty resides with the people and if their representatives, who have the constitutional authority to write law, redelegate that lawmaking authority to others in the executive branch, then the people no longer have the direct means to remove the de facto lawmakers for failure to respond to public demands. In extreme situations, the elected representatives have delegated lawmaking to unelected executive branch officials. Though the principle of nondelegation is important for democratic governance and accountability, the Constitution is silent on whether Congress is permitted to delegate its powers. In fact, since the New Deal era, the principle of nondelegation has not constrained Congress from ceding its legislative power in key areas of policy.

In 1991, the U.S. Supreme Court resolved that the nondelegation doctrine "does not prevent Congress from seeking assistance, within proper limits, from the coordinate branches. Thus, Congress does not violate the Constitution merely because it delegates in broad terms, leaving a certain degree of discretion to executive or judicial actors" (*Touby v. U.S.* 1991). But what are the "proper limits"? The Court has placed few restrictions on Congress as it delegates. Generally, and with few exceptions, the courts have allowed Congress to delegate broad authority to the executive and judicial branches if Congress does so as a means of exercising its own legislative power. That is, if Congress can legislate in a particular area of policy, it can also delegate in that area. As long as Congress "laid down by legislative act an intelligible principle to which the person or body authorized to take such action is directed to conform," the delegation of power is permissible (*J.W. Hampton, Jr. & Co. v. U.S.*, 1928).

This "intelligible principle" standard that the Court articulated in *Hampton* can be capacious, permitting very broad grants of discretion to bureaucratic agencies in the executive branch to implement laws. The enabling legislation for many executive branch agencies and independent commissions includes broad delegations of legislative power, such as to "set just and reasonable rates" or "regulate in the public interest."[8] In a series of cases in 1935 and 1936, the Court struck two impermissible delegations of legislative power, but more recent Court rulings have redefined the nondelegation doctrine (*West Virginia v. Environmental Protection Agency* (2022) and *Loper Bright Enterprises v. Raimondo* (2024)). The president's role and the role of executive branch agencies in shaping and implementing legislation had grown apace with the broad grants of delegated power. But by overturning *Chevron* (1984), *Loper Bright* (2024) limits the degree of judicial deference afforded executive branch agencies as they use their own expertise to promulgate rules implementing statutes. It is important to note, however, that in *Loper Bright*, the Court reaffirmed its commitment to *Skidmore* deference. Unlike *Chevron* deference, which obligates courts to defer to agency interpretation of vague or ambiguous statutes, *Skidmore* deference invites courts to give due respect to an agency's interpretation when the agency demonstrates sound reasoning, consistency with past practice, "and all those factors which give it power to persuade, if not power to control." (Jackson, Robert H. in *Skidmore v Swift & Co*, 1944) Nonetheless, a likely consequence of *Loper Bright* (2024) will be to firmly insert courts into virtually all areas related to delegation.

Congress derives its power from enumerated, implied, and inherent powers, the full range of areas in which Congress may legislate (and therefore, presumably, delegate) is expansive. It is virtually impossible to legislate in a broad, more complex array of policy areas without also delegating in those areas, but after *Loper Bright* (2024) delegated authority must be increasingly specific. Presuming such specification is possible, any expansion of congressional activity concurrently expands the executive power over those same policy areas. Put differently, as the domain of congressional policymaking grows, so too does the domain of policy areas in which Congress delegates, which ensures that presidential control over those areas expands as well. As noted, post-*Loper Bright* the role of the courts in policymaking is also enhanced.

Why would Congress willingly give up control over policy outcomes to another branch of government? Certainly, members of Congress have an interest in making good policy (Fenno 1978), taking positions on key issues, and claiming credit for those policies when seeking reelection (e.g., Mayhew 1974). Therefore, delegating discretion to agencies to write regulations and implement policies must serve the self-interest of legislators. Political scientists have explored this decision to delegate extensively. Many scholars agree that members of Congress would prefer to write detailed legislation themselves, ensuring that the implementation of that legislation would not "drift" away from members' policy preferences. However, most of the time members lack the resources, information, and capacity to write such detailed legislation constraining the implementation of policy.

Technological advances often require the specialization and expertise that members of Congress typically lack, so they must turn to those in the bureaucracy with informational advantages. In addition, because legislators are driven by reelection, the degree to which their constituents care about and pay attention to a particular issue matters. Therefore, issue salience, which indicates constituents' awareness, interacts with complexity. When issues are less salient, politicians are more likely to delegate broad discretionary authority. Conversely, when an issue is highly salient and less complex, members' interest in delegating declines due to heightened awareness and concern among constituents (Gormley 1986). Members of Congress perform a "political transaction cost analysis" to determine the value of delegating broad discretion or writing detailed legislation themselves (e.g., Epstein and O'Halloran 1999). The result is a division of labor, shared with the executive branch, in which congressional delegations of discretion can serve the interests of members of Congress under conditions of uncertainty, fluidity, and incomplete information.

As Congress delegates, though, its members have several means by which they can retain some control over the action of the executive branch agencies. Congress can write legislation with detailed substantive controls to constrain actions of the executive branch even before any implementation occurs. Although they might not offer policy details in legislation, legislators affix detailed procedures to constrain executive branch implementation. McCubbins, Noll, and Weingast (1989) highlighted the importance of several *ex ante* controls that are regularly deployed by legislators. Statutory limitations and procedural requirements within the Federal Register Act, the Administrative Procedures Act, the Freedom of Information Act, various notice and comment requirements, additional reporting requirements, and subsequent amendments tied to the aforementioned acts all aim to control bureaucratic agencies by increasing the cost of bureaucratic noncompliance. In creating or otherwise benefiting from most of these requirements, Congress can more effectively ensure executive branch compliance with congressional preferences (e.g., Bawn 1995; MacDonald 2007).

There are also *ex post* controls. For example, Congress also has the "power of the purse," which affects the appropriation of funds to the executive. In that respect, executive agencies rely on Congress for both their reauthorizations and their annual appropriation bills, without which agencies have neither the authority nor the funding to act.[9] With limitation riders, Congress can further restrict the areas or manner in which funds are spent (Fisher 2001; MacDonald 2010). Congress can also impose "sunset provisions," limiting the longevity of the measure to a predetermined period of time. If the agency with authority to implement the measure is faithful to congressional preference in its implementation, presumably, the delegation would be reauthorized when it would otherwise be due to sunset.

Importantly, Congress can also oversee the agencies charged with implementing policy. Congressional oversight takes many forms, but it usually involves formal hearings in which members of the House or Senate subcommittees or committees with jurisdiction over the agencies hear from agency leadership about the agent's actions (or inactions), policies, or other key topics of interest to members of Congress. Perhaps the most controversial deployment of congressional oversight occurs when reporting requirements in legislation obligate agencies to update Congress on their regulatory activities and authorize Congress to veto agency decisions. The constitutionality of these "legislative veto provisions" was successfully challenged in *Immigration and Naturalization Service v. Chadha* (1983), but Congress continues to incorporate detailed reporting requirements in bills.

One of the newest tools of *ex post* congressional control has similarities to the legislative veto. Whereas the legislative veto typically operated at the congressional committee level, the 1996 Congressional Review Act (CRA) requires majority votes in both chambers of Congress. The CRA gives Congress 60 days to rescind an agency regulation by a majority vote on a Resolution of Disapproval in both chambers. The effect of the Resolution of Disapproval is not only the revocation of the offending rule, as it also prohibits the agency from promulgating a substantially similar rule in the future. This powerful tool of congressional control over agencies remained relatively dormant for several years until the Trump administration and Republicans in both chambers of Congress deployed it to revoke a series of rules promulgated at the very end of the Obama administration. From 1996 to 2017, the CRA had been deployed just one time to target a Clinton administration rule regarding OSHA standards. Early in 2017, Congress used the CRA to strike 13 Obama-promulgated rules within President Trump's first 60 days in office.

It is virtually impossible for Congress to avoid delegating authority to the executive branch. The executive branch therefore has partial agency in the development of the details required to implement policy. The partial agency, to use Madison's terminology, that the president has over lawmaking does not preclude members and senators from monitoring the executive branch implementation of policy.

Conclusion

As dire circumstances arise, citizens and government officials expect and demand energy and dispatch from the president. Congress faces a quandary with respect to the executive branch. As Congress delegates authority to the executive branch through the lawmaking process, the president is given greater authority to act. But failing to delegate does not preclude presidential action, especially as dire circumstances arise. Further, if presidents are invigorated by the tremendous potential implied by their energy and dispatch, they might direct their efforts to a wider and wider array of circumstances, including those far from dire. The exercise of presidential authority, especially as reflected in unilateral presidential actions, clearly implicates issues of democratic accountability and control. As Howell and Moe (2020, 194) write, "No aspect of executive politics invites more controversy than the exercise of unilateral powers." When a president says, as Trump did, "Article II says I can do anything I want" (CNN 2019), other political actors, citizens, and scholars and journalists reconsider the limits of presidential powers, even if they disagree about where those limits are and struggle to constrain the actual exercise of those powers. In *Trump v. United States* (2024), the Supreme Court focused ever greater attention on the issue, but it did not fully determine the limits on presidential powers in a wide array of potential circumstances.

In the face of unilateral powers, how can democratic accountability be managed? In *The Spirit of Laws*, Montesquieu argued that a separation of branches would prevent the concentration of dangerous amounts of power and influence in a single body. As noted in the previous section, Madison displayed a nuanced reading of Montesquieu. In *Federalist #47*, Madison argued that the separate branches would operate with "partial agency in" the other branches. In *Federalist #48*, Madison wrote that "the political apothegm [separation of powers] . . . does not require that the legislative, executive, and judiciary departments should be wholly unconnected with each other." Put more bluntly, wholesale reliance on a witty aphorism offers little guidance for the structuring, let alone the functioning, of a democratically founded government.

By the end of *Federalist #48*, Madison imagined how constitutional limits on paper might relate to constitutional limits in practice: "The conclusion which I am warranted in drawing . . . is, that *a mere demarcation on parchment* of the constitutional limits of the several departments, *is not a sufficient guard* against those encroachments which lead to a tyrannical concentration of all the powers of government in the same hands" (emphasis added). One hundred sixty-five years after Madison, Justice Jackson wrote that the Constitution "enjoins upon the branches separateness but interdependence, autonomy but reciprocity. Presidential powers are not fixed, but fluctuate, depending on their disjunction or conjunction with those of Congress" (Jackson, concurring in *Youngstown Sheet & Tube Co. v. Sawyer*, 1952). Justice Jackson seems to have embodied the nuances in Madison's views on separated branches.

In the absence of accepted formulas dictating boundaries for the three branches of government, we are left with fluid lawmaking and policy implementation processes in which there are regular contestations over policy. Fiorina (1982a) argued that complete congressional control of the placement of a policy is limited by a mismatch of capabilities and incentives. This mismatch occurs because Congress's lack of a centralizing control mechanism over the bureaucracy is a function of Congress's own decentralized institutional structure (1982a, 345). In this decentralized context, the electoral incentive to be mindful of policy drift on specific policy dimensions—and not broad, collective goals—drives members' behavior. Conversely, the president has the incentive to control national policy across dimensions, but lacks the specific mechanisms to do so. Congressionally delegated authority exists only within limits, and congressional monitoring is ongoing. Additionally, independent agencies, and even executive branch agencies, have the means to insulate themselves from presidential control. The president, in Fiorina's metaphor, is an admiral without command of the vessels in the fleet. Congressional committees are in command of the ships, but the ships do not resemble a fleet acting in concert.

How can Congress command the ships without an overriding or coordinating policy goal? The committee system and the decentralization of Congress play a particularly important role. Our current era of politics is marked by heightened presidential power, an expansive federal bureaucracy, and citizens' enhanced expectations of positive government. Although Congress cannot control multidimensional policies across any broad range of areas, we contend that members have the incentive to be attuned to specific policy dimensions of multidimensional policies as those policies move toward implementation. Even when broad authority has been delegated, Congress continues to oversee and contest policymaking via *ex ante* and *ex post* controls. Although often denigrated, members and senators appreciate the importance of congressional oversight. Muller and Boller (2022) argue that "the 'fire-alarm' analogy is misleading" because it overlooks the incentives for "congressional entrepreneurs" to monitor implementation and policymaking in the executive branch.[10] As we have seen in the earlier sections of this chapter, members and senators do monitor and respond to formal statements of policy made by the president.

Textbook presentations of the separation of powers often suggest entirely separate realms of operation for the three branches. These simplified presentations ignore Madison's views on the separation of the branches. Such presentations also wholly fail to recognize the roles and impact of congressional delegation and oversight.[11] During the policymaking process, Congress regularly delegates authority to the executive branch. Such delegation enhances presidential powers because it attaches additional congressional authority to the existing constitutional prerogatives of the president. Presidents enjoy greater latitude to act when Congress delegates authority to the executive branch. Of course, even in the absence of congressional delegation, presidents still maintain their independent constitutional powers, but for many of the president's powers there are clear claims to concurrent authority.

The role of unilateral presidential actions is best understood in light of the policymaking process. Each unilateral action we examine in this work has a policy implication. Managing democratic accountability in the face of unilateral presidential actions will only occur within the realms of the policymaking processes. Inevitably, the executive, legislative, and judicial branches contend with one another for public policymaking power. Modern congresses have worked with the president in the policymaking process, but equally important, they have responded to the actions taken by presidents. Bargaining alone is insufficient to explain presidential success across many policies. Indeed, there is ample evidence of unilateralism in the modern presidency, even as presidents may bargain with Congress on certain issues. Presidents "go it alone" on many policies, but as they do so, they may invite congressional reaction on specific issue dimensions. We contend that the president is more than a bargaining agent relative to Congress, but less than the unilateral policymaker that some portray the office to be. Similarly, Congress is more than the president's lapdog, but less than the final arbiter when it comes to lawmaking and public policy.

In the next chapter, we use a spatial model to show how presidents can react to either limited delegated authority or silence, delay, and obstruction within Congress. One implication of the model is that when structuring legislation, members of Congress may effectively invite presidential unilateralism as a way to avoid hard votes on multidimensional policy proposals.

THREE

A Theory of Strategic Responsiveness

> [P]residents care intensely about securing changes that promote
> their institutional power, while legislators typically do not. They
> are unlikely to oppose incremental increases in the relative power
> of presidents unless the issue in question directly harms the special
> interests of their constituents.
>
> —Moe quoted in Howell 2003, 111

Formal models of institutions highlight the roles of actors' preferences and
opportunities. The notion that political actors have policy preferences is
widely held, and our work follows these long-established traditions.[1] Generally, scholars delimit strategic opportunities in a formal model by "the
rules of the game," largely structured by the institution being modeled.
Institutional rules might determine jurisdictional claims for committees
or affect the distribution of agenda-setting power across political actors. A
long line of literature shows how institutional rules can affect the distribution of proposal power, the influence of agenda control, and the determi-
nation of policy adjustments, including the resistance to policy change or
gridlock.[2]

In this chapter, we consider both institutional rules *and* behavioral tendencies when we discuss opportunities for legislators and the president.
Preferences and institutional rules can affect behavioral tendencies, but
behavioral tendencies can also stand apart because institutional rules do
not readily constrain all behavioral tendencies. Consider the selection from
Moe at the start of this chapter. One reason legislators do not regularly

oppose presidential encroachments is that legislative undertakings typically require coordinated efforts that are prone to freeriding. Freeriding is a behavioral tendency with a strong rational underpinning. Institutional rules and structures can affect freeriding, but they are unlikely to eliminate the motivations underlying freeriding or the practice thereof. Even in the absence of observed freeriding, the underlying tendencies toward freeriding remain.

Position-taking by legislators includes blame avoidance and vote explanation, which are the two behavioral tendencies of most interest to us in this chapter. The importance of vote explanation and blame avoidance for understanding legislators' behaviors is well established. Legislators appreciate blame avoidance, as they are concerned about how they can explain their legislative activities to constituents (e.g., Fenno 1978; Bianco 1994; Grose et al. 2014; Denzau, Riker, and Shepsle 1985). As presented by Mayhew (1974, 132), position-taking underscores that "electoral payment is for positions rather than for [policy] effects." Additionally, when credit-claiming opportunities for large legislative packages are rare, legislators avail themselves of opportunities for blame avoidance and vote explanation. Blame avoidance and vote explanation persist regardless of the institutional structures in force (committee systems, agenda procedures, etc.) and regardless of the distribution of legislators' ideal points in the legislative body. In those senses, the behavioral tendencies, vote explanation and blame avoidance, stand apart from other important elements of a legislature's makeup.

In Chapters 1 and 2, we highlighted two competing views of presidential unilateralism. Advocates of the unitary theory of the executive see the president as an equal player in all ways to the other branches, including, for instance, in determining whether a provision of a legislative act is constitutional. Critics of the unitary executive theory fear presidential overreach and the associated imbalance in the separation of powers. Sometimes the expressed concerns of overreach depend upon who holds the presidency and what policies are at stake. In the spatial model developed in this chapter, we consider how preferences and opportunities affect the countervailing dynamics of policymaking and policy implementation. In particular, we connect policymaking to the need of legislators to explain their legislative activities to their constituents via blame avoidance and vote explanation (e.g., Fenno 1978).

Concerns for blame avoidance and vote explanation create an overall status quo bias that is grounded behaviorally at the individual level. Earlier references to a status quo bias in legislatures might note that at the final stage of a congressional agenda, the final proposal must face the status quo. Other references might note how large gridlock intervals favor the status quo.

Extant models of policy gridlock focus on the ways that *competing preferences* can create policy stalemates (e.g., Krehbiel 1991). Here we note that legislators' concerns around blame avoidance and vote explanation create *individual-level* motivations to resist change to a status quo. The possibility of regret is so prominent that decision theorists have formalized a notion of a regret premium (e.g., Bell 1983) and have introduced regret as an argument in utility functions (e.g., Bell 1982). Here each vote on a legislative proposal embodies subsequent decisions related to blame avoidance and vote explanation. To maintain as much flexibility as possible when it comes to blame avoidance and vote explanation, legislators hesitate to support proposals that force key constituent groups to make trade-offs or compromises.[3] As noted in a 2021 *Roll Call* op-ed, "[P]oliticians rarely regret voting 'no'" (Rothenberg 2021). Our spatial model illustrates how presidents can react with unilateral efforts in the face of status quo bias among legislators.

Tools of Unilateralism

The tools of presidential unilateralism, and in particular signing statements, memoranda, and executive orders, reveal that bill signings do not solely affirm legislative efforts or conclude the struggle over policymaking. For example, presidents' signing statements often assert flexibility in policy implementation. Pious's (2009, 459) concerns are clear, as for modern presidents:

> constitutional architecture has not become more explicit, and presidential power has not been better enumerated, defined, or confined. Instead, presidents have been able to exploit the silences, ambiguities, and incomplete constructions and have vastly expanded their prerogative powers, even at times developing novel interpretations of what seemed to be routine.

In such instances, a presidential signing statement highlights the *start* of the struggle over policy implementation. In his portrayal of the presidency in a separated system, Jones noted that "lawmaking is continuous" and that there is "no formula for presidents' participation in lawmaking" (1994, 183, 182).

Recall that signing statements allow presidents to convey their personal views of the legislation that has just been signed into law. Although some signing statements are entirely anodyne, used to thank supporters or highlight key components of the measure that reflect the president's policy preferences, many times, a statement includes the president's objections to specific provisions of the statute, such as the amount of an appropriation or the inclusion of procedural requirements during implementation. Sometimes the statements go beyond criticism by revealing the president's intentions not to comply with specific provisions of the law, to interpret the provision as advisory, or to indicate that the implementation of the offending provision(s) will proceed in a manner consistent with presidential preference.

Cooper (2002) details numerous instances when presidents used signing statements to move policy in a manner that would not have survived legislative scrutiny. In the context of the 2005 Detainee Treatment Act, Kelley and Marshall note that "where the president could not get Congress to budge, he used the signing statement to turn a policy loss into a win" (2008, 2) by directing agency implementation without regard to congressional preferences. In Kelly and Marshall's (2008) unidimensional setting, policy losses for one actor yield policy gains for another as in a zero-sum conflict. Indeed, in any one-dimensional model, policy struggles quickly become zero-sum conflicts once the most extreme policies have been addressed.[4]

In the next section, we present a spatial model of policy development with presidential-congressional interactions explicitly allowing the president to take unilateral actions. After presenting a brief review of one-dimensional models of congressional-presidential interactions, we develop a multidimensional model of those same interactions. In our multidimensional spatial model, unilateral tools allow presidents to disaggregate complex, multidimensional legislation by taking unilateral actions along specific issue dimensions. In particular, we analyze situations where the disaggregation of multidimensional policies via presidential unilateralism may secure policy gains for both Congress and the president.

In this way, control mechanisms attached to one branch can yield a positive-sum benefit for another branch. Some unilateral policy adjustments can yield Pareto improvements, meaning that no one is made worse off and at least one actor is made better off. However, in a multidimensional setting, Pareto adjustments can still lead to policy losses along *some* issue dimensions as policy gains are made along other issue dimensions. To wit: adjustments unilaterally made by a president can trade policy gains on some dimensions with losses on others. Under such a situation, even if made better off, a legislator might still need to explain the policy trade-offs to constituents who are more focused on specific issue losses rather than overall multidimensional policy gains. Being made better off overall does not imply that no one has suffered a policy loss on *some* issue dimension. As a result, legislators resist some but not all unilateral actions through *ex post* oversight activity.

Legislators' Choices in the Face of Unilateral Actions

The vast majority of spatial models portraying legislatures or the separation of powers are unidimensional. Unidimensional models are relatively straightforward, and they offer powerful visualizations. In Figure 3.1, there are three key actors: the median legislator, L_m, a veto pivot, V, and the president, P. The placements of L_m, V, and P in Figure 3.1 indicate their ideal points along the issue dimension. The underlying presumption is that policies yield utility and that some policies are better for a legislator than others. Given that an actor's utility simply reflects her preferences, her ideal policy must yield her maximal utility. Moving away from one's ideal point, either to the left or to the right, creates a utility loss for them. As is common for spatial models, we presume that actors have single-peaked and symmetric utility functions. With those assumptions, it is relatively easy (and helpful) to establish preferred-to-sets once we identify an ideal point and a status quo. A preferred-to-set indicates those alternatives that some actor prefers to a status quo. For instance, in Figure 3.1, $P_V(SQ)$, the preferred-to-set for V given the status quo SQ, spans SQ and SQ'. The ideal point, V, is equidistant from SQ and SQ' by construction because V's utility function is symmetric. Preferred-to-sets illustrate a set of choice options for players. No actor willingly submits to alternatives that make her worse off, so choices beyond $P_V(SQ)$ would fail to secure V's support.

Using just two actors, C_m and V, to represent a legislative body can appear sparse, but Figure 3.1 allows us to introduce Black's (1958) median voter theorem (BMVT). Given BMVT, we know that the median legislator's ideal point cannot be majority rule defeated by any other legislative proposal. The median legislator combined with the legislators to her left comprise a majority. Similarly, if she joins their cause, she and the legislators to her right also constitute a majority. The median legislator is sitting in the catbird seat, as the late sportscaster Red Barber would say. As such, the median legislator's ideal point is the only undefeatable alternative

$$\mathbf{C_m} \qquad\qquad \mathbf{SQ`} \qquad \mathbf{V} \qquad \mathbf{SQ} \qquad \mathbf{P}$$

Figure 3.1. A One-Dimensional Spatial Model with Veto Bargaining

in the legislature. Rather than portraying every legislator in the chamber, BMVT justifies highlighting only the median legislator.

How does veto bargaining come into play? P would like to move SQ to the right, but C_m would like to move SQ to the left. One might imagine gridlock, but the presence of the veto and the override allows C_m to offer any alternative within V's preferred-to-set. Policies to the left of SQ` would be vetoed by P, and because those policies are beyond $P_V(SQ)$ the veto would not be overridden because V prefers SQ to points to the left of SQ`. If C_m offers alternatives within $P_V(SQ)$, the president might veto them, but those vetoes will be overridden because V prefers anything within $P_V(SQ)$ to the status quo SQ. Considering all the veto-proof alternatives within $P_V(SQ)$, C_m prefers the leftmost alternative at SQ`. Given the array of preferences and the "rules of the game," the veto override yields policy gains to C_m.

If we add unilateral actions to the institutional rules, the situation in Figure 3.1 changes. The president could use a signing statement, memorandum, or executive order to affect the implementation of the legislation passed. As affected by unilateral actions, the final policy would shift back toward the president's ideal point somewhere in the red zone highlighted in Figure 3.2.

How far would the president shift policy? Scholars have argued that it would depend on the costs and effectiveness of congressional oversight as well as the costs associated with passing newer, more detailed legislation that yields less discretion to the president (e.g., Ainsworth et al. 2012; Kelley and Marshall 2008). Given the array of preferences in Figure 3.2, with unilateral tools, the president regains policy ground that had been lost in the presence of the override. The one-dimensional spatial model illustrates the policy costs for Congress when the president employs unilateral tools and zero-sum conflicts dominate the interbranch relations. Of course, the one-dimensional model cannot illustrate the trade-offs actors face in the presence of a multidimensional policy space. Without policy trade-offs, there are no roles for blame avoidance or vote explanation because every policy adjustment is restricted to be zero-sum. Also, unidimensional models cannot illustrate the aggregation and disaggregation of distinct policies into complex legislation. And, of course, very few legislative packages are one-dimensional.

C_m		$SQ^`$	V	SQ	P

Figure 3.2. A One-Dimensional Spatial Model with Veto Bargaining and Unilateral Tools

Blame Avoidance and Vote Explanation
When Politics Is Multidimensional

Although we adopt the long-held notion that legislators must explain their votes, more precision is needed for the expression. To wit: legislators must explain their support for a multidimensional policy package to separate audiences that are themselves focused on specific issue dimensions of the new, multidimensional legislation. Elected officials seldom need to explain an entire statute. Indeed, it would be hard for a legislator to master all the intricacies of all legislation. Whether they have mastered the legislation at hand or not, legislators lack the time to explain all the policy trade-offs inherent in a complex piece of legislation, and over-explanation is typically a losing proposition for legislators (e.g., Bianco 1994). Instead, legislators must explain any narrow aspect of a statute that a particular audience finds troublesome. Simple explanations are generally preferred to complex ones.

A key *behavioral* claim that we introduce in our model is that legislators pursue alternatives that allow them to explain their support for *discrete* elements of a multidimensional bill to select audiences, often called attentive publics in the congressional literature. Attentive publics embrace traceability, linking legislator's actions to legislative policies (Arnold 1990), which prompts vote explanation and blame avoidance. Suppose scholars considered these behavioral tendencies, blame avoidance and vote explanation, collectively and incorporated them into the canonical spatial models of legislative decision-making. Diermeier and Krehbiel argue that scholars of institutions should first "define and hold fixed *behavioral postulates*" (2003, 127). How might the canonical spatial model change with a behavioral postulate built from blame avoidance and vote explanation?

Legislators often employ mechanisms that minimize concerns about blame by guarding against the disaggregation problem. For example, amendments to peel off certain goods or sectors from a tariff bill are frequently disallowed a priori, and budget amendments are tightly controlled by the party leadership. When a legislator's hands are tied, it is easier to avoid blame. Mechanisms used to limit discretion often impede the disaggregation of a compromise policy bundle (e.g., Weaver 1986). That is, an entire set of tariffs, military base closures, or proposed federal pay raises must be voted up or down, having these mechanisms operate as a type of closed rule that eliminates the ability to alter the policy package. Legislators establish mechanisms or external bodies, such as the Base Realignment and Closure commission, to guard against the disaggregation problem, which allows legislators to avoid blame.

The blame avoidance literature in political science dates to at least the 1980s, when Weaver (1986) and McCubbins and Schwartz (1984) wrote about legislators' desires to avoid blame. More recently, Curry and Lee (2020, ch. 6) assess such legislator practices empirically. With blame avoidance, the upside is limited, but the downside is eliminated. Blame avoidance does not eliminate policy change, but it does create a status quo bias. Tversky and Shafir write that "when one option is better than another in all essential respects, there is no conflict and choice is easy. However, when each option has significant advantages and disadvantages, people often experience conflict that makes choice aversive and compels . . . delay" (1992, 358). These matters are more complicated if the advantages and disadvantages occur along separate issue dimensions and affect different groups of constituents. On the individual level, blame avoidance and a concern for vote explanation limit one's willingness to engage in policy trade-offs. Our references to literature from behavioral economics and political psychology do not mean that we reject the basic model of rational choice. Rather, we mean to take behavioral tendencies seriously and strive to incorporate two types of behavioral tendencies into the canonical spatial model.[5] In the end, we develop and employ a stronger definition of rationality.[6]

When trade-offs are complicated, legislators' concerns about vote explanation and blame avoidance undergird a status quo bias. When legislation is passed, explaining a vote often means explaining one's support for a narrow slice of a larger piece of legislation. Trade-offs generally imply compromise, and Anderson, Butler, and Harbridge-Yong (2020) highlight how difficult compromise is when electoral concerns are prominent.[7] Arnold (1990, 76) suggests that the "potential for retrospective voting keeps legislators worried about the effects they produce, or at least about those [effects] that citizens might trace back to legislators' actions." The most attentive publics know specific aspects of legislation but not all aspects of legislation, and voters can only trace what they know. Legislators, therefore, must be prepared to justify particular aspects of legislation to different audiences.

A Multidimensional Spatial Model

For our spatial model, we focus on two actors, a president, P, and a legislator, L, in a two-dimensional policy space. Actors' preferences are reflected in their utility functions, which are single-peaked and symmetric. The opportunities to affect policy are determined by the rules of the game and behavioral postulates. As noted earlier, those behavioral postulates include the strong desire by L to avoid blame and readily explain votes.

Suppose the president and legislature, P and L, bargain over policy in a two-dimensional policy space. The utility functions for P and L maintain the standard assumptions, so their preferences are separable. Separability simply means that an actor's preferences on one issue dimension are unaffected by the policy levels in other issue dimensions. Our assumptions about the utility functions for P and L ensure that each actor has circular indifference curves. An actor's ideal point lies at the center of her indifference curves. Any two points on the same indifference curve yield the same utility to the associated actor. Any points on smaller indifference curves yield greater utility than points on larger indifference curves. As in the one-dimensional case, distance is straightforwardly associated with utility. The closer a policy is to an actor's ideal point, the higher the utility it yields for that actor. Of course, as with the one-dimensional models, an ideal point for an actor yields the highest utility.

Let $\mathbf{x} \in R^2$ represent a policy in a two-dimensional space. The set of points that P and L prefer to $\mathbf{x}$ are defined by their preferred-to-sets $\boldsymbol{P}_P(\mathbf{x})$ and $\boldsymbol{P}_L(\mathbf{x})$. To distinguish the separate dimensions of $\mathbf{x}$, we use $\boldsymbol{P}_P(x_1)$ and $\boldsymbol{P}_L(x_1)$ to define policies that P and L prefer to $\mathbf{x} = (x_1, .)$. That is, given $\mathbf{x}$, $\boldsymbol{P}_i(x_1)$ defines the set of policies that i prefers to $\mathbf{x}$ "along the x_1 axis." $\boldsymbol{P}_i(x_2)$ defines the set of policies that i prefers to $\mathbf{x}$ "along the x_2 axis." We use $\boldsymbol{P}_i(x_1)$ and $\boldsymbol{P}_i(x_2)$ to define the *no-regret zone* (NRZ) for player i. The $NRZ_i(\mathbf{x})$ is the set of points that ensures that player i suffers no policy loss on any dimension, ensuring that blame is indeed avoided and vote explanation is easy.[8]

It is helpful to contrast preferred-to-sets and no-regret zones. For any player and any status quo, the no-regret zone is always a proper subset of the preferred-to-set, but the basis for no-regret zones is entirely different from the basis for preferred-to-sets. In bargaining settings, preferred-to-sets make behavioral sense when players trade policy gains in one dimension for policy losses in another dimension. In Figure 3.3, any point inside

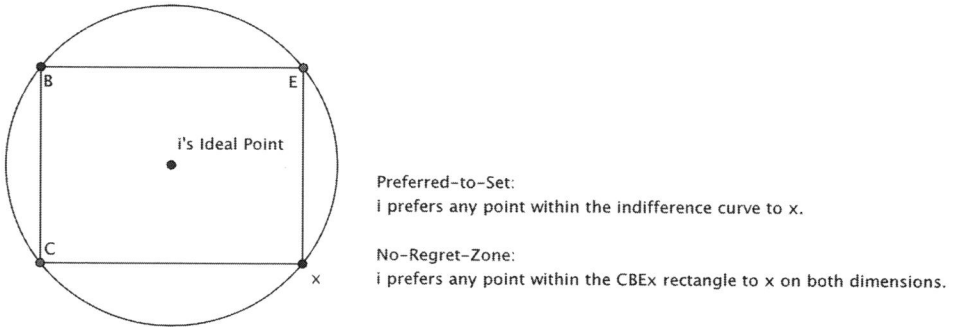

Figure 3.3. No-Regret Zones Contrasted with Preferred-to-Sets

of the indifference curve yields greater utility for i than policy **x**. Focusing only on the points inside of the indifference curve, note the points to the right of the vertical line segment xE. Player i loses utility on the horizontal dimension. Nonetheless, i's overall utility increases because of the offsetting gains on the vertical dimension. The same is true for points to the left of line segment CB. For points below segment Cx, losses on the vertical dimension are offset by gains on the horizontal dimension. The same holds true for points above the line segment BE. However, for points inside of the CBEx rectangle, i secures policy gains on both the horizontal and vertical dimensions. If gains are made on every dimension, there can be no regrets, even if the new policy is somehow disaggregated dimension by dimension. If one trades gains on one dimension for losses on another, regrets might arise as one tries to explain the vote dimension by dimension to different groups of constituents. No legislator wants to say, "We lost on your dimension, but as a society overall we're better off." No-regret zones are consistent with concerns for blame avoidance and vote explanation. If we accept the latter (blame avoidance and vote explanation), we are compelled to accept the former (no-regret zones).

There is a growing body of work focused on ways in which decision-makers reduce a large set of alternatives to smaller sets. Lleras et al. (2017) review several different formal models in which decision-makers maintain a behavioral pattern to winnow the number of alternatives they face. Cherepanov et al. (2013) and Patty and Penn (2014) independently developed similar approaches to the issue. For Cherepanov et al. decision-makers employ a rationalization for their choices, and in Patty and Penn decision-makers repeatedly apply the same principle to a series of choices. In either event, a decision-maker "must be able to give a connected, logical and continuous account of himself, his conduct and opinions, and all his mental processes are unconsciously manipulated and revised to that end" (Cherepanov et al., 2013, 775, quoting Jones (1908)). "Rationalization occurs because people feel 'a necessity to provide an explanation'" (Cherepanov et al., 2013, 775). Decision-makers are choosing both a policy alternative and a psychological grounding for their choice. Any number of rationalizations or principles could be employed, but in this chapter the operating behavioral principles are blame avoidance and vote explanation.

$P_i(\mathbf{x})$ and $NRZ_j(\mathbf{x})$ are helpful concepts because they inform our predictions about the choices made by i and j. No-regret zones reflect players' status quo biases, and such biases are rational when constituents demand vote explanations from legislators on separate dimensions of a multidimensional policy and legislators desire blame avoidance. The only way to ensure a satisfactory explanation of alternatives to the status quo is to restrict attention to proposals that are in the no-regret zone. Prominent findings in the political science and behavioral economics literatures reinforce our use of no-regret zones. First, blame avoidance and vote explanation underpin the no-regret zone.[9] Second, constituents appear to be more sensitive to losses than gains. Arnold (1990, 51) demonstrates the point: "Citizens are far more likely to pursue traceability chains [of policy responsibility] when they incur perceptible costs than when they reap an equal measure of benefits . . . [because] . . . costs produce more intense preferences than do benefits." Policy points within a preferred-to-set can yield losses along some dimension. Policy points within a no-regret zone ensure gains on every dimension.

Figure 3.4 illustrates the preferred-to-sets and no-regret zones for P and L. The intersection of their preferred-to-sets, $P_P(\mathbf{x}) \cap P_L(\mathbf{x})$, is denoted by the lens-shaped area. Both actors prefer points in $P_P(\mathbf{x}) \cap P_L(\mathbf{x})$ to $\mathbf{x}$. As such, any trade from $\mathbf{x}$ to an alternative within $P_P(\mathbf{x}) \cap P_L(\mathbf{x})$ yields a Pareto improvement. Pareto improvements ensure that one actor is made strictly better off and no other actors are made worse off. The contract curve, the line segment connecting P and L, defines the Pareto set for trades between P and L and provides the baseline prediction for the vast majority of spatial models. For any outcome not in the Pareto set, gains from trade can be made by adopting some policy in the Pareto set. For any outcome in the Pareto set, mutually beneficial trades are no longer possible. For status quo points along the contract curve, $P_P(\mathbf{x}) \cap P_L(\mathbf{x}) = \Phi$, meaning no more mutually beneficial trades are possible. The bargaining over alternatives on the contract curve in Figure 3.4 is akin to the zero-sum bargaining in the

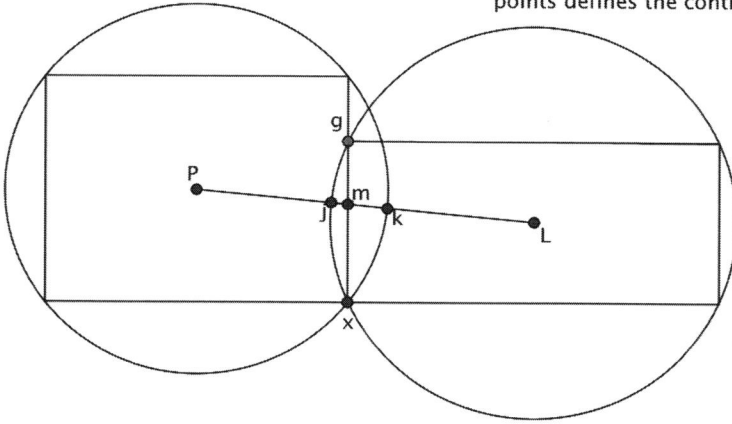

Figure 3.4. Preferred-to-Sets, No-Regret Zones, and the Contract Curve for P and L

one-dimensional models in Figures 3.1 and 3.2.

Of all the points in $P_P(x) \cap P_L(x)$ in Figure 3.4, only those along the xg line segment are in the intersection of P's and L's no-regret zones, $NRZ_P(x) \cap NRZ_L(x)$. If P and L are concerned about blame avoidance and vote explanation, we can predict trades along the xg line segment. Of all the points along segment xg, only m is on the contract curve. Our assumption that players are concerned about disaggregation allows us to make a more precise prediction, m, than the traditional spatial models, which predict the entire jk line segment. By construction, the intersection of actors' no-regret zones is a subset of the intersection of those actors' preferred-to-sets.

We now state our first proposition.

Proposition 1: If P and L focus on their no-regret zones, for a typical array of ideal points and a status quo, one dimension will dominate the bargaining process in the two-dimensional ideological space.

We present Proposition 1 without proof, as Tsebelis and Money (1997) establish a parallel claim in their spatial model of bicameralism with traditional preferred-to-sets. Depending on the extremity of the status quo, policy gains on both dimensions can occur, as noted in our second proposition.

Proposition 2: Only when the status quo lies "beyond" the contract curve in all directions can P and L stay within their no-regret zones and make gains on both dimensions.

For a formal sense of "beyond" the contract curve, consider the x_1, x_2 coordinates for the ideal points for P and L, (x_{P1}, x_{P2}) and (x_{L1}, x_{L2}). A status quo is beyond the contract curve along the first dimension if x_{SQ1} is either less than $MIN\{x_{P1},x_{L1}\}$ or greater than $MAX\{x_{P1},x_{L1}\}$. For a status quo to be "beyond" the contract curve in all dimensions, the aforementioned inequalities must hold for every dimension. That is, x_{SQi} is either less than $MIN\{x_{Pi},x_{Li}\}$ or greater than $MAX\{x_{Pi},x_{Li}\}$ for every possible dimension i. For a status quo "within" the contract curve on all dimensions, x_{SQi} must be between the highest and lowest ideal levels for each dimension i for P and L. That is, $MIN\{x_{Pi},x_{Li}\} < x_{SQi} < MAX\{x_{Pi},x_{Li}\}$ must hold for every dimension i.

Of course, a status quo can be extreme in some dimensions and moderate in others. For any status quo "within" P's and L's ideal points on some dimension, P and L will want to move the policy in different directions on that dimension. Given that they seek opposing policy shifts, both cannot make gains. Only when altering status quo policies that are extreme along every dimension is regret not a concern. The appendix to this chapter provides more information regarding extreme status quos. For now, one can simply focus on the fact that with extreme status quo points, the differences between no-regret zones and preferred-to-sets are reduced; but for more moderate status quo points the differences between no-regret zones and preferred-to-sets remain sharp.

Some of the differences between the no-regret zones and preferred-to-sets foundations for spatial models can be illustrated and formalized. First, we define the notion of NR Stability when there are two actors, P and L.

Definition: A policy alternative x is NR Stable if P and L cannot mutually agree to shift x while remaining in their respective no-regret zones.

Proposition 3: If x is within the contract curve on all dimensions i such that $MIN\{x_{Pi},x_{Li}\}<x_{SQi}<MAX\{x_{Pi},x_{Li}\}$, then x is NR Stable.

For example, alternative e in Figure 3.5 is NR Stable. There is no alternative that P and L can move to while staying within their no-regret zones.

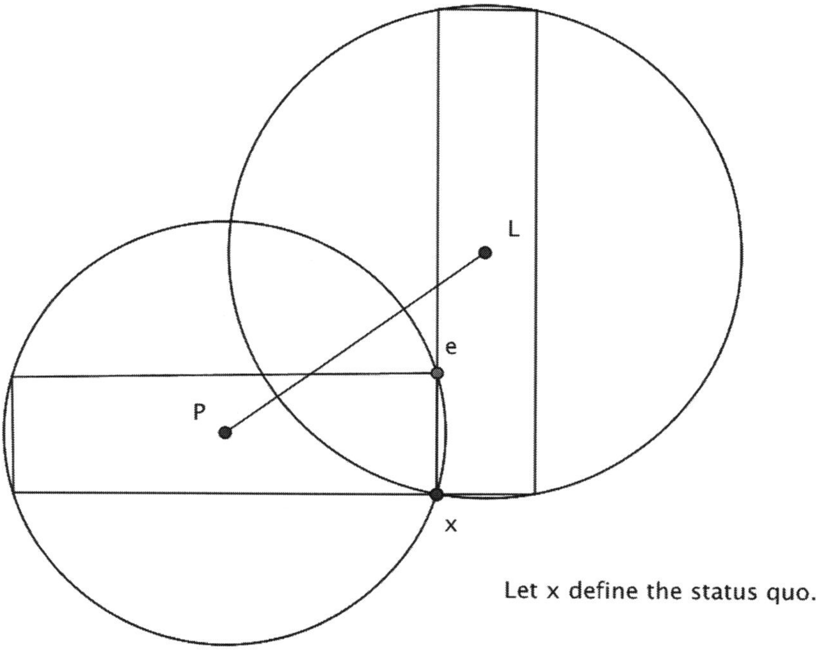

Let x define the status quo.

Figure 3.5. All Points in $NRZ_p(x)NRZ_L(x)$ are Pareto Inferior

Figure 3.5 also illustrates the possible Pareto inferiority of policies within $NRZ_p(\mathbf{x}) \cap NRZ_L(\mathbf{x})$ as none of the points on the line segment xe are on the contract curve. Given the policies in $NRZ_p(\mathbf{x}) \cap NRZ_L(\mathbf{x})$, L prefers e, and P prefers the bisector of xe. Agenda control, which is not a major focus here, will likely affect which element from the xe line segment will prevail. If both players are sensitive to blame avoidance and vote explanation, then movements along xe will appear incremental in contrast to larger movements to Pareto-efficient outcomes along the contract curve. Here we see incremental movements because players insist on policies in their no-regret zones. Other scholars have also noted the occurrence of incremental policy movements. For instance, Krehbiel (1998) shows how pivots can expand gridlock intervals and produce incremental movement under certain conditions. Herzberg (1992) and Tsebelis (2002) note that veto players limit the scale of policy movement.[10] Ainsworth and Hall (2011) illustrate how incremental policy shifts limit legislative sabotage efforts, address the uncertainty that legislators have about policy impact, and limit the counter-mobilization efforts of groups and activists outside Congress.

Where might presidential unilateralism fit into this model? If a player insists on only approving policy within his or her no-regret zone, Pareto gains might be forsaken. The movement from alternative x in Figure 3.5 to some point along the line segment xe remains woefully inefficient. Efficiency would require movement to the contract curve, but movement to the contract curve PL would require one or both actors to adopt a policy beyond their no-regret zone. Given that there is a brake on policy adjustments, one could think of this as a form of gridlock. The gridlock in Krehbiel (1998) occurs because policy status quos are already within the Pareto set of the pivotal actors who have opposing preferences. Here gridlock occurs because the individual actors themselves are focused on blame avoidance and vote explanation for different audiences who are themselves focused on different issue dimensions.

Let CC represent the set of points on the contract curve for P and L. By definition, every policy in CC is Pareto efficient, and every policy not in CC is Pareto inefficient.

Proposition 4: If $NRZ_p(x) \cap NRZ_L(x) \cap CC = \Phi$, then either $NRZ_p(x) \cap P_L(x) \cap CC = \Phi$ or $NRZ_L(x) \cap P_p(x)CC = \Phi$.

In other words, Proposition 4 indicates that Pareto-inferior outcomes can result when just one player rejects policies outside of his or her no-regret zone.

In the appendix to this chapter, we show that when $NRZ_p(x) \cap NRZ_L(x) \cap CC = \Phi$, as is the case in Figure 3.5, neither player has an incentive to focus on preferred-to-set thinking if the other player is insisting on his or her no-regret zone. This is a powerful finding. One player's rationalization (blame avoidance) creates an incentive for the other player to adopt the very same rationalization. In other words, rationalizations (Cherepanov et al. 2013) or principles (Patty and Penn 2014) are not necessarily independent across players. A status quo bias stemming from L's concerns for blame avoidance and vote explanation create a focus on NRZ_L, ensuring that P has incentives to focus on P's own no-regret zone, NRZ_p. Neither player has any incentive to independently "step above the fray."

Now suppose a player is capable of unilateral actions—even after an initial agreement has been reached. Moe and Wilson (1994, 14) argue that presidents possess residual rights, thereby allowing independent, unilateral actions. How can this occur? Residual rights are referenced most often in the contracts literature. Negotiated agreements and contracts are seldom fully specified. That is, contracts handle many contingencies, but they cannot readily handle the universe of contingencies. A *fully specified contract* would imagine every possible contingency that might affect contractual obligations, but two hurdles arise making such specificity all but impossible. First, there are informational asymmetries and unknown unknowns (as opposed to probabilistic uncertainty). For example, imagine all the contracts and agreements that failed to consider the implications of a worldwide pandemic in 2020 lasting over two years. Second, the transaction costs associated with exploring all the possible contingencies are tremendous in a complicated world. At some point, the costs associated with specifying more and more contingencies are not justified. In short, a fully specified contract is highly unlikely.

Laws are akin to negotiated agreements or contracts between the legislative and executive branches. A legislature delegates specific authorities to the president and executive branch for implementation. The laws themselves are not fully specified, and they are not self-implementing. Indeed, the entire federal bureaucratic structure involves rulemaking to give appropriate specificity to goals stated in laws. Presidents strive to guide the rulemaking process (Potter 2017), and unilateral efforts are often directed at bureaucratic agencies in the executive branch. The president, as a constitutional actor, can operate unilaterally with either implied constitutional authority or with authority specified by law. The presence of residual rights is consistent with the Hamiltonian view of an executive moving with energy and efficiency to secure wide-ranging benefits.

Given his residual rights, could P capture Pareto gains that were previously ignored? Suppose P and L agree to move the status quo $\mathbf{x}$ to $\mathbf{x}'$ in Figure 3.6. After the adoption of $\mathbf{x}'$, P can use unilateral tools to move policy while still staying within $P_\mathrm{L}(\mathbf{x}') \cap P_\mathrm{p}(\mathbf{x}')$. Movement could be primarily along the vertical dimension or some blend of the vertical and horizontal dimensions. The unilateral actions can make incremental changes or larger policy shifts. Suppose the unilateral policy shifts are beyond $\mathrm{NRZ}_\mathrm{p}(\mathbf{x}')$ but within which $P_\mathrm{p}(\mathbf{x}')$. How is that justified? Two things come to mind. First, the shift in P's reasoning, being initially focused on P's no-regret zone and then on P's preferred-to-set, is perfectly rational. P had no incentive to embrace the broader preferred-to-set earlier as long as L was insistent on focusing on L's own no-regret zone. Recall Proposition 4. Whenever L rejects policies beyond NRZ_L, it is rational for P to reject policies beyond NRZ_p. Second, when using unilateral tools to move $\mathbf{x}'$, P can stay within $P_\mathrm{L}(\mathbf{x}') \cap P_\mathrm{p}(\mathbf{x}')$ to limit legislative backlash.

How might legislators respond to unilateral actions? In Figure 3.6, unilateral action roughly halved the distance from L to $\mathbf{x}'$ along the vertical

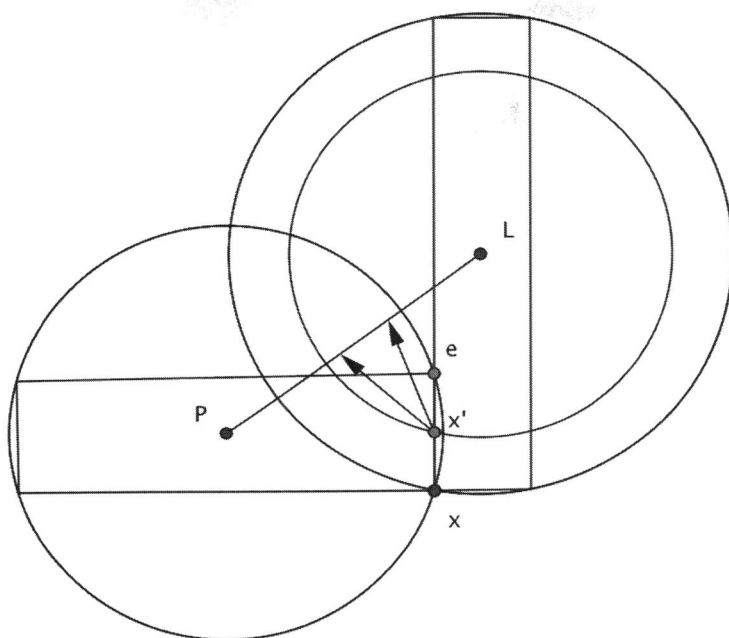

Figure 3.6. Unilateral Actions by the President to Alter Policy x'

dimension. Whether those gains on the vertical dimension can assuage legislators concerned about the policy losses along the horizontal dimension will depend on legislators' audiences' reactions. Engineering collective, statutory efforts to counter unilateralism remains challenging (Moe and Howell 1999), especially if unilateralism led to Pareto gains. By insisting on policies in their no-regret zones, legislators secure gains from blame avoidance and easier vote explanation, knowing that the president might subsequently take unilateral actions to make Pareto improvements. Legislators value Pareto improvements but are sensitive to how those gains are achieved. In the scenario laid out, unilateral efforts yielded Pareto gains. However, legislators can still explain their votes, avoid blame, and maybe even claim credit for fighting the president on those dimensions that did suffer policy losses due to unilateral adjustments.

Policy multidimensionality is a defining characteristic of contemporary lawmaking. What Congress aggregates to accommodate supermajoritarian requirements, the president can disaggregate via unilateral tools. With signing statements, the president creates winners and losers for specific dimensions of a multidimensional bill. Executive orders are typically narrowly focused relative to the enabling statutes. The Pareto gains that might be secured through unilateral efforts still entail policy trade-offs, as losses on one or more dimensions are coupled with gains on one or more other dimensions. When legislators foresee focused policy losses due to the executive branch's implementation, we predict legislative pushback. For many reasons, the pushback is unlikely to entail new legislation. Two reasons bear repeating. First, for a status quo $\mathbf{x}'$, the president can keep unilateral policy shifts within $\boldsymbol{P}_{\mathrm{L}}(\mathbf{x}') \cap \boldsymbol{P}_{\mathrm{p}}(\mathbf{x}')$, thereby reducing the incentives for new legislation. Second, legislative efforts require collective efforts, and often supermajoritarian ones. Of course, not all legislative pushback requires herculean collective efforts. In the next section, we reexamine the issues of delegation and discretion and debates about presidential and congressional authority. We also consider the possibility that legislative oversight hearings are prompted by presidential unilateralism.

Discussion

As instruments of unilateral action, signing statements have engendered public reprobation when sensitive policies, like the treatment of detainees suspected of terrorism (e.g., Savage 2006a, 2006b), are at stake. Executive orders during the Obama and Trump presidencies generated similar criticism within some circles. More generally, unilateral actions are viewed as powerful tools that allow the president to gain greater control over policy implementation. While many scholars have examined how specific instruments of unilateral policymaking operate, few have considered how members of Congress might behave *in anticipation of* and *in reaction to* unilateral efforts. Scholars recognize that the effectiveness of unilateral presidential control over policy depends on the actions of the other branches in government. Howell (2003) notes that "the limits of unilateral powers are as wide or as narrow as Congress . . . permits" (23) and that "Congress's ability to constrain the president is principally a function of its members' preferences" (65). In particular, Howell considers how the possibility of new legislation and veto overrides affect a president's willingness to act unilaterally.

What is the full array of congressional responses? The Howell (2003) and Moe and Howell (1999) formulation of presidential unilateral politics is remarkably useful, but its focus on supermajoritarian means—new legislation and veto overrides—does not fit the situations we explore here.

Congressional oversight is committee based, which dramatically lowers the supermajoritarian collective action hurdles inherent with legislation and veto overrides. Simply put, although new legislation and veto overrides often require supermajorities, congressional oversight by committees does not. If an executive order or signing statement is a means by which presidents can direct bureaucratic implementation, then congressional committees can use the directives in the orders and statements to guide their own oversight activities.[11] To explore this possibility, we consider scenarios when Congress responds to presidential unilateralism and when it chooses to ignore it. We presume that both the president and Congress act strategically. After negotiating over policy, the president can take unilateral actions, and Congress can subsequently react to presidential unilateralism on particular dimensions of that policy.

Unilateral actions by a president and oversight from congressional committees are both connected to the political control of bureaucracies. For too long, oversight was deemed a neglected function, unable to affect policy or enhance legislators' careers (McGrath 2013, 351–52; MacDonald and McGrath 2013; cf. Lewallen 2020). We propose that members of Congress respond to objections in presidential signing statements with increased oversight. Two factors reinforce the importance of oversight. First, *ex post* oversight by Congress in response to presidential unilateralism is partly a consequence of the costs Congress incurs in crafting new statutes explicitly limiting policy drift. Second, *ex ante* controls inserted into legislation by legislators are not necessarily triggered, and they might not be efficacious even if they are triggered. *Ex ante* controls are especially difficult for Congress to structure if presidential preferences on each dimension of a complex bill were not fully revealed. Put differently, legislators cannot predict or guard against every possible circumstance of presidential unilateralism, nor can Congress expect reporting requirements, for instance, to be effective *ex ante* constraints on executive discretion.

In a May 2017 signing statement attached to an appropriations bill, President Trump (2017c) commented:

> Numerous provisions authorize congressional committees to veto a particular use of appropriated funds. . . . These are impermissible forms of congressional aggrandizement in the execution of the laws other than by enactment of statutes. My Administration . . . will not treat spending decisions as dependent on the approval of congressional committees.

By issuing a signing statement with specific objections, Congress is alerted to areas of possible noncompliance, and Congress can exercise *ex post* oversight to counteract drift away from its preferred policies (e.g., Ainsworth et al. 2012). Congressional oversight does not automatically negate presidential influence. However, unilateral efforts and oversight do exemplify the ongoing interbranch struggle to guide policy implementation.

Questions of Delegation and Discretion

How does our model fit within the extant literature on delegation, discretion, and oversight? Numerous scholars consider delegation as a strategic and anticipatory calculation rather than as congressional acquiescence to executive policymaking (Epstein and O'Halloran 1994, 1999; Huber and Shipan 2000, 2002; Huber et al. 2001; Kiewiet and McCubbins 1991). As we noted earlier, however, delegation is an action that operates like a binary switch. It's either on or off.

Discretion indicates the range of free movement as the executive branch implements congressional statutes. Typically, discretion that one entity delegates to another simply allows the executive to adjust to unfortunate and unforeseen exogenous shocks (e.g., Gilligan and Krehbiel 1987). Of course, that discretion also allows some policy slippage, especially in the absence of an unfortunate exogenous shock. In the model in this chapter, the legislator does not grant discretion, per se, to the president; but the legislator does recognize that the president might nonetheless take unilateral actions to adjust policy implementation. The president's residual powers and the fact that negotiated legislative agreements are not necessarily Pareto efficient means that unilateral presidential actions are quite likely.

Presidential versus Legislative Dominance

Many scholars explore the tension between congressional and presidential control of agency decision-making. The presidential control literature suggests presidents are advantaged in the "politics of structure" whenever conflicts arise between the executive and Congress over issues of institutional design (e.g., Moe 1989, 1993; Moe and Wilson 1994; Howell 2003). Moe (1993) and Howell (2003) argue that presidents retain important residual decision rights, reflecting their opportunities for centralized control and unilateral action. Similarly, Huber and Shipan (2002) consider the president to be a privileged actor with respect to Congress, while Lewis (2003) and Howell (2003) note the advantages presidents have over policy outcomes because of their ability to shape the design and guide the actions of agencies.

The delegation and congressional dominance literatures tend to emphasize congressional effectiveness in achieving desired policy results due to the design of administrative arrangements and congressional budgetary authority (e.g., McCubbins, Noll, and Weingast 1987, 1989; Epstein and O'Halloran 1994, 1999; Huber and Shipan 2002; Balla 1998; Balla and Wright 2001; Bawn 1995, 1997). Absent other *ex ante* constraints, once authority is delegated, all that remains is *ex post* control on those dimensions where discretion has been granted. As such, the design of administrative arrangements and budgetary control are intricately tied to congressional oversight. As legislators consider questions of administrative design and budgetary support for agencies, the ability to monitor executive actions remains paramount (e.g., Bawn 1995, 1997). Simply put, congressional oversight remains part of the tussle.

Berry (2009), Francis and Sulkin (2013), and MacDonald and McGrath (2016) connect the presidential and congressional control literatures. Berry (2009) explores whether legislative veto provisions prompt presidential signing statements. Francis and Sulkin (2013) suggest that presidents craft signing statements with an eye toward legislative support coalitions.[12] Work by MacDonald and McGrath (2016) demonstrates the role of committees in engaging in "retrospective oversight," taking advantage of opportunities for policy coordination under conditions of unified government and monitoring noncompliance under divided government. In a particularly important contribution that reflects the dynamism of the policymaking environment, Bolton and Thrower (2016) find that legislative capacity (which they characterize as Congress's ability to overcome costs associated with crafting legislation that constrains executive discretion) affects the issuance of executive orders. Specifically, they demonstrate that when congressional capacity is high, the costs associated with writing constraining legislation for an ideologically distant president are lowered, thereby limiting unilateral executive actions (which are typically—though not exclusively—issued under statutory authority).

Unilateral Actions and Oversight

Many scholars investigate the effects of divided government on a wide array of legislative activities, including congressional oversight (see, e.g., Aberbach 1990, Mayhew 2005). Most scholars argue that Congress is more apt to give the executive branch broad discretionary authority when both actors hold similar policy preferences. Conversely, under divided government, Congress is less likely to delegate control (Epstein and O'Halloran 1999; Huber and Shipan 2002). Unilateral actions complicate these claims because if the president and Congress share preferences, there could be less incentive for presidents to modify policy through unilateral efforts. Alternatively, Kelley and Marshall (2010), exploring signing statements, and Howell (2003), exploring executive orders, have found that more unilateral actions are taken under unified government than under divided because congressional reaction to presidential unilateralism under unified is less likely.

Bolton and Thrower's (2016) work demonstrates the nuances associated with this dynamic in the context of executive orders, finding that when legislative capacity is high and in alignment with presidential preference, more executive orders are issued. However, they also find that under conditions of diminished legislative capacity, an ideologically divergent president can make policy gains by issuing executive orders. The model introduced in this chapter suggests that there might be another compatible explanation for unilateral actions by a president during unified control. Specifically, the multidimensionality of legislation might generate supermajority support in Congress, but legislators' adherence to blame avoidance and vote explanation limits policy adjustments within the legislature. Pareto-inefficient legislation invites presidential "improvement" on specific dimensions through unilateral actions.

Conclusion

It is widely accepted that for the separation of powers to be meaningful, members of the separate branches must show some resilience and willingness to resist encroachment. We concur with that general sentiment; but we add a behavioral twist to the structural, institutionalist arguments surrounding the separation of powers. In this chapter, we showed how congressional behaviors create room for unilateral actions by the president. Indeed, members of Congress behave in anticipation of unilateral actions by the president. Leaving room for others to operate unilaterally in a separation of powers context might seem odd. However, the fact that members of Congress work to avoid blame and engage in vote explanation in especially visible ways on salient issues has been long established. We simply place those regular congressional behaviors within a separation-of-powers context. Numerous scholars have argued that members of Congress could create a brake on unilateralism undertaken by the president. We concur with that understanding, but we contend that congressional behaviors can also encourage presidential unilateralism. In particular, we argue that congressional behaviors leave room for unilateralism; presidents do undertake unilateral efforts; and members of Congress do push back when unilateral efforts create policy losses that are electorally problematic.

Senator Robert C. Byrd (D-WV) opined, "Congress functions less and less . . . as a truly independent and deliberative body. . . . [C]oncerned with . . . petty partisanship . . . [i]t seems more and more willing to delegate portions of legislative authority" (2005, 40). Leaving potential gains on the table, knowing that another actor will react seems an unlikely sign of congressional abdication. Blame avoidance during the legislative phase of policymaking and credit claiming for oversight and pushback during the implementation phase of policymaking are central parts of the story developed in this chapter. As a hedge against constituents' unfavorable retrospective assessments of elaborate statutes due to specific policy losses, legislators must be able to explain their votes for comprehensive measures with a focus on the particulars. We demonstrated how unilateral actions could disaggregate issues that had been previously aggregated by legislative statute and how no-regret zones could be used to model negotiations between legislators and the president. Legislators can insist on policies in their no-regret zones, knowing that presidents will adjust policies that the legislators themselves can continue to reevaluate and perhaps redirect through legislative oversight efforts or with new legislation. Legislators get to claim credit for some policy gains, avoid blame when difficult policy trade-offs are made, and reassert themselves in the politics of structure, fighting the imperial executive if there are strong reactions to a president's unilateral actions.

The compulsion to react to presidential unilateralism is tempered by the recognition that legislators are not typically focused on a desire to protect their institutional powers (see, e.g., Levinson and Pildes 2006). For legislators, electoral concerns remain prominent even as presidents usurp and encroach on congressional authority. Indeed, Matthews's discussion of a legislative, institutional patriotism norm seems out of place in the 21st century (Mathews 1960). For presidents, concerns about institutional prerogatives remain prominent. Their limited terms provide limited time to move policy. Moe and Wilson (1994, 27) sum up the reasoning when they write, "[P]residents care intensely about securing changes that promote their institutional power, while legislators typically do not. They are unlikely to oppose incremental increases in the relative power of presidents *unless the issue in question directly harms the special interests in their clientele"* (quoted in Howell 2003, 111, emphasis added).

The canonical view of unilateral actions presents signing statements, executive orders, and memoranda as effective devices for presidents to rein in bureaucratic drift, move policy closer to presidential preferences, influence future judicial decisions, and assert presidential power in the coordinate construction of the constitution (cf., Halstead 2008). We suggest that the story is more nuanced. If legislators are obliged to explain their support for a multidimensional package of legislation to separate audiences, legislative bargaining can fail to secure all possible gains otherwise available during the crafting of legislation. By explicitly modeling vote explanation, we uncovered interbranch policy gains most immediately available through presidential unilateralism.

In the next two chapters, we explore empirical trends related to some of the key issues raised here. Signing statements with a large number of objections focused in different policy areas hint at multidimensionality. To highlight losses along specific policy dimensions, we focus on committee claims and policy areas. Legislation emanating from particular committees (or policy areas) is most apt to be the focus of unilateral actions that create policy losses. In the fifth chapter, we use an even more granular set of data, distinguishing between defense-related objections and all other types. In the next two chapters, we use time series models to examine focused legislative pushback to narrow unilateral efforts while controlling for an array of covariates associated with the ebb and flow of policymaking activities.

Appendix: Further Discussion of No-Regret Zones

To be certain, employing no-regret zones in a spatial model is noncanonical, and it is unlikely that we can imagine and respond to all concerns. Notably, economists have explored noncanonical formal models to a much greater extent than political scientists. With a keen sense of the social sciences, Rabin argues that behavioral economists concerned about psychology or elements of bounded rationality must be more than malcontent "flaw finders" (2013, 617): "[T]he heart of modifying existing . . . theories is to formulate credible and systematic alternatives" (Rabin 2013, 617). As long as blame avoidance and vote explanation are reasonable assumptions, no-regret zones are reasonable. Indeed, we can show that blame avoidance need not be systemic, intrinsically affecting all actors. As long as some actors adhere to no-regret reasoning, other actors have an incentive to behave similarly. For these other actors, it is entirely rational to behave "as if" they were embodying no-regret reasoning.

The mechanisms underpinning no-regret reasoning are very simple. Multidimensional proposals are disaggregated into their component dimensions, and the operative choice space for i is reduced from $P(x_i)$ to $NRZ(x_i)$. There is a growing body of literature in economics that follows a similar path. Harstad and Selten (2013) review work by Selten and various coauthors that imagines firms addressing goals related to profit maximization sequentially rather than holistically. Harstad and Selten also note work by Rubinstein and various coauthors that separates comprehensive decisions into component dimensions. Crawford (2013, 524) provides a nice overview of these models, concluding that "in most settings, there is an enormous number of logically possible models . . . that deviate from neoclassical models. . . . [Accordingly, it] is essential to have some principled way of choosing among the alternatives." For us, the principled way of choosing among models stems from the oft-noted prevalence of blame avoidance and vote explanation, which indicates the importance of formally incorporating it into canonical spatial models.

The remainder of this appendix is divided into four sections. The first three sections address potential critiques of the modeling approach. The last section highlights results from the model. We offer comments on rationality, institutional and behavioral constraints on decision-making, spatial modeling, and cooperative and noncooperative game theory.

Rationality and NRZs

Is adherence to NRZs rational? In short, yes. Rationality itself has different definitions, but common to many of them are the following: (i) a rational decision-maker has some means to compare every x and y from the set of available alternatives, and (ii) a rational decision-maker maintains some notion of consistency in the choices made from different pairs of x, y, z . . . from the set of available alternatives X. The first condition is typically referred to as *comparability* or *completeness*. If X is the set of available alternatives, then for any elements x and y $\in$ X, either xRy or yRx. The second condition is typically addressed via *transitivity*, but weaker conditions are also used (e.g., Sen 1970). For transitivity, if x, y, and z $\in$ X and if xRy and yRz, then xRz.

Transitivity and comparability yield an order. As a binary relation, xNRy can be read as "x is better in all ways than y." NR is transitive, irreflexive, and asymmetric, but NR is not necessarily complete.[13] As such, NR is a strict partial order. Numerous scholars have explored choice in the face of incompleteness (e.g., Binder 2014; Sen 2004; 1973). Whenever there are "value conflicts"[14] wherein no single standard of valuation exists, incompleteness is possible. Sen (2004, 55) distinguishes between "tentative" and "assertive" incompleteness. Tentative incompleteness might exist until one secures more information (Sen 2004, 55) or during an early stage of a "multi-stage exercise" (Sen 2004, 56). Assertive incompleteness is much more profound. Consider Sophie's choice from William Styron's novel of the same name (1979). Some have suggested that, ultimately, Sophie made a choice (e.g., Shepsle 2010). The incompleteness was interpreted as only tentative. Others argue that "not comparing one's children forms part of one's identity as a parent" (Binder 2014, 961). In that interpretation, incompleteness is assertive rather than tentative. As the late mother-in-law of one of the authors stated, 'I love my children differently because they are each so different.' She opined and deeply felt that there was no single standard of value (or love) when considering her own children.

If there are no constraints on an individual's choice, the individual's ideal point is the only rational alternative to choose. Setting aside instances in which one has dictatorial powers, a chosen $\mathbf{x}$ from within $P(\mathbf{x})$ is often thought to be the product of institutional constraints (e.g., Shepsle 1986). We fully recognize the role for institutional constraints, but we also see the U.S. Congress and other legislatures as "historical composites, full of tensions and contradictions" (Schickler 2001, 267) wherein legislators' behaviors within Congress are affected by the electoral environments far removed from Congress. In sum, there is no reason one should not consider individual-level behavioral constraints, especially given the long-established behavioral traditions in political science. Indeed, behavioral assumptions imbue cooperative game theory, even though there are no means to detail those behaviors. Bargaining by individuals and coalitions is imagined. Narratives (and equilibrium concepts) imagine offers met with counteroffers. Behaviors are not always explicitly specified, but they are deeply embedded in the models.

Consider the uncovered set. It presumes non-myopic behavior and particular agenda structures. Consider too the following justification of the uncovered set: "outcomes that lie outside the uncovered set are *unlikely* to be seriously considered by *sophisticated* decision-makers, who know that such proposals are *unlikely* to survive" cleverly structured agendas (Bianco et al. 2004, 258, emphasis added). The uncovered set and other solution concepts seem to imply narratives and rationalizations. Herein we are offering particularly clear behavioral assumptions (blame avoidance and vote explanation) that are used to rationalize individuals' choices.

When more than one decision-maker plays a role in determining policy, it is important to emphasize that i $\in NP_i(\mathbf{x})$, even under constrained optimization, does not always yield a single option. For instance, when there are multiple options within a Pareto set, there is not always an established basis for choice among the Pareto alternatives. Alternatives in the uncovered set are not always Condorcet alternatives. If there are reasonable justifications, social scientists can model institutional and behavioral constraints to play a role in winnowing the alternatives.

Of course, the model developed herein does not fully detail the strategy sets for L and P. But that is the nature of cooperative game theory and many spatial models. The decision-maker adhering to NRZ($\mathbf{x}$) reasoning and choice is simply using a stronger, more restrictive decision calculus than the decision-maker adhering to $P(\mathbf{x})$ reasoning and choice. Formally, any element in NRZ($\mathbf{x}$) is also in $P(\mathbf{x})$, but not every element in $P(\mathbf{x})$ is in NRZ($\mathbf{x}$). In either situation, a decision-maker is partitioning the universe of choices into those deemed "justifiably equivalent" to $\mathbf{x}$, "more justifiable than" $\mathbf{x}$, and "not as justifiable" as $\mathbf{x}$. Any definition of rational choice, whether from $P(\mathbf{x})$, NRZ($\mathbf{x}$), or from some other binary relationship, embodies behavioral assumptions. No-regret reasoning is consistent with legislators' focus on electoral uncertainty, desire to avoid blame, and interest in explaining their votes. Is the NRZ reasoning too restrictive? Matthews (1989) considers a type of president who rejects any offer the proposer favors to the status quo. Matthews's work, in which a "recalcitrant president" rejects all proposals, is not tied to empirical regularities and is in some ways more restrictive than NRZ reasoning. Assumptions, like no-regret reasoning, need not have empirical content, but there is no reason to adhere only to those assumptions *devoid* of empirical content (e.g., Morton 1999). Alesina and Passarelli (2019) reconsider the Downsian two-candidate election by adding loss aversion. Their modeling strategy is grounded in the empirical regularities (endowment effects and status quo bias) tied to loss aversion. There are clear empirical patterns suggesting that legislators act "as if" they restrict their choices in manners consistent with NRZ($\mathbf{x}$) choices.

As a final note on rationality, we consider the advantages and disadvantages of stronger constraints on choice. Stronger constraints can yield more information in that predictions are tighter. Recall X, the set of alternatives available to a decision-maker. A uniform lottery over X–$\mathbf{x}$ could be used to choose an alternative to $x \in X$. The lottery $L(X-x)$ yields a choice, but it is not particularly helpful. $P(x)$ is stronger in the sense that it is more restrictive than $L(X-x)$. $P(x)$ is also more informative than $L(X-x)$. Likewise, $NRZ(x)$ is stronger and more informative than $P(x)$. However, as choice mechanisms become stronger and more informative, they are also more apt to risk empirical invalidation because the expected set of alternatives to x becomes smaller and smaller.

Why Not Highlight Institutional Constraints Rather Than Behavioral Ones?

Shepsle states that the "relationship between social choices and individual values is a mediated one. Standing between the individual . . . and the social choices are institutions" (1986, 51). We counter with three points. First, the leverage provided by institutional structures and rules limits the applicability of a model to *those* institutions. For example, rules that protect committee jurisdictions in the House do not apply in the same fashion in the Senate. Of course, behavioral constraints are similarly limiting. In settings where legislators stand tall, never fearing the electoral implications of vote explanation, no-regret reasoning is not as helpful. However, if we have reason to believe that legislators are always running scared, then the behavioral constraints implied by no-regret reasoning can be widely applied. We are certainly not the first political scientists to suggest that "the internal politics of Congress and its performance as an institution are deeply affected by how its members win and hold office" (Jacobson 1987, 40). The long list of scholars noting that members of Congress focus on electoral vulnerability includes such luminaries as Fenno (1978) and Mayhew (1974).

Second, our focus on behavioral constraints does not preclude attention to institutional constraints. Third, although institutional rules and procedures can prevent cycling over policy alternatives, those same rules and procedures are themselves often the product of group choice that is itself vulnerable to cycling. The instability of policy choice may lead to instability over the choice of rules and procedures. Fourth, if legislative scholars want to explore policy trade-offs in a multidimensional setting, they have limited means to address blame avoidance. If blame avoidance is a key concern for legislative scholars, it should be modeled much more explicitly than extant spatial models allow. We developed no-regret reasoning and no-regret zones simply to highlight legislators' sensitivities to blame avoidance and vote explanation.

Why Use a Spatial Model?

Most scholars exploring separation-of-powers issues, including unilateral actions, have used spatial models, so there are good reasons to maintain the same modeling format to allow for a more straightforward comparison of results. Spatial models also readily highlight potential Pareto inefficiencies. Of course, one could specify a sequence of choices to determine subgame perfect equilibria. We leave that to subsequent work, partly to bypass the debates on who moves first and to make progress in other areas of analysis. One could likely develop a noncooperative game-theoretic model in which legislators establish a weight, $\beta \in [0, 1]$, placed on policy gains and another weight, $\alpha \in [0, 1]$, placed on vote explanation. To date, scholarship has been dominated by models in which $\beta = 1$ and $\alpha = 0$, implying that policy gains are the only concern so that trading losses in one policy dimension for gains in another dimension carries no risks for legislators. To imagine circumstances in which $\beta < 1$ and $\alpha > 0$, indicating that vote explanation and blame avoidance play some role in legislators' lives, we use no-regret reasoning in our models.

$P_i(x)$, $NRZ_j(x)$, Extreme Status Quos, and NR Stability

By construction, for any status quo $\mathbf{x}$, $NRZ_i(\mathbf{x})$ is a proper subset of $\boldsymbol{P}_i(\mathbf{x})$. Furthermore, $\boldsymbol{P}_i(\mathbf{x})$ is strictly convex because of the standard assumptions made about the set of allowable utility functions. To wit: utility functions are single peaked and symmetric, thereby yielding circular indifference curves. In contrast, $NRZ_i(\mathbf{x})$ is convex but not strictly convex. To show how predictions from the no-regret zones are narrower than those from preferred-to-sets, we examine the sizes of no-regret zones in relation to preferred-to-sets for two individuals.

Claim: Given that $NRZ_i \subset \boldsymbol{P}_i$ and $NRZ_j \subset \boldsymbol{P}_j$, $(NRZ_i \cap NRZ_j) \subset (\boldsymbol{P}_i \boldsymbol{P}_j)$.

The proof has four parts. (i) Suppose $NRZ_i \cap NRZ_j = \emptyset$, which would happen whenever $\mathbf{x}$ lies along the contract curve. The empty set $\emptyset$ is a subset of every set, so $(NRZ_i \cap NRZ_j) = \emptyset \subset (\boldsymbol{P}_i \cap \boldsymbol{P}_j)$. (ii) Suppose $NRZ_i \cap NRZ_j = NRZ_i \subset NRZ_j$. That is, $NRZ_i = NRZ_j$, which is only possible when actors i and j share ideal points. Therefore, $NRZ_i = NRZ_j \subset \boldsymbol{P}_i$ and $NRZ_j = NRZ_i \subset \boldsymbol{P}_j$. Additionally, $\boldsymbol{P}_i = (\boldsymbol{P}_i \cap \boldsymbol{P}_j) = \boldsymbol{P}_j$. (iii) Suppose $NRZ_i \subset NRZ_j$, ensuring that $NRZ_i \neq NRZ_j$. In this case, NRZ_i is subsumed by

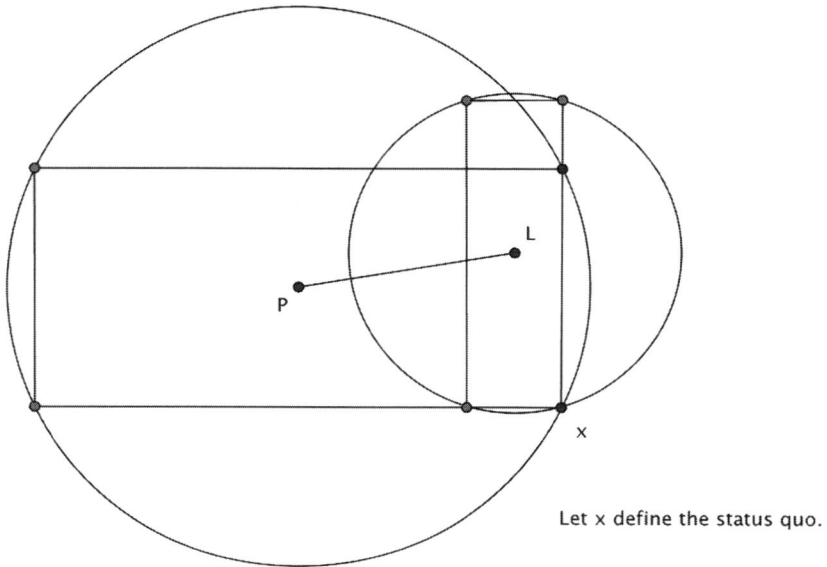

Figure 3.7. Pareto Optimal Moves within NRZ$_P$(x)NRZ$_L$(x)

NRZ$_j$. Therefore, $P_i \subset P_j$ and $P_i \cap P_j = P_i$. Of course, NRZ$_i \subset P_i = P_i \cap P_j$. (iv) Suppose NRZ$_i \cap$ NRZ$_j \neq \varnothing$ and NRZ$_i$ is not a proper subset of NRZ$_j$. This scenario is illustrated in Figures 3.7 and 3.8. By definition, no part of NRZ$_i \cap$ NRZ$_j$ can lie outside of $P_i \cap P_j$. Recall that $P_i(\mathbf{x})$ is strictly convex, whereas NRZ$_i(\mathbf{x})$ is convex but not strictly convex. ■ In sum, no-regret reasoning indicates a smaller set of options preferable to **x** than traditional preferred-to reasoning.

Figure 3.7 illustrates a status quo that is extreme on all dimensions in relation to the P and L ideal points. Note that NRZ$_P(\mathbf{x}) \cap$ NRZ$_L(\mathbf{x})$ is a proper subset of $P_P(\mathbf{x}) \cap P_L(\mathbf{x})$. In addition, a portion of the contract curve near to L lies within NRZ$_P(\mathbf{x}) \cap$ NRZ$_L(\mathbf{x})$. The intersection of the no-regret zones is smaller than the intersection of the preferred-to-sets, and only a small portion of the contract curve lies within NRZ$_P(\mathbf{x}) \cap$ NRZ$_L(\mathbf{x})$.

Next we show that insistence on no-regret reasoning by one player can be enough to create Pareto-inferior outcomes. In Figure 3.8, if P is willing to trade policy gains in one dimension for losses in another while L is not, the set of viable alternatives to **x** expands. $P_P(\mathbf{x}) \cap$ NRZ$_L(\mathbf{x})$ is the narrow lens-shaped area in Figure 3.8 with line segment xe defining its western edge.

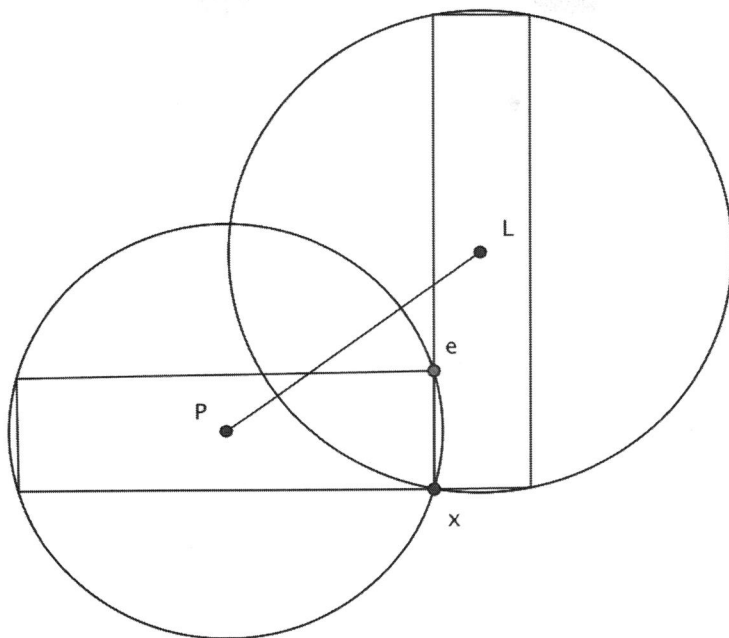

Figure 3.8. Contrasting $P_i(x)NRZ_j(x)$ to those in $NRZ_i(x)NRZ_j(x)$

Proposition A.1: If $NRZ_L(x) \cap P_p(x) \cap CC = \varnothing$, then P will never strictly prefer proposals in $P_p(x) \cap NRZ_L(x)$ to those in $NRZ_p(x) \cap NRZ_L(x)$. In contrast, L will strictly prefer some of the proposals in $P_p(x) \cap NRZ_L(x)$ to those in $NRZ_p(x) \cap NRZ_L(x)$.

Proposition A.1 indicates that a single player cannot necessarily break the gridlock of no-regret reasoning by focusing on her own preferred-to-set instead of her no-regret zone without a loss of utility to herself.

We now consider NR Stability, which relies on dimension-by-dimension decision-making. For N individuals where n is odd, if the ideal points are entirely unique, then there is a single pivotal individual on each issue dimension. Pivotal players are often designated to have special agenda-setting powers, gatekeeping powers, veto powers, monopoly proposal powers, or some other institutional advantage. Alternatively, here, the pivotal player on dimension m_j is simply the individual with the median ideal point along the jth dimension. Let m_j represent the individual with the median preference on the jth dimension and let the $(m_1, m_2, \ldots m_j, \ldots, m_m)$ vector represent those individuals whose ideal points are the medians for the 1st, 2nd, . . . , and mth issue dimensions.

> **Definition**: With m dimensions and N-odd individuals, if $\mathbf{x} = (m_1, m_2, \ldots m_j, \ldots, m_m)$, then the policy alternative $\mathbf{x}$ is NR Stable.

Without proofs, we add some final propositions.

> **Proposition A.2**: No-regret reasoning yields the core whenever the core is nonempty.

> **Proposition A.3**: NR Stable outcomes are within the yolk and the uncovered set.

> **Proposition A.4**: In the presence of no-regret reasoning, an NR Stable point always exists.

No-regret decision-making yields a stable point and does not suffer from the inheritability problem (Riker 1980). Inheritability problems occur when the institutional structures that lead to stability are themselves the product of group choices. Just as a group might cycle over policy alternatives, that same group can cycle over institutional structures that affect the selection of policy alternatives.

Scholars have long recognized that dimension-by-dimension decision-making leads to a stable outcome. What we have shown is that widely accepted behavioral assumptions, blame avoidance and vote explanation, lead inexorably to a stable point that is identical to the dimension-by-dimension stable point.

> **Proposition A.5**: When players are pivotal along some dimensions due to special institutional powers and when they are *not* also the medians along those dimensions, Proposition A.3 might not hold, and the NR Stable point may lie beyond the Pareto set.

Proposition A.5 indicates that institutional structures can indeed interact with our behavioral assumptions.

FOUR

The Evidence

Oversight and Presidential Unilateralism

> For nearly two centuries, Presidents have issued signing statements
> addressing constitutional or other legal questions upon signing
> bills into law (signing statements). Particularly since omnibus bills
> have become prevalent, signing statements have often been used
> to ensure that concerns about the constitutionality of discrete
> statutory provisions do not require a veto of the entire bill.
>
> —President Obama's Memorandum on
> Signing Statements, March 9, 2009

In 2015, tragic mass shootings occurred throughout the United States, including the killing of nine worshipers at Mother Emanuel AME Church in Charleston, South Carolina, and the shootings in San Bernardino, California, which left 16 dead. As often occurs in the wake of these tragedies, the salience of gun control legislation increased as did the pressure on members of Congress to act. With a majority of the public supporting modest gun control measures, pressure was applied through district-level demands, party leadership, interest groups, and sometimes by the president (Blackman and Baird 2014). In December 2015, Democrats proposed the Assault Weapons Ban Act, but with Republicans in control of the House and Senate, the bill failed.

A month after the bill was introduced, President Obama acted independently. On January 4, 2016, his administration announced a series of executive actions "to reduce gun violence and make our communities safer"

(White House 2016). These actions, however, were not sweeping executive orders; rather, they included three agency rulemaking announcements regarding background checks and increased enforcement of regulations. There was also one policy memorandum instructing the Department of Defense, Department of Justice, and Department of Homeland Security to "prepare jointly a report outlining a research and development strategy designed to expedite the real-world deployment" of gun safety technology (Obama 2016). The next day, President Obama (2016) gave a press briefing announcing the actions:

> Now, I want to be clear. Congress still needs to act. The folks in this room will not rest until Congress does. Because once Congress gets on board with common-sense gun safety measures we can reduce gun violence a whole lot more. But we also can't wait until we have a Congress that's in line with the majority of Americans. There are actions within my legal authority that we can take to help reduce gun violence and save more lives—actions that protect our rights and our kids.

The "actions within . . . [his] legal authority" were largely perfunctory announcements regarding commonplace rulemaking, but the policy being addressed was sensitive and politically problematic.

Although the actions that President Obama announced were limited, the Senate Appropriations Subcommittee on Commerce, Justice, State, the Judiciary and Related Agencies held oversight hearings on the propriety of the measures. Appropriations Subcommittee chair Senator Richard Shelby (R-AL) expressed his concern not only with the policy, but also with the unilateral nature of the actions taken:

> I'm very concerned with the recent executive actions by the president for two main reasons. First, President Obama I believe is far too willing to end-run Congress through executive action. The president has said that he believes that when Congress doesn't act the way he wants us to, then he must act alone. Our Constitution won't allow for this kind of unilateral action and the American people will not stand for it. Whether through executive amnesty to thousands of illegal immigrants or increased gun control measures, the president has unwisely I believe acted alone. However, what the president fails to remember is that we have a system of checks and balances, a system that was created to ensure that power was not

concentrated in a single branch of the federal government. The president I believe has ignored the founders' system and accelerated the use of executive fiat in an alarming—to an alarming new level. (US Senate 2016)

Senator Shelby concluded his introductory remarks with a warning for U.S. attorney general Loretta Lynch:

Madam Attorney General, the department is on notice. This subcommittee will have no part in undermining the Constitution and the rights that it protects. (US Senate 2016)

Senator Shelby presented President Obama's actions as both dangerous and unprecedented, and he noted his subcommittee's role in monitoring the administration's actions.

What was ordinary governance and what was extraordinary? This case reveals several dynamics between the executive and legislative branches over policy placement. We highlight two key observations. First, Senator Shelby articulated policy-level objections, as he was alert to even modest changes in gun control policy. Recall that the measures were limited relative to the legislative proposals Congress had previously rejected. Rulemaking by executive agencies is part of standard governance, as agencies have engaged in rulemaking for as long as Congress has granted agencies the authority to write rules (e.g., Potter and Shipan 2019). Also, any proposed rules must satisfy Administrative Procedure Act requirements for formal and informal rulemaking. And the policy memorandum, directing several agencies to engage in research on gun safety technology, was only tenuously related to an increase in governmental regulations of guns. Nonetheless, a shift away from the status quo generated objections from members of Congress who identified policy losses as a result of unilateral actions by a president.

Second, Senator Shelby forcefully objected to what he perceived as "executive fiat" by these unilateral actions. During this hearing, Shelby linked the announcement of proposed rulemaking and the policy memorandum on research and development of gun safety mechanisms to "executive amnesty to thousands of illegal immigrants." Curiously, the reference to the Deferred Action on Childhood Arrivals raises difficulties similar to the objections to the executive actions on guns. President Obama's action protecting Dreamers from deportation was not an executive order; rather, it was the announcement of an agency guidance document issued by the

Department of Homeland Security. The memorandum initiating the policy identified the authority to establish the program as within the prosecutorial discretion of the president to pursue (or defer) deportations for immigrant youth. Again, the policy direction rather than the tools employed were likely the main concern.

Many media outlets and public officials contemporaneously and subsequently mischaracterized Obama's action as an executive order (see, e.g., Cohen 2012; Klein 2021; McDonnell Nieto Del Rio 2021) thereby overestimating its consequences for both policymaking and constitutionalism. Indeed, properly identifying the specific unilateral actions is not a straightforward exercise, as policy memoranda, agency guidance documents, executive orders, and others are all examples of a more general category of actions presidents can take without congressional review. Both the legal authority and the obligations each instrument places on agencies vary, but members of Congress can investigate those instruments to learn of and critique specific policy preferences of presidents. That is, the tools of unilateralism differ with respect to legal status and policy implementation authority, but they each convey meaning to Congress. And Congress, in turn, can respond strategically to their issuance.

On January 2, 2013, President Obama signed the National Defense Authorization Act (NDAA), which strengthened whistleblower protection for defense and nondefense contractor employees. At the same time, Obama issued a signing statement that was perceived by Senators McCaskill (D-MO) and Grassley (R-IA) and Representatives Cummings (D-NC) and Issa (R-CA) as "undermining congressional intent." In their January 17, 2013, letter to the White House, they admonished the president, "[T]he Legislative Branch has the Constitutionally-mandated authority and responsibility to oversee the Executive Branch . . . [and] we encourage you to enforce the law as written."[1] Clearly, the signing statement caught the attention of members well positioned to respond to presidential unilateralism—the chair and ranking member of the House Committee on Oversight and Government Reform, the chair of the Senate Sub-Committee on Contracting, and the ranking member of the Senate Judiciary Committee.

The president's insistence that he would interpret the law "consistent with . . . [his] authority to direct the heads of executive departments to supervise, control, and correct employees' communications with the Congress in cases where such communications would be unlawful or would reveal information that is properly privileged or otherwise confidential" indicated to the bipartisan group of legislators that executive noncompliance with specific provisions of the NDAA was likely. Debates about Obama's use of executive orders related to the Affordable Care Act and immigration were less bipartisan than the NDAA debates; but the possibility of congressional reaction remained real. Indeed, the threat of legal action against Obama by the Republican-controlled House of Representatives hung over Obama's use of executive orders for much of his second term in office.[2] Threats of congressional oversight when executive implementation counters congressional intent indicate that the struggle over policy implementation is an ongoing process.

In light of the executive-congressional interactions illustrated by the executive actions on gun control, the NDAA implementation, and broader debates over unilateral action, we suggest that this action is one element of the struggle over policy placement (Korzi 2011; Ostrander and Sievert 2013). Courts and independent agency action also play roles (Rudalevige 2021; Potter 2019). These struggles illustrate how ideology, policy placement, and presidential actions frequently become intertwined, regardless of the constitutional debates about institutional prerogatives and the separation of powers that might or might not emerge (Garber and Wimmer 1987; Lee 2009).

Writing about scholarship on unilateral actions, Howell (2003, 134) suggests that considerable work remains:

> Missing . . . is a sustained analysis of the political forces that dictate when presidents will act administratively, when they will pursue legislation, when they entertain both strategies simultaneously, and when they forego action entirely. Insights abound, but no single theory holds them together.

We suggest that a sustained analysis of reactions to unilateral actions is also absent. If "all three branches . . . have the power and duty to interpret the Constitution and . . . the meaning of the Constitution is determined through dynamic interactions of all three branches," then models of presidential unilateral actions must include more than just the president (Calabresi and Yoo 2003, 668–669). Thus, unilateralism cannot be studied in isolation. Congressional resilience in the face of presidential unilateralism and congressional behaviors taken with awareness of the opportunities for unilateral action are important dimensions of the competition between partisans and branches of government as they contest the implementation of policy.

Presidential versus Legislative Dominance

Many scholars explore the tension between congressional and presidential control over policy, with a particular focus on agency-level decision-making. The presidential control literature suggests presidents are advantaged in the "politics of structure" whenever conflicts arise between the executive and Congress over issues of institutional design (e.g., Howell 2003; Moe 1989, 1993; Moe and Wilson 1994). Moe (1993) and Howell (2003) argue that presidents retain important residual decision rights, reflecting their opportunities for centralized control and unilateral action. Similarly, Huber and Shipan (2002) consider the president to be a privileged actor with respect to Congress, while Lewis (2003) and Howell (2003) note the advantages presidents have over policy outcomes because of their ability to shape the design and guide the actions of agencies. The delegation and congressional dominance literatures, however, tend to emphasize congressional effectiveness in achieving desired policy results due to the design of administrative arrangements and congressional budgetary authority (e.g., Balla 1998; Balla and Wright 2001; Bawn 1995, 1997; Epstein and O'Halloran 1994, 1999; Huber and Shipan 2002; McCubbins, Noll, and Weingast 1987, 1989; Potter and Shipan 2019).

Berry (2009) and Francis and Sulkin (2013) connect the presidential and congressional control literatures. Berry (2009) explores whether legislative veto provisions[3] prompt presidential signing statements. Francis and Sulkin (2013) argue that the stature of a legislative support coalition restricts how presidents craft a signing statement.[4] Thrower (2013) explores interbranch competition with a game-theoretic model of the interactions between the president, Congress, and the Supreme Court. In each of these three works, the authors highlight the strategic interdependencies across the branches of government. Although we focus on presidential unilateralism, we consider multiple actors in separate branches of government.

Congress provides the institutional backdrop for several pieces exploring the use of executive orders. Mayer (2001) provides a detailed look at presidents' extensive, wide-ranging use of executive orders, but he does not empirically examine congressional reactions to executive orders. Rudalevige (2021) examines how executive orders are created and points to their creation as a route by which executives are constrained from acting unilaterally. Bailey and Rottinghaus (2014) consider the authority invoked by a president's executive order. Depending on the relative strength of Congress, a president uses statutory or nonstatutory authority. Deering and Maltzman (1999) deem executive orders as means to circumvent a recalci-

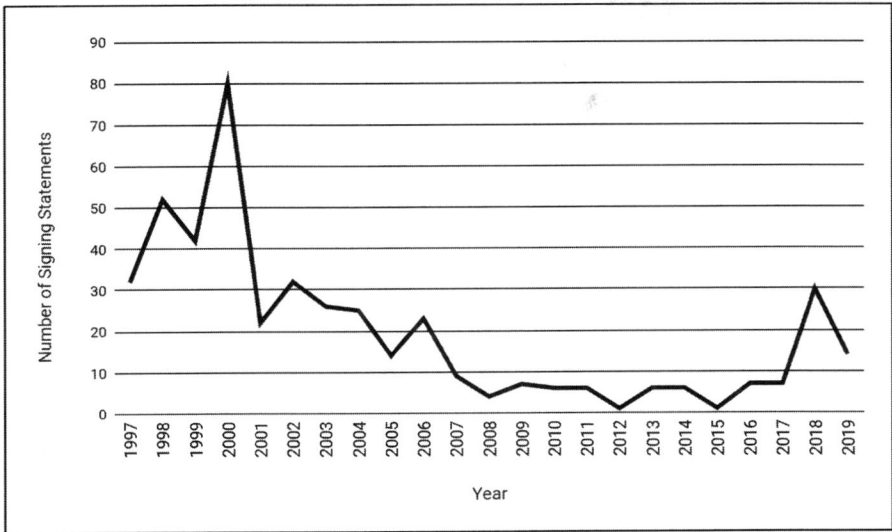

Figure 4.1. Annual Number of Signing Statements, 1997–2019

trant Congress, but a president, in their view, still must anticipate congressional reaction. In these works, the issuance of executive orders is modeled empirically, but there is no assessment of actual congressional reaction. Actions and counteractions are considered but not directly evaluated.

Presidential signing statements, executive orders, policy memoranda, and congressional oversight are all connected to the political control of bureaucracies. For too long, oversight was deemed a neglected function, unable to enhance legislators' careers (Aberbach 1990; MacDonald and McGrath 2016; McGrath 2013, 351–52). Some scholars have suggested that as members of Congress adjust to the strategic deployment of signing statements, such statements will gradually become less useful (e.g., Ostrander and Sievert 2013). Indeed, as seen in Figure 4.1, the use of signing statements peaked around 2000, declined during the Barack Obama presidency, and reemerged during Donald Trump's presidency.

Ostrander and Sievert (2013) make an important point. Within a competitive framework, one should imagine opponents developing strategies to counter one's own successful actions. If signing statements were effective, members of Congress and other political actors would have incentives to develop countermeasures. That said, signing statements affect the "dual principal" or "competing principal" problem, which creates opportunities for bureaucratic drift away from congressional preference. Some congressional countermeasures require collective efforts that are vulnerable to failure due to freeriding. If, for whatever reason, members of Congress fail to counter presidential unilateralism, guidance from presidential directives dominate the placement of policy. Additionally, successful countermeasures are not themselves forever invincible. Consider an analogy. If a tennis player has a monstrous first serve but little else, a worthy opponent learns how to keep a few serves in play to challenge the serving powerhouse. The player who had relied so heavily on a powerful serve does not discard it but does have the incentive to develop additional tools to win matches.

Like those tennis players, presidents and members of Congress parry and counter one another. Given that signing statements reemerged during Donald Trump's presidency, one might speculate that the congresses during the Trump years for some reason were not well situated to parry Trump's signing statements. However, the signing statements alone tell an incomplete story. The total number of objections in signing statements and the average number of objections per statement are more meaningful indicators of the extent of presidential objections as well as indicators of the likelihood of noncompliance on specific issues or policy dimensions of the legislation. Those trends, illustrated in Figures 4.2 and 4.3, peaked in the mid-2000s, show a decline while Obama was president, and then had a resurgence under Trump's presidency.

The unique objections in signing statements provide a more meaningful measure of unilateralism and also a better sense of the policies at stake.

Hypotheses

As our theoretical model developed in Chapter 3 anticipates, not all signing statement objections spur congressional pushback. Signing statement objections and congressional reactions are issue (or dimension) specific. Presidents can use signing statements to trade policy gains on one dimension for losses on another. We hypothesize that concentrated losses in a narrow policy area spur more oversight than diffuse losses spread over numerous policy areas.

As presidents make objections within particular signing statements, some of those objections implicate specific policy issues and would therefore be more likely to trigger congressional reaction. Other, more generalized objections, such as those pertaining to reporting requirements, or broad critiques of legislative intrusion on presidential implementation authority, will likely receive less attention from congressional committees

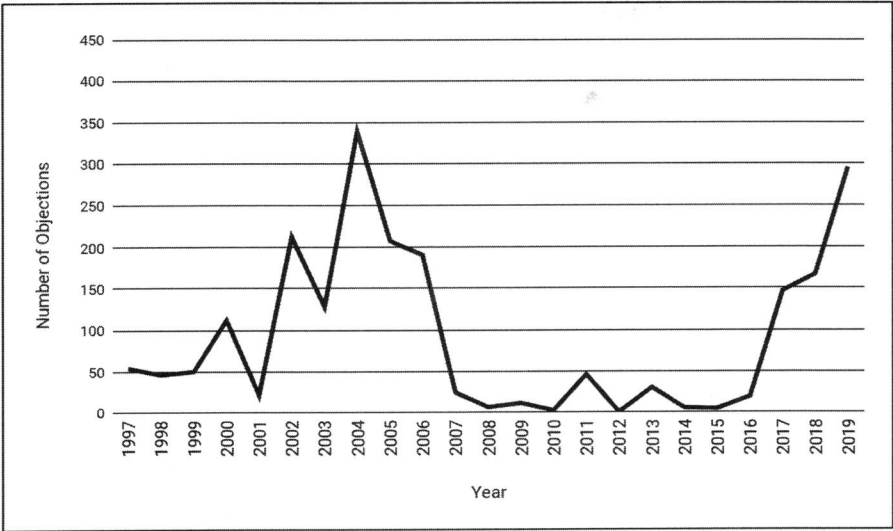

Figure 4.2. Annual Number of Signing Statement Objections to Provisions of Law, 1997–2019

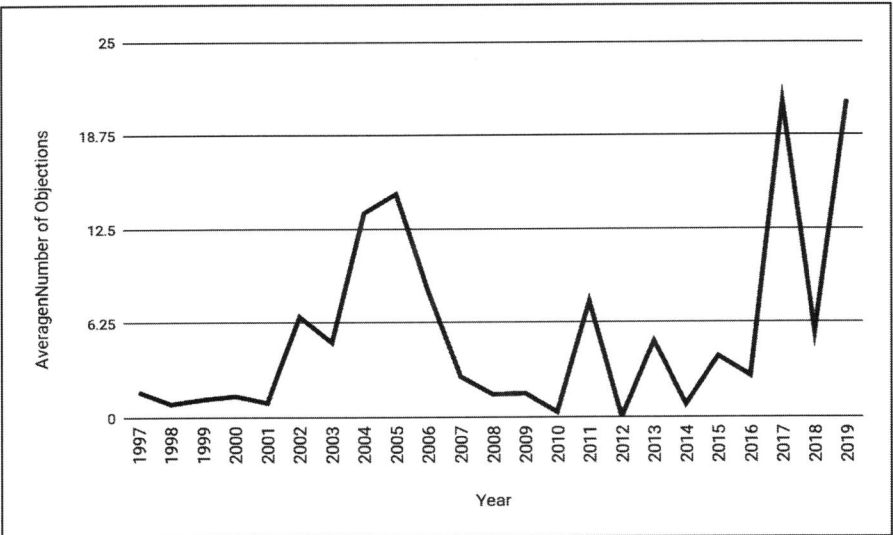

Figure 4.3. Average Number of Objections per Signing Statement, 1997–2019

as they do not generate specific policy loss for members in the same way that dimension-specific objections would. As we have noted previously, presidents have incentives to reinforce the message to executive-level agencies that the president's interpretation of statutes will drive implementation. The broad, generalized statements of objection to procedural requirements imposed by a statute are likely to be anticipated by the legislative coalition, as well as by the committees with oversight authority. Those assertions of presidential prerogative fit a larger, long-standing, and cross-partisan pattern in a way that issue- or dimension-specific objectives do not.

Therefore, we anticipate that oversight will be triggered by a nontypical, rather than an anticipated, presidential response. In some cases, presidents may have expressed their likely objections on issue-specific dimensions by issuing statements of administration policy (SAPs) (Kernell 2005; Kernell and Rice 2005; Rice 2010). The degree to which Congress satisfies the preferences of the president, as articulated in the SAP, indicates how much remains to be objected to in the signing statement. That is, the number and nature of the objectives in a signing statement is a measure of the president's satisfaction with the negotiated result. If Congress is universally accommodating, little remains for the signing statement to address (if one is issued at all), and little uncertainty remains regarding presidential implementation (Ainsworth et al. 2014). More likely, Congress has accommodated the president on some dimensions but not others. This pattern generates presidential objections on specific dimensions to which Congress may be motivated to respond. Irrespective of the issuance of an SAP, then, oversight should follow issue-specific objections more than broad, institutional authority-related objections. Thus, we expect the following:

> *H1*: A higher number of objections to specific provisions of bills should be connected with future, higher levels of oversight activity.

Budget Spending and Oversight

Bargaining between branches that have separated powers involves distributing portions of the policy "pie" (Cameron 2000). Specific allocations of the "pie" may include policy gains (and losses) or key elements of distributive politics such as district- or state-level funding (Evans 2004). The size of the "pie" to be distributed has implications for district-level credit-claiming by members. As the policy proportions in that pie change,

Congress varies its attention to the budgetary process in different policy areas because budgetary tools remain powerful tools to control executive activity (Art 1985).

Rule changes affect the extent to which Congress exercises its control through the budgetary process. The elimination of earmarks in 2011 removed a principal means by which coalitions for distributive politics emerged and accommodated particular members' demands (Courser and Kosar 2021; Evans 2004). When earmarks were eliminated, district-level funding and pork barrel politics remained, but the locus of the bargaining shifted from the legislative branch to the executive (Courser and Kosar 2021; Hudak 2014). Presidents or, more specifically, agencies—and not legislative coalitions—held the authority to allocate portions of the "pie." District-level funding, then, was conditioned by members' ability to negotiate, cajole, demand, and request allocations upon policy implementation, or through lettermarks (Courser and Kosar 2021).[5] Congressional *ex post* oversight provides a mechanism, entirely under the purview of legislators, by which members claim credit, stake claims to district-level spending, and hold the executive branch accountable. Thus, legislators devote more attention to those agencies whose funding has proportionally increased.

H2: As the percentage of the budget spent on differing policy areas increases, legislators engage in more oversight in those areas.

Presidential Approval

The political circumstances surrounding the negotiations over congressional policy likely differ from the circumstances surrounding unilateral action. Legislative action requires collective efforts to secure votes for final passage, while signing statements, executive orders, and policy memoranda are unilateral actions. As members of Congress compromise, accommodate, haggle, logroll, and strongarm to achieve policy gains and avoid policy losses on bills, they have limited means by which to shape the measures independent of other members in the chamber. Legislation that is presented to the president is the totality of those accommodations, compromises, logrolls, and so forth. As seen in Chapter 3, what Congress aggregates the president can disaggregate. As a unitary last mover (at least in the absence of a veto override), the president is in the sole position to capture specific policy gains and losses through unilateral action. The dynamics that shape the presidential decision to shift policy unilaterally on specific dimensions is distinct from the legislative context.

As noted in Chapter 3, members of Congress can anticipate unilateral action and might even rely on it to aid their own blame avoidance strategies. While unilateral actions are not strictly elements of legislative bargaining, they are part of coordinated strategies deployed by presidents as they pursue their policy agendas (see, e.g., Kernell and Kim 2006). As presidents bargain with Congress, their bargaining position is conditioned by their standing with the electorate, among other considerations (Ponder 2017). Popular presidents have bargaining advantages with Congress in a way that unpopular presidents do not (Canes-Wrone 2001; Kernell 2006). But popularity is also considered in light of contemporaneous political polarization in Congress. Presidential leadership on a particular issue may commit co-partisans to the president's position but may also galvanize opposition in Congress (Lee 2009). Among other things, the heightened political polarization has had the effect of breaking down "regular order" in Congress. The rise of entrepreneurial bipartisan "gangs" that move legislation along reduces the role of committees in fashioning legislation (Binder and Lee 2015).

As committees are sidelined from policy development, they may have incentives to reassert committee influence as legislation is implemented through *ex post* oversight (Lewallen 2020). In addition, as noted in Chapter 3, limited congressional action on specific policies on which presidents have taken a public position invites unilateralism. For example, actions by the Obama and Trump administrations reveal the incentives presidents have for unilateralism, especially in the face of congressional inaction or objections. Belco and Rottinghaus recorded instances when presidents used executive orders successfully to preempt or short-circuit concurrent legislative efforts (2017). In 2011, President Obama launched the "We Can't Wait" initiative that sought to exercise unilateral powers in the face of congressional stonewalling. In a 2011 *60 Minutes* interview President Obama stated: "I'm not going to wait for Congress. So wherever we have an opportunity and I have the executive authority to get things done, we're just going to go ahead and do them" (Kroft 2011). And, in 2014, President Obama stated, "I've got a pen to take executive actions where Congress won't, and I've got a telephone to rally folks around the country on this mission" (Keith 2014).

On issues such as mortgage and college loan relief, tax credits for veteran job creation, and regulatory changes for small businesses, Obama issued executive orders and new regulations that circumvented Congress. Similarly, President Trump took numerous unilateral actions as he faced a Democratic House, unwilling to move his legislative agenda on immigration, health insurance, and myriad other issues. Predictably, in both contexts, such unilateralism may generate significant oversight activity in Congress. The conditions under which congressional committees might be motivated to engage in oversight activity will at least in part be driven by the public's regard for the president and the degree to which the president's standing generates electoral payoffs for members' attention to policy implementation. To capture political circumstances, we consider presidential approval and year-to-year emphasis on a series of policy areas, including defense, healthcare policy, the wars in Iraq and counterterrorism, and law and crime policy.

H3: A less popular president experiences more congressional oversight.

Data

The dataset in this chapter spans each month from 1997 to 2018 and includes data on congressional oversight activity, signing statement objections, executive orders, congressional budget spending, and more. Using data from the Policy Agendas Project and excluding appropriations hearings, we gathered data on our dependent variable: the total number of oversight hearings held during each month, year, and policy area from 1997 to 2018. By organizing our data by the policy areas in the Policy Agendas Project instead of committees, we can use policy-related controls that are largely orthogonal to events in Congress. Appendix A of the online appendixes contains summary variables for all measures that we use in this book.[6]

There is some disagreement about what constitutes an oversight hearing. Smith (2003) states that any hearings that are not about legislation or the creation of a new government program or agency are, by definition, about oversight. McGrath (2013, 358) narrows the definition of an oversight hearing because the Policy Agendas Project data would otherwise include many hearings that do not focus on the "review or control of policy implementation" (Dodd and Schott 1979, 156). We follow McGrath's (2013) operationalization and filter the hearings data from the Policy Agendas Project using keywords related to oversight.[7] By being more restrictive when constructing our dependent variable, we are more likely to underestimate congressional sensitivity to unilateral actions than if we used Smith's (2003) definition of oversight hearings. Figure 4.4 shows the number of oversight hearings by month and year in the House and Senate.

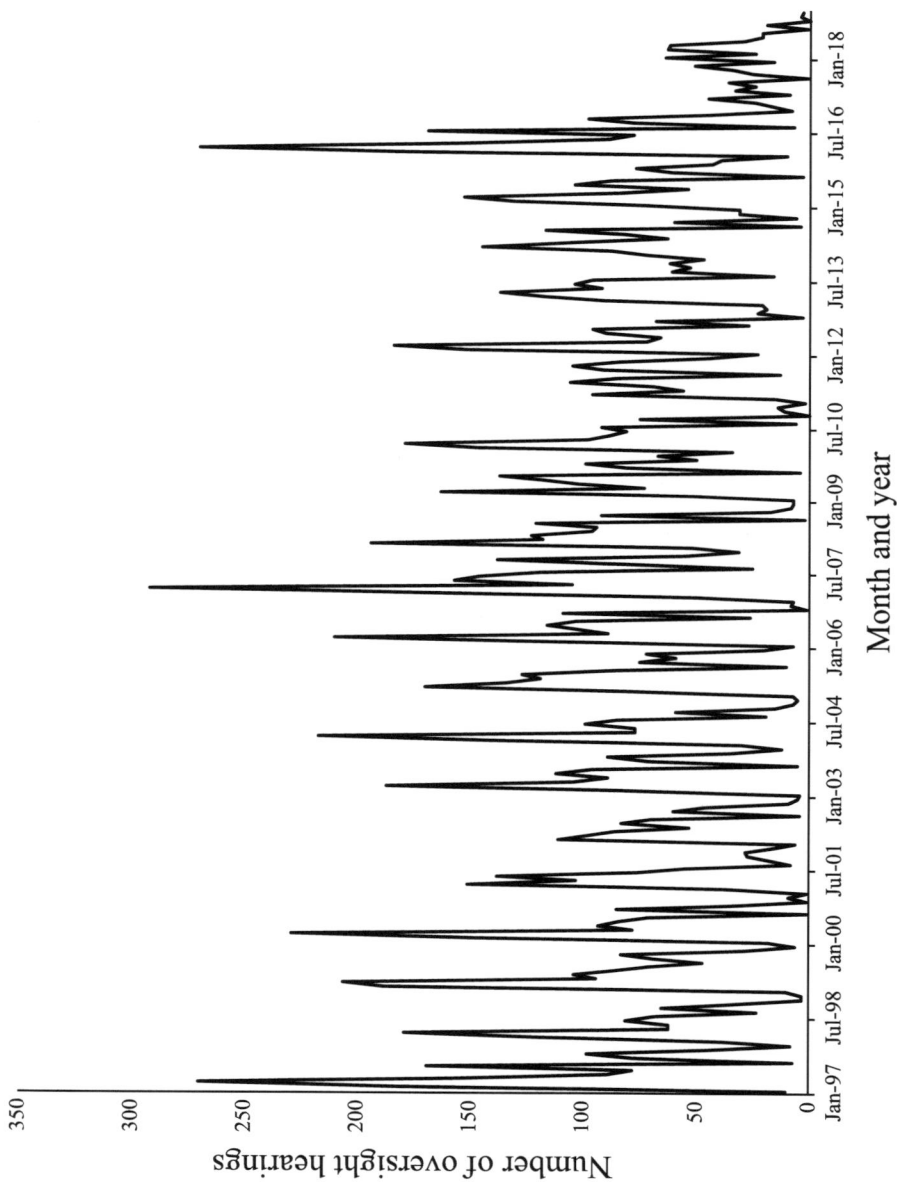

Figure 4.4. Oversight by Month, 1997–2018

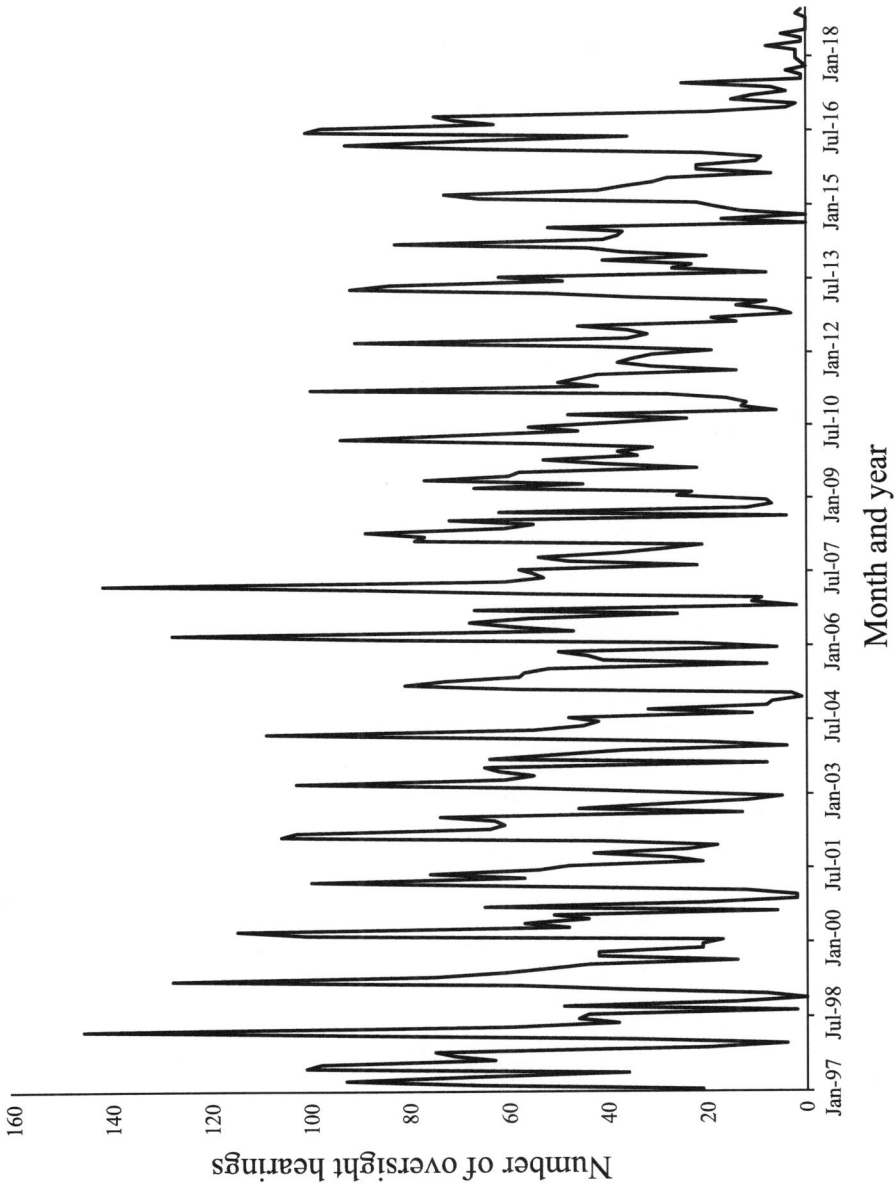

Number of oversight hearings

Month and year

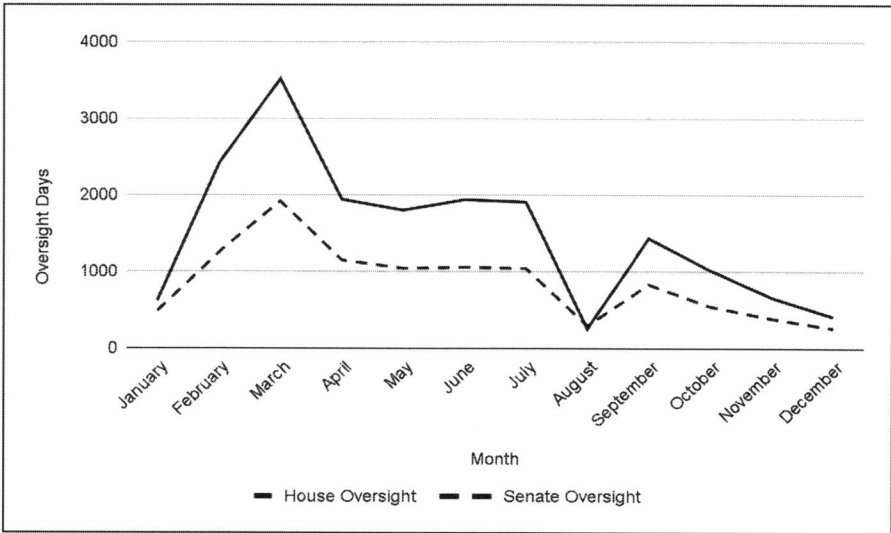

Figure 4.5. Aggregate Oversight by Calendar Month from 1997–2018

Both figures display stationarity, which is important for our econometric tests. Additionally, the figures indicate that the House engages in more oversight than the Senate.

In Figure 4.5, we look for seasonal variations in oversight. Recess months (August and to a lesser extent December and January) have little oversight activity, but from February through July both chambers conduct oversight hearings. After the August recess, oversight activity resumes for September, October, and November but not at the peak levels seen in the spring and summer.

Signing Statements

To investigate whether the contents of signing statements might invite congressional oversight activity, we identified all bills from 1997 through 2018 on which the president placed a constitutional signing statement.[8] We read the signing statements and ascertained the number of objections to provisions of law, recording them by month, year, and policy area. Signing statements can contain a variety of objections, including constitutional concerns, expressions of concern about the cost or scope of congressional action, and objections to specific policy provisions. There were 437 signing statements issued from 1997 to 2018. Regarding objections, Bill Clinton raised 262, George W. Bush 1,130, Barack Obama 117, and Donald Trump 329. On average, signing statements contained 4.21 objections (1.27 for Clinton; 7.29 for Bush; 3.08 for Obama; and 8.89 for Trump). After we read each signing statement, we connected it to its relevant public law. From there, we drew upon bill categorization data from the Policy Agendas Project to connect signing statements and public laws to policy areas.

Descriptive statistics related to signing statements highlight some key issues. As indicated in Figure 4.6, there is substantial variance in the number of objections in signing statements by policy area of the bill on which the signing statement was placed. Defense-related objections clearly dominate, and this holds for each president in our data.

Aside from defense, there is considerable variation in objections by presidents across policy areas. Linking the substance of unilateral actions to the substance of oversight hearings is a monumental task. Reading the signing statements and recording their objections was key to our ability to link objections in signing statements to oversight hearings. We recorded objections in signing statements by month and year. As seen in Figure 4.7, there is annual periodic variation and secular variation over the entire time span. Signing statements typically spike once or twice in the second half of the calendar year.

We employed one-, two-, three-, four-, and five-month lags for signing statement objections. Lags were employed because we expect that the effect of objections in signing statements will occur within the few months immediately after statements are placed on bills. Distributed lags are appropriate because we have very little temporal aggregation in our data and there are severe institutional constraints that prevent immediate congressional responses to presidential actions.[9] In a well-behaved time series, we anticipate that the impact of these lags should dissipate over time. Thus, we anticipate a naturally dissipating impact from our signing statements variables as time progresses.

Executive Orders

For good reason, executive orders are the most commonly studied instrument of presidential power among scholars of American political institutions (see, e.g., Howell 2003; Mayer 2001; Rudalevige 2021). Presidents can make policy using executive orders without concurrent congressional approval, which warrants their scholarly examination as a key feature of unilateralism. We identified all nonclassified executive orders from 1997

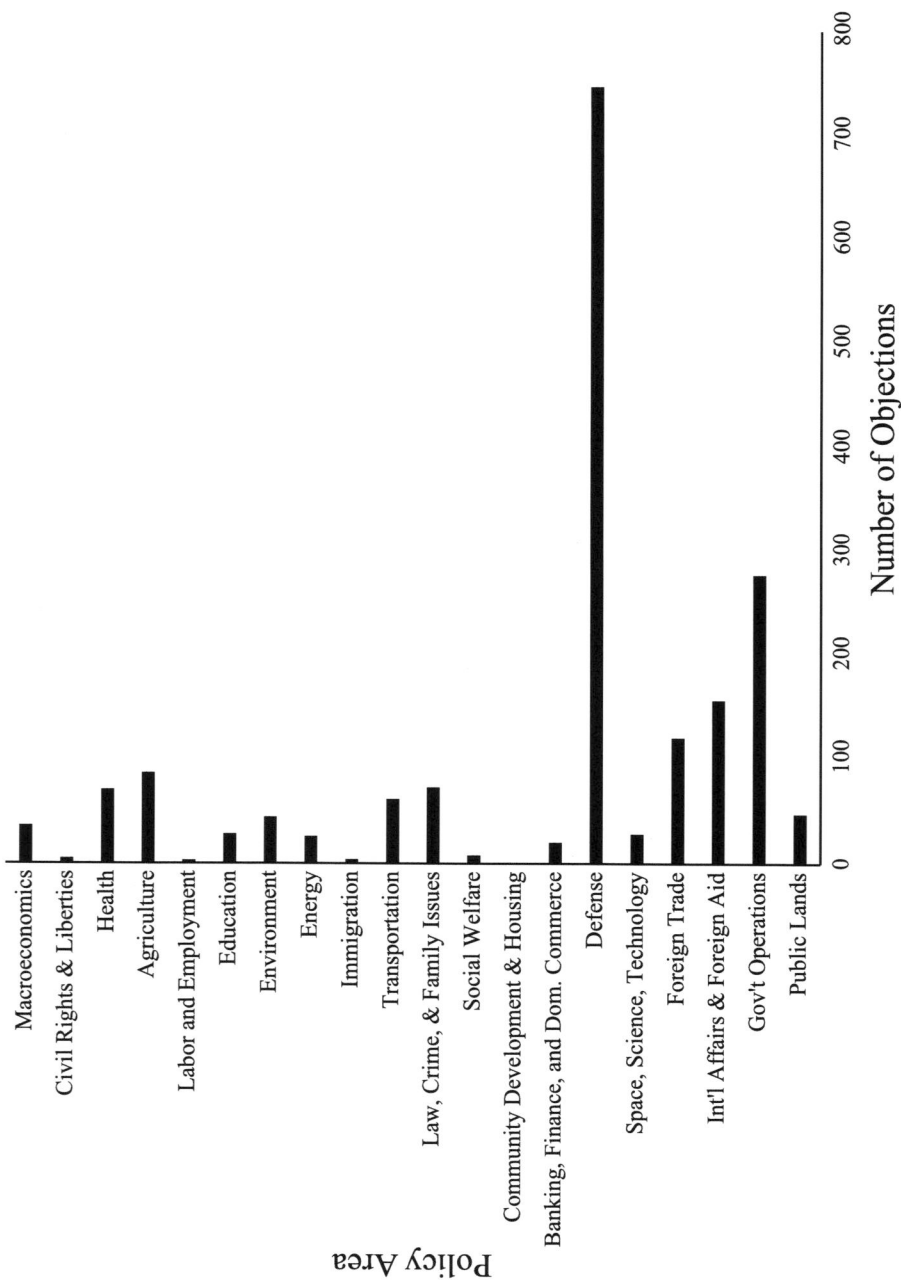

Figure 4.6. Number of Objections in Signing Statements by Policy Area, 1997–2019

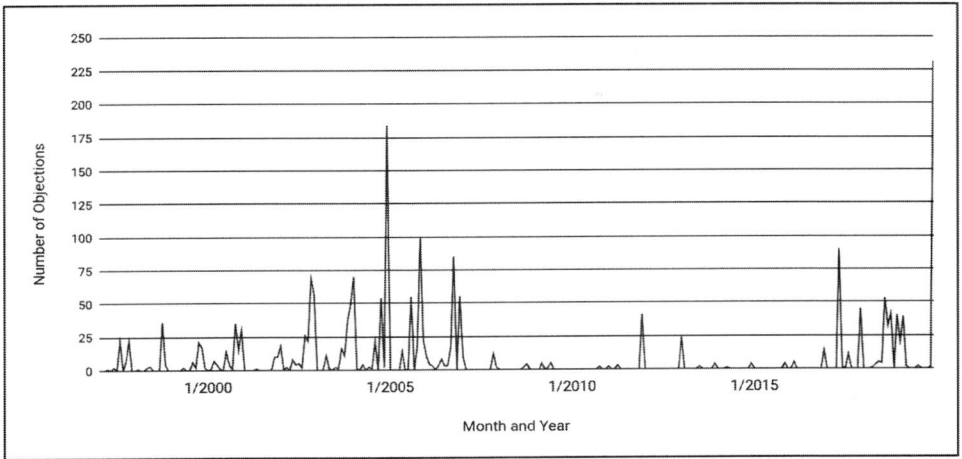

Figure 4.7. Number of Signing Statement Objections by Month, 1997–2019

through 2018 and used policy area categorization data on each order from the Policy Agendas Project to connect public laws to policy areas. Following Rudalevige (2021) and Lowande (2014), we recorded the number of executive orders by month, year, and policy area. We do not distinguish between significant and insignificant executive orders, as scholars use these documents to query the extent to which presidents can make policy independently (see, e.g., Lowande 2014; Rudalevige 2021). By not making this distinction, we stack the deck against obtaining statistically significant results, as Chiou and Rothenberg (2014, 2017) suggest that Congress is more apt to respond to significant presidential actions.

There were 820 executive orders issued from 1997 to 2018—164 by President Clinton, 291 by President Bush, 273 by President Obama, and 92 by President Trump. In Figure 4.8, we display the number of executive orders by year from 1997 through 2018.

Figure 4.8 demonstrates that the use of executive orders peaked in 2001 but has remained between 30 and 40 annually, with a resurgence under President Trump in 2017. In Figure 4.9, we illustrate the use of executive orders by policy area, and see that there are three policy areas in which executive orders get used more frequently: defense, international affairs, and government operations. It makes sense that there are more executive orders about government operations because of the fundamental purpose of executive orders: to issue directives to the bureaucracy as part of managing the daily operations of the federal government. In addition, we see that

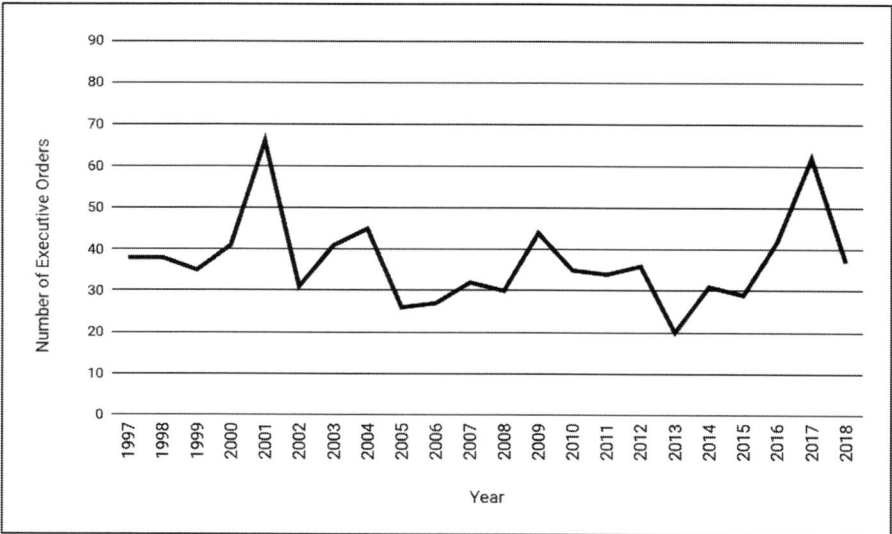

Figure 4.8. Annual Number of Executive Orders, 1997–2018

there are somewhere between 20 and 40 executive orders issued in many of the remaining policy areas.

As with our signing statements variables, we employ one-, two-, three-, four-, and five-month lags for our executive order variables.

Policy Memoranda

Policy memoranda are increasingly used as instruments of presidential power, and subsequently scholars of American political institutions have begun to study them (see, e.g., Lowande 2014; Lowande and Gray 2017; Sievert and Ostrander 2017). These scholars suggest that presidents shifted away from using signing statements and executive orders, as those devices attracted congressional and public attention much more readily than other comparatively "under the radar" devices like policy memoranda. These scholars gently admonish American political institutions scholars about the danger of examining just one or even two devices by which unilateral policymaking can occur.

We heed this admonition and include policy memoranda in our analysis because presidents can make policy using policy memoranda without congressional approval, just as they can with executive orders. We use a multistep process to identify policy memoranda. We begin with Lowande's

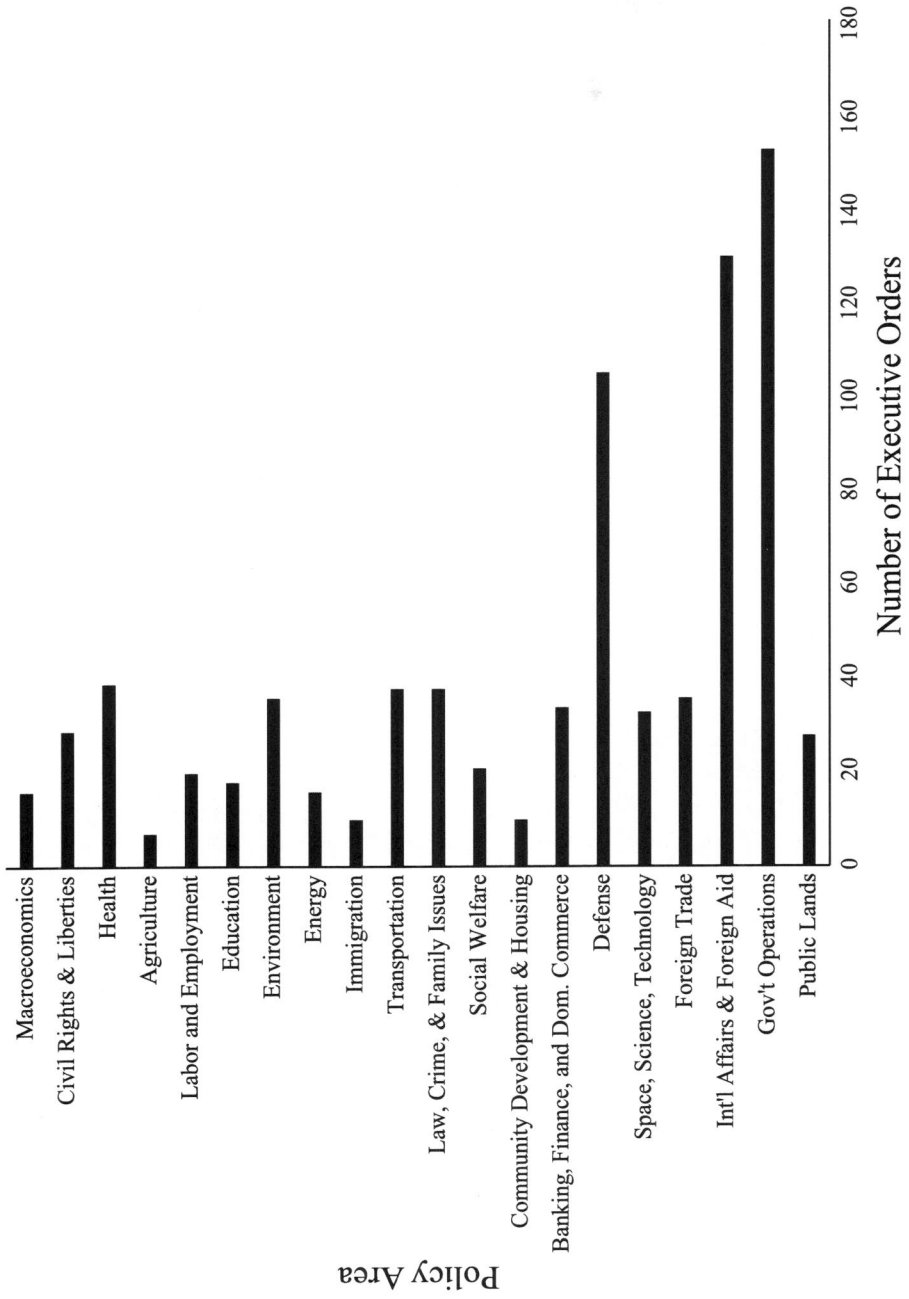

Figure 4.9. Number of Executive Orders by Policy Area, 1997–2018

(2014) list of policy memoranda, as this runs from 1997 to 2013. We then follow Lowande's (2014) selection criteria to extend the policy memoranda list to 2018.[10]

Next, we coded each of these policy memoranda according to the policy areas identified in the Policy Agendas Project, as policy areas were not present in Lowande's original data collection. We use the primary policy area of each memorandum, as we want to discern the ultimate policy area for each document. In the majority of cases, identifying the primary policy area for each memorandum was relatively straightforward. However, in approximately a third of the policy memoranda there is language directing official X to perform action Y based on statute Z, where Action Y can be linked with a policy area from the Policy Agendas Project. Our coding of these memoranda requires attention. A case can be made that these memoranda involve the "government operations" issue area, as the document orders an official to perform a particular action. Conversely, a case can also be made that the focus of these memoranda is on the policy area of a particular action rather than the act of ordering an official to perform a specific act.[11] With these memoranda, we coded the primary policy area for these policy memoranda as the policy area of the specified action, but we note the secondary policy area as government operations. We also note secondary policy areas for the remaining policy memoranda where those exist.

We decided upon this decision rule because our goal is to examine the effects of policy memoranda in discrete policy areas. Moreover, executive orders carry a permanence in a way that policy memoranda do not (see, e.g., Lowande 2014; Lowande and Gray 2017). Consequently, policy memoranda require a level of action that does not always extend to executive orders. We consider policy memoranda as part of the rulemaking process, making sure that an agency implements statutes in a way that the executive intends. To use an analogy here, policy memoranda constitute directions to a fleet, while Congress directs its attention toward specific ships.

Once we coded each policy memorandum for its primary policy area, we recorded the number of policy memoranda by month, year, and policy area. As with executive orders, we make no distinction between significant and unimportant policy memoranda. There were 484 policy memoranda issued from 1997 to 2018—38 by President Clinton, 129 by President Bush, 257 by President Obama, and 60 by President Trump. In Figure 4.10, we display the number of policy memoranda by year from 1997 through 2018.

Figure 4.10 shows that the use of policy memoranda has increased over time, particularly since Obama took office in 2009. There is a clear, seemingly permanent structural increase in the use of these memoranda that

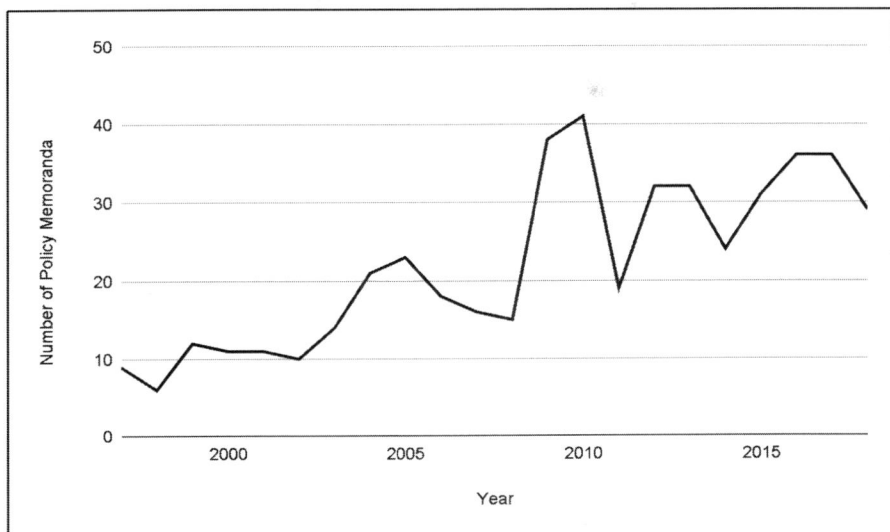

Figure 4.10. Annual Number of Policy Memoranda, 1997–2018

spanned Trump's presidency such that there are around 30 memoranda annually during this period. In Figure 4.11, we show the use of policy memoranda by policy area, and we observe that three policy areas predominate relative to all others: defense, international affairs, and government operation. Additionally, we see that there are fewer than 20 policy memoranda issued in most of the remaining policy areas.

As with our signing statements and executive orders variables, we use one-, two-, three-, four-, and five-month lags for our policy memoranda variables.

Policy-Relevant Factors

We utilized four policy variables to test hypothesis two. First, we gathered Office of Management and Budget (OMB) data on the percentage of the federal budget during the previous fiscal year that was devoted to defense spending. We interacted this variable with the defense policy area, since any effects of defense spending should manifest themselves in that policy category, rather than across all policies. Second, we acquired OMB data on the percentage of the budget during the previous fiscal year that was devoted to Medicare or Medicaid spending. We interacted this variable with the healthcare policy area, since the effects of Medicare or Medicaid

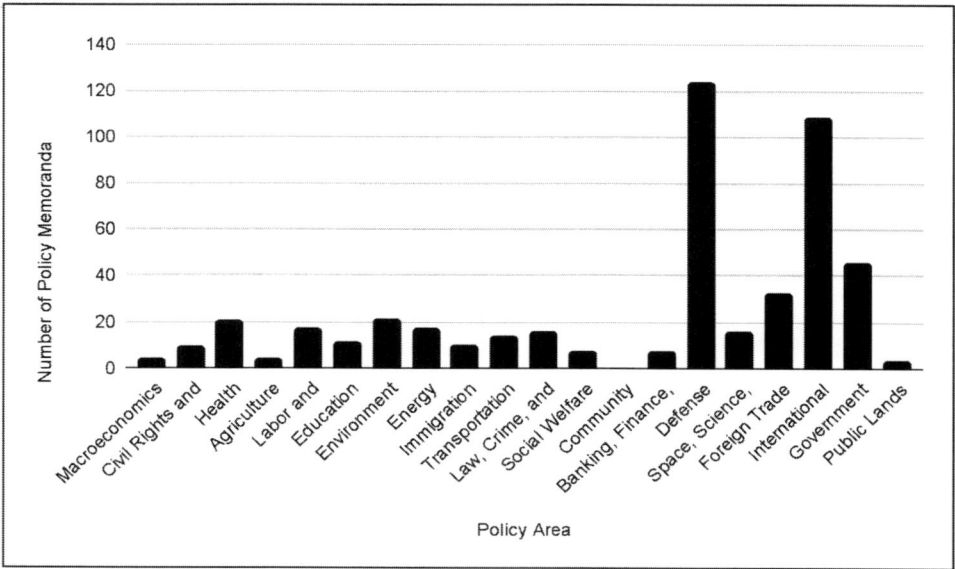

Figure 4.11. Number of Memoranda by Policy Area, 1997–2018

spending should be confined to that policy area rather than being spread across all policies.

Third, we acquired data on the number of violent and property crimes per 100,000 people across the entire country during the previous reporting year from the Federal Bureau of Investigation. We interacted this variable with the Law, Crime, and Family Issues policy area, since we expect the effects of heightened crime on oversight activity to be limited to that policy area rather than public policies in general.

We expect a positive sign on all of the interactive terms, as Congress should be more likely to hold oversight hearings on (i) defense when spending in this policy area takes up a higher percentage of the federal budget, (ii) health care when spending in this policy area takes up a higher percentage of the federal budget, and (iii) law, crime, and family issues when the crime rate is high. Finally, we tested whether the war in Iraq and counterterrorism policy affected oversight activity, as a sizable portion of the controversy over the use of signing statements surrounded the Detainee Treatment Act (Kelley and Marshall 2008; Savage 2006b). To consider these effects, we constructed a binary variable for the International Affairs and Defense policy areas in the months and years after the September 11, 2001, attacks.

We employ two additional variables to control for the effects of fiscal issues on oversight activity. First, we use the percentage of discretionary spending during the previous fiscal year. We consider spending to be discretionary if it is neither mandated by law nor a mandatory payment to individuals, such as Social Security or Medicare. Second, we measure the size of the federal budget deficit (or surplus) as a percentage of the total budget during the previous fiscal year. We acquired data for both variables from the OMB.

Institutional Considerations

To test our third hypothesis, we considered the effects of presidential popularity on oversight activity, as Congress might hesitate to confront a popular president. We measure these effects by using the average approval rating for the president's job performance in the Gallup poll taken during the previous month. We then filtered the series for autocorrelation.

Many scholars investigate the effects of divided government on a wide array of legislative activities, including congressional oversight (see, e.g., Aberbach 1990; Mayhew 2005).[12] If the president and Congress hold similar policy preferences, then we anticipate that Congress is more likely to give the executive branch broad discretionary authority in implementing statutes. Conversely, when at least one house of Congress has a majority of members from the president's opposition party, then Congress is less likely to delegate that control (Epstein and O'Halloran 1999; Ainsworth and Harward 2009; Huber and Shipan 2002). We consider the effects of ideology by examining the distance between the president and the median member of each chamber, using bridge ideal point scores (Bailey 2013, 2021). These scores are comparable across institutions and time by accounting for actors in one institution who take positions on votes in another institution (through amicus briefs, Supreme Court cases, tweets, roll-call votes, or public statements), votes from an earlier time period, and votes being related to ideology (Bailey 2013, 2021). Thus, these scores represent a methodological and conceptual improvement over roll-call-based voting measures.

We utilize four additional institutional controls in the analysis. First, we considered the number of days that the House and Senate were in session per month and year, as Congress is less able to conduct oversight hearings as the number of days in session decreases. Second, we used a binary variable to account for the effects surrounding the second session in each Congress. Third, we include bill counts in the House and Senate because we expect that legislators face time constraints making it difficult to pass bills and engage in oversight simultaneously. Finally, we separated House and Senate oversight activity in our modeling to investigate whether systematic differences exist between the chambers.

Methodology

We are primarily interested in understanding how unilateral actions, as displayed in executive orders and signing statements, affect the number of oversight hearings. We aggregated our data by month, year, and policy area to generate a panel dataset with 5,280 observations that has some properties of a repeated cross-sectional (RCS) dataset. RCS designs recognize that the cross-sectional units can vary in composition over time. That is, features of a policy area (say, its most active legislators or the committees that hold hearings related to it) vary over time, so we cannot use simple differencing or lagged dependent variables that reflect the unit (i.e., policy) level. Multilevel ARFIMA procedures account for the two types of autocorrelation that plague RCS (as well as cross-sectional time series or panel datasets) (Lebo and Weber 2015). First, for a given time period t, policy i might correlate with policy j, but for t + 1, 2, 3, . . . that correlation generally dissipates. Second, within a single policy area i, autocorrelation over time is likely.

ARFIMA employs fractional integration to filter out the influence of past values on a series. The mean of Y_t is filtered to create a stationary series that is free of autocorrelation (Lebo and Weber 2015). The same filtering is used for the X_t and Z_t variables.[13] The Z variables only vary over time, whereas X variables also vary within time units. Combining ARFIMA with multilevel modeling (Lebo and Weber 2015) allows us to nest policy area activities within our units of time. A multilevel model that allows for varying intercepts and slopes fully leverages the structure of our data, since the systematic variance in oversight activity comes from both temporal and policy levels.[14] Additionally, we can include variables (like presidential approval) that do not vary across policy areas within time units.

Our multilevel ARFIMA model enables us to gain a limited degree of causality given that we use observational data (see, e.g., Hainmueller and Hangartner 2019) to estimate the links between oversight activity and the objections in signing statements as well as the issuance of executive orders. Additionally, the processes by which signing statement objections, executive orders, and policy memoranda are generated fundamentally differ from those that produce oversight. If these data-generating processes were similar, then the average change in oversight would be the same for those policy areas where objections in signing statements, executive orders, or policy memoranda were articulated and those areas where signing statement objections, executive orders, or policy memoranda did not arise (see Oosterbeek, van Praag, and Ijsselstein 2010; Mares and Moffett 2019). Absent an ARFIMA model, we would not be able to estimate the relationship between the use of unilateral policy instruments and oversight activity that allows any room for causal inference. Finally, there is no concern about self-selection issues, as policy areas cannot choose to opt out of congressional oversight.

Results

Table 4.1 shows the results for the House and Senate models and separates the variables into five groups—objections in signing statements, executive orders, policy memoranda, policy-related variables, and institutional controls. When assessing the impact of the estimated coefficients, one should keep in mind that key variables are filtered.

Given that the dependent variables are filtered and have means of zero, small coefficients can still indicate considerable impact. Our key variables of interest are the objections in signing statements, executive orders, and policy-related variables. That said, our third hypothesis allowed us to sign key institutional control variables. More specifically, each additional day that Congress is in session increases our filtered oversight activity by slightly less than one-quarter of a day in the House and one-tenth of a day in the Senate. The ideological difference measures and the measure for the second session of a Congress do not attain statistical significance in the models. Bill count is statistically significant. For every additional 100 bills in the House, there are 5.3 additional days of oversight activity, while that same increase in bill volume in the Senate is associated with 3.5 more days of oversight hearings. During the years we analyzed, legislating does not preclude oversight.

Policy Issues and Oversight

Salience of policy issues exerts significant effects on oversight activity when interacted with the associated policy areas in Congress. As seen in the *Defense Policy* variable, each chamber is less likely to perform oversight on defense policy than on other policy areas. The decreases in oversight

TABLE 4.1. Congressional Oversight, Signing Statements, Executive Orders, and Policy Memoranda, 1997–2018

Independent Variable	House of Representatives	Senate
Objections in Signing Statements		
Signing Statement Objections $_{T-1}$	−.056**	−.014
	(.018)	(.013)
Signing Statement Objections $_{T-2}$	.020	.004
	(.018)	(.013)
Signing Statement Objections $_{T-3}$	.082***	.080***
	(.018)	(.013)
Signing Statement Objections $_{T-4}$	.085***	.060***
	(.018)	(.013)
Signing Statement Objections $_{T-5}$	.066***	.047***
	(.018)	(.013)
Number of Executive Orders		
Number of Executive Orders $_{T-1}$	.647***	.248*
	(.134)	(.096)
Number of Executive Orders $_{T-2}$	1.222***	.615***
	(.134)	(.096)
Number of Executive Orders $_{T-3}$	1.250***	.969***
	(.134)	(.096)
Number of Executive Orders $_{T-4}$	.798***	.361***
	(.134)	(.096)
Number of Executive Orders $_{T-5}$	.584***	.384***
	(.134)	(.096)
Number of Policy Memoranda		
Number of Policy Memoranda $_{T-1}$	.690***	.240+
	(.183)	(.131)
Number of Policy Memoranda $_{T-2}$	.441*	.250+
	(.183)	(.131)
Number of Policy Memoranda $_{T-3}$	.282	.0002
	(.185)	(.133)
Number of Policy Memoranda $_{T-4}$	−.009	−.157
	(.185)	(.133)
Number of Policy Memoranda $_{T-5}$	−.112	−.233+
	(.186)	(.133)
Policy-Related Variables		
Budget Deficit	.0005	.0002
	(.0004)	(.0003)
Discretionary Spending	.107	.040
	(.129)	(.072)
Defense Spending	−.082	−.060
	(.181)	(.104)
Healthcare Spending	−.186	−.079
	(.128)	(.074)
Crime Rate	−.004	−.002
	(.004)	(.002)

Defense Policy	−17.690***	−10.480***
	(2.734)	(1.958)
Healthcare Policy	5.895*	17.820***
	(2.364)	(1.693)
Law and Crime Policy	−3.706*	−1.321
	(1.698)	(1.216)
Defense Policy*Defense Spending	1.230***	.713***
	(.152)	(.109)
Healthcare Policy*Healthcare Spending	−.178	−.764***
	(.117)	(.084)
Law and Crime Policy*Crime Rate	.009*	.003
	(.004)	(.003)
Iraq/Counterterror Policy	.074	.077
	(.595)	(.324)

Institutional Controls		
Presidential Approval	−.012	.004
	(.028)	(.016)
Days in Session	.241***	.114***
	(.026)	(.014)
House Bill Count	.053*	−
	(.018)	
Senate Bill Count	−	.035*
		(.015)
President-House Ideological Difference	.052	−
	(.540)	
President-Senate Ideological Difference	−	.038
		(.252)
Second Year	.301	.095
	(.248)	(.141)
Constant	2.899	1.590
	(5.659)	(3.242)

Random Effects, Variance and Standard Deviation		
Time Intercept	2.679	.707
	(1.637)	(.841)
Policy Area Intercept	17.319	8.878
	(4.162)	(2.980)
N	5180	5180
Number of Time Units	259	259
Number of Policy Areas	20	20
Log-Likelihood	−14961.75	−13185.60

Note: The values in parentheses denote standard errors. The values in parentheses in the Random Effects section correspond to the standard deviation. * denotes $p < .05$, ** denotes $p < .01$, and *** denotes $p < .001$, all two-tailed tests. + denotes $p < .05$, one-tailed test.

are demonstrable, as we observe 18 fewer days in the House and 10 fewer days in the Senate devoted to oversight. Congress is more likely to perform oversight on health policy relative to other policy areas, as we observe six more days in the House and 18 more days in the Senate devoted to oversight.

The policy interactions with spending deserve more attention because they offer a more nuanced interpretation of policy areas and oversight. For instance, the defense interaction variable is positive and significant in both chambers even though *Defense Policy* itself is negative. Each 10% increase in the defense spending interactive term is connected to a 12.3-day increase in oversight activity in the House and a 7.1-day increase in the Senate. Health policy spending yields a different dynamic. Although the chambers focus attention on health policy oversight, that attention wanes as health spending increases. Each 10% increase in healthcare spending is associated with an 8-day decrease in oversight in the Senate. Given that the constitutive term in each chamber for defense policy was negative and statistically significant and the constitutive term for health policy was positive and statistically significant in both chambers, we explore the crossover effects displayed in Figure 4.12.

For defense policy, we observe increases in oversight on defense policy as defense spending increases. At 16% of the federal budget (for the House) and 17% of the budget (for the Senate), there are clear crossover effects. At high levels of defense spending, the interactive element overcomes the general structural bias against defense policy oversight indicated by the constitutive variable *Defense Policy*. Once we exceed those spending thresholds, we observe a positive connection between defense spending and congressional oversight activity. In the dataset, the minimum level of defense spending as a percentage of the federal budget is 14.82%, with a maximum of 20.53% of the budget. In fact, the only years in which defense spending as a percentage of the federal budget is less than 16% is from fiscal year 2016 onward, or the last 15 full months of Obama's second term and the Trump years in the dataset. In all other years, we observe a positive overall relationship between defense spending and oversight activity when viewed in this way.

When we examine healthcare policy, we see positive effects on oversight when spending on health is less than 21% of the federal budget in the Senate and 16% in the House. Recall that we see no statistically significant relationship in the House when we examine the interactive term. Once we exceed the 21% threshold in the Senate, we observe a negative connection between healthcare spending and oversight activity in the Senate. In the dataset,

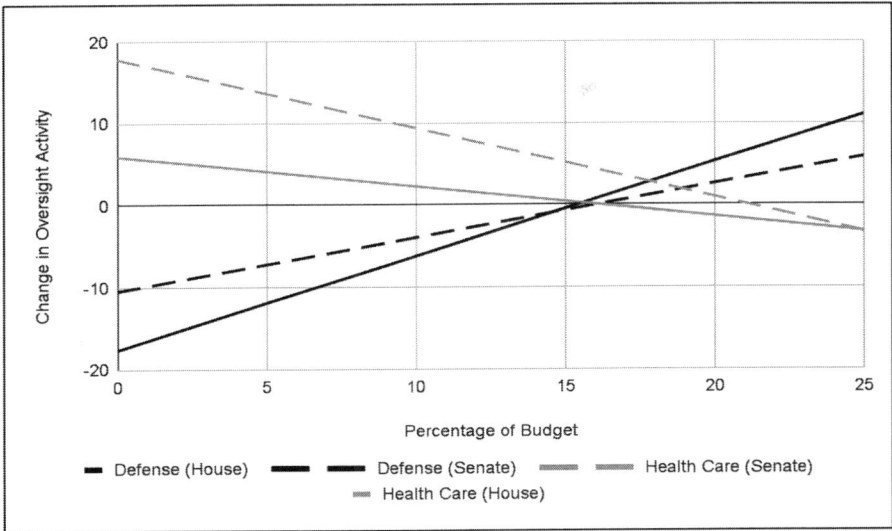

Figure 4.12. Crossover Effects on Oversight for Defense and Healthcare Policy by Chamber

the minimum level of healthcare spending is 16.87%, with a maximum of 24.83% of the federal budget. From 2013 onward, healthcare spending is 23% or more of the federal budget. These fiscal years correspond to the last half of Obama's second term and the Trump years in the dataset. In all other years, we observe a positive overall relationship between healthcare spending and oversight activity when visualized in this fashion.

The crime policy interaction is not statistically significant. The effects of the September 11 attacks exhibit no statistically significant effect in either the House or the Senate. Finally, broader fiscal policy issues, such as the deficit or discretionary spending, exerted no discernible effect on oversight activity in either the House or the Senate.

Unilateral Action and Oversight

Signing statements and executive orders remain our primary variables of interest. Even after controlling for a wide range of concerns, our key variables of interest show considerable statistical and substantive impact. Figure 4.13 illustrates the effect of 10 additional objections to varying provisions of law, relative to the effects of issuing 10 additional executive orders and 10 issuing additional policy memoranda in each the House and Senate.

House

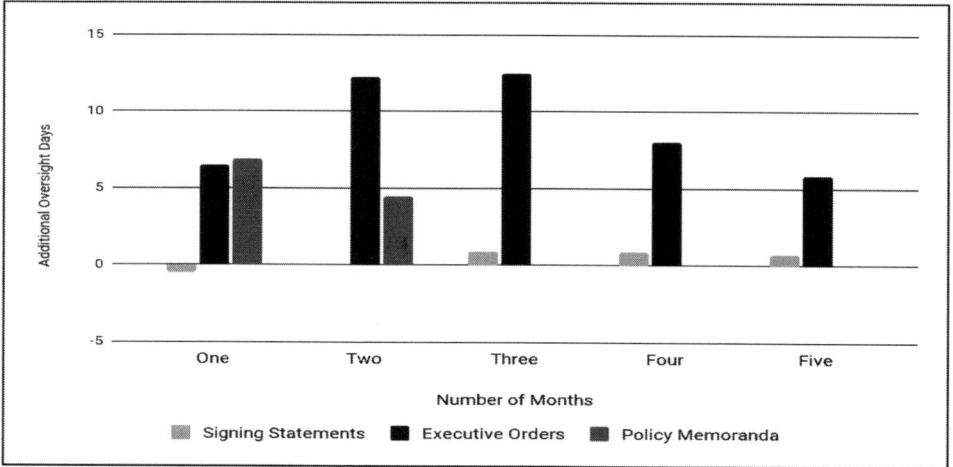

Senate

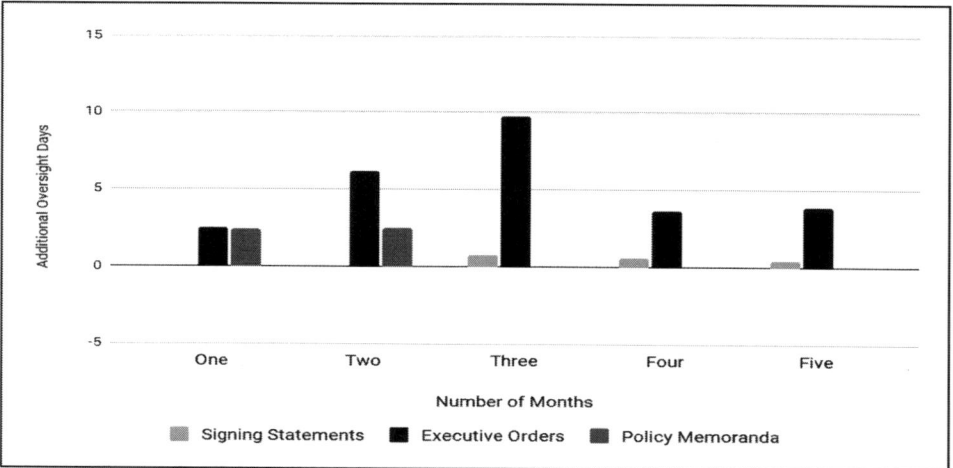

Figure 4.13. Effect of Signing Statements, Executive Orders and Policy Memoranda on Oversight Activity

In Figure 4.13, we see that objections in signing statements in the first two months have either no effect or a negative effect on oversight. By the third month, an increase in objections yields an increase in oversight activity, particularly in the House. For every 10 additional objections to varying provisions of law, there are associated 0.82-day (House) and 0.80-day (Senate) increases in oversight three months after the signing statement was issued, 0.85-day (House) and 0.60-day (Senate) increases in oversight four months afterward, and 0.66-day (House) and 0.47-day (Senate) increases in oversight five months afterward.

The effects from executive orders are stronger than those from objections in signing statements. For every 10 additional executive orders, there are increases in oversight by two days (Senate) and six days (House) one month after the orders were issued. This volume of oversight increases significantly in the second and third months, as every additional 10 executive orders is associated with increases of six days (Senate) and 12 days (House) two months after the orders were issued, increases of 10 days (Senate) and 13 days (House) three months after the orders were issued, increases of four days (Senate) and eight days (House) four months after the orders were issued, and increases of four days (Senate) and six days (House) five months after the orders were issued.

The effects of policy memoranda on oversight are more pronounced in the first two months after they are issued. For every 10 additional policy memoranda, there are increases in oversight by seven days (House) and two days (Senate) one month after the memoranda were issued. And, there are subsequent rises in oversight by four days (House) and three days (Senate) for every 10 additional policy memoranda issued two months prior.

We found similar results across the chambers for the time constraints that days in session create. However, ideology and presidential approval do not matter when compared to issue-specific objections in signing statements and institutional constraints as measured by days in session. Overall, our key variables operated as we hypothesized and show clear substantive significance.

Consistent with our discussion of traceability (e.g., Arnold 1990), presidents' unilateral actions generate congressional response through increased oversight activity. Our findings are significant and noteworthy because we have demonstrated a link between the contents of a unilateral policy instrument and congressional responsiveness to that content.

We also see immediate, demonstrable congressional responses via oversight for both executive orders and policy memoranda. Although reactions to objections in signing statements start more slowly and remain less dramatic, there are still statistically and substantively significant congressional responses.

Possible Limitations

Two empirical issues deserve attention. First, it is possible that our specifications by month, year, and policy area in Table 4.1 drive the results (see Ho et al. 2007; Head et al. 2015). To investigate whether this happens, we removed one year, one month, one policy area, and one variable (or set of variables as appropriate) at a time from the analyses. Then, we re-executed the models with the remaining independent variables. When we examine these models by looking at the signing statements lags, 95.56% (129/135) of the models contain results that mirror those in this chapter. Moreover, 100% (135/135) of the models furnish results that have identical signs and significance patterns when we examine the executive order lags. Additionally, 65.19% (88/135) of the models contain results that either mirror the results in this chapter or are helpful to the argument when we examine the policy memoranda lags.[15] Also, 96.32% (131/136) of the models contain results that have identical signs and significance patterns when we examine all other variables in the models. The remaining cases that deviate from these patterns have little systematic patterning indicative of a broad divergence from our results. Thus, we have little reason to believe that there is a common, systematic set of specifications that drive the results.[16]

Second, it is possible that oversight is connected with higher levels of objections to provisions in law in signing statements or enhanced numbers of executive orders or policy memoranda.[17] To examine whether reverse causality is present, we used each of our unilateral policy instruments as response variables in place of oversight while retaining the lag structures of all remaining covariates in Table 4.1. When we substitute oversight for signing statements, we find that oversight is significant in four of the 10 lags, including three in the Senate (at two, three, and four months), and one in the House (three months). Also, when we substitute oversight for executive orders, oversight is significant in eight of the 10 lags, only not being significant in the Senate at two and four months. Further, when we substitute oversight for policy memoranda, oversight is positive and significant in five of the lags, of which four are in the House (one, three, four, and five months), and one in the Senate (at four months). Altogether, these findings furnish evidence that reverse causality might occur with respect to the statistical relationships discussed in this chapter.

One possible reason for reverse causality lies in omitted variable bias (see, e.g., Greene 2018). To verify whether our models have this issue, we examine whether public perception of the most important policy problem drives oversight activity in addition to our phenomena of interest. We utilize data on the percentage of Americans from 1997 to 2018 who identify a policy problem within each of the major policy areas in the dataset as the primary policy problem in that year based on Gallup polls.[18] If omitted variable bias is present, then the relationships will change between our key independent variables and our dependent variable. When we include this measure in each of our House and Senate models, the statistical relationships that we find remain unchanged in terms of signs and significance patterns with one exception: the binary indicator for law and crime policy remains statistically significant at $p < .05$ with a one-tailed test. Because the statistical relationships do not otherwise change, we retained the models in this chapter without that measure.[19]

Nonetheless, the possibility of reverse causality does require further investigation. One way by which we can do so is to examine the policy area in which we observe the highest number of objections in signing statements, the most prevalent issue in which the president issues executive orders, and the most common issue in which the president promulgates policy memoranda: defense policy. Our examination of defense policy in the next chapter will allow us to examine the causal relationships that we articulated in this chapter more closely.

Conclusion

In this chapter, we demonstrated several things. First, Congress, regardless of chamber, varies its oversight activity depending on the policy area in question in response to our measures of issue salience and budgetary pressures. Second, we uncover mixed evidence for the effects of institutional factors on oversight activity. On the one hand, the number of days that Congress is in session during each month affects oversight activity. However, bicameral differences or the effects of being in the second year of the legislative session are not associated with changes in oversight activity.

In the previous chapter, we showed how blame avoidance among legislators creates opportunities for unilateral actions by presidents. Indeed, we suggested that legislators can anticipate unilateral actions and then claim credit by responding to those unilateral actions that are most problematic in terms of policy losses. Oversight, an increasingly important congressional activity (e.g., Lewallen 2020), increases after presidents employ unilateral policymaking instruments. In particular, we discovered that objections in signing statements yield higher levels of oversight activity, regardless of the chamber examined. In addition, we found that higher numbers of executive orders and policy memoranda are associated with higher levels of congressional oversight, regardless of chamber. These findings are important because we have demonstrated a direct link between the policy focus of unilateral instruments and congressional responsiveness to the information conveyed in those actions. This chapter provides direct evidence that objections in signing statements and the issuance of executive orders and policy memoranda result in pushback from the House, Senate, and Congress as a whole. Despite remonstrances of unconstitutional presidential overreach via unilateral actions, the congressional responses uncovered in this chapter are policy focused rather than constitutionally grounded.

In the next chapter, we focus on defense policy, as this policy area garners significant attention from presidents, legislators, scholars, journalists, and the public. By focusing on defense-related bills, we consider congressional sensitivity to presidential unilateralism as a "most difficult case." Defense is by far the most common issue area to generate policy objections from presidents. It is also an issue area, like foreign affairs, where many scholars have argued that Congress gives the president a large measure of discretion. In this "most difficult case," we find that Congress *still* responds with increased oversight to the president's disaggregation of policy.

FIVE

Is Defense Policy Different?

It is the nature of war to increase the executive at the expense of
the legislative authority.

—Alexander Hamilton, *Federalist #8*

On August 2, 2017, President Trump signed the Countering America's
Adversaries Through Sanctions Act (CAATSA), which placed sanctions
on Russia, Iran, and North Korea. At the same time, Trump issued two
signing statements that received bipartisan condemnation from Senators
Durbin (D-IL), Gardner (R-CO), McCain (R-AZ), Schumer (D-NY), and
House minority leader Nancy Pelosi (D-CA). Senator Durbin declared,
"The president['s] signing statement is nothing like I've ever read before"
(CNN 2017). Senator Gardner stated, "Look, whether it was President
Bush, President Obama, or President Trump, I've never been a fan of
signing statements" (Nussbaum and Schor 2017). He added, "I think that
they're a way for any president to usurp the role of the legislative branch.
And that's why I've always been concerned, regardless of who issued them,
on any matter" (Nussbaum and Schor 2017). Senator McCain (2017) was
more pointed in his criticism: "The concerns in the President's signing
statement are hardly surprising, though misplaced. The Framers of our
Constitution made the Congress and the President coequal branches of
government. The bill has already proven the wisdom of that choice."

Unsurprisingly, Democratic Party leaders in Congress were even
more critical of President Trump's signing statements on this bill. Senator
Schumer (2017) argued, "The President's extended signing statement . . .

demonstrates that Congress is going to need to keep a sharp eye on this Administration's implementation of this critical law and any actions it takes with respect to Ukraine." Finally, Nancy Pelosi (2017) stated, "President Trump's signing statement raises serious questions about whether his Administration intends to follow the law, or whether he will continue to enable and reward Vladimir Putin's aggression."

In his first statement on the bill, the president chided Congress for having included "a number of clearly unconstitutional provisions" (Trump 2017a). Trump continued, "My Administration will give careful and respectful consideration to the preferences expressed by the Congress in these various provisions and will implement them in a manner consistent with the President's constitutional authority to conduct foreign relations." In his second statement, Trump (2017b) added, "Since this bill was first introduced, I have expressed my concerns to Congress about the many ways it improperly encroaches on Executive power, disadvantages American companies, and hurts the interests of our European allies." In an apparent dig at Congress, Trump (2017b) stated that "the bill remains seriously flawed, particularly because it encroaches on the executive branch's authority to negotiate. Congress could not even negotiate a healthcare bill after seven years of talking." In his final parting shot, Trump stated, "As President, I can make far better deals with foreign countries than Congress" (Trump 2017b).

All to say, these statements indicated to members of Congress from both political parties that executive noncompliance with specific provisions of the CAATSA was likely. Threats of congressional oversight if executive branch implementation countered congressional intent indicated that the struggle over policy implementation would likely continue. The signing statements on the CAATSA demonstrate how policy disaggregation can characterize presidential unilateralism. At the beginning of the second statement, President Trump (2017b) wrote:

> I favor tough measures to punish and deter bad behavior by the rogue regimes in Tehran and Pyongyang. I also support making clear that America will not tolerate Russian subversion and destabilization. . . . My Administration has attempted to work with Congress to make this bill better. We have made progress and improved the language to give the Treasury Department greater flexibility in granting routine licenses to American businesses, people, and companies. . . . Yet, despite its problems, I am signing this bill for the sake of national unity.

By addressing countries individually and by separating American business interests, the signing statement hints at the disaggregation of what Congress had combined.

In light of the executive-congressional interactions illustrated by the CAATSA and its implementation, we suggest that presidential unilateralism in the form of signing statements exemplifies the struggle over policy placement (Korzi 2011; Ostrander and Sievert 2013a). The CAATSA offers another illustration of how ideology and presidential actions become intertwined, especially as constitutional debates about institutional prerogatives and the separation of powers emerge (see, e.g., Garber and Wimmer 1987; Howell 2003; Lee 2008; Bolton and Thrower 2015; de Figueriredo et al. 2008).

For our purposes, the CAATSA also illustrates the potential for congressional responsiveness to unilateral presidential action applied, in part, to defense policy. In the previous chapter, we saw that many more signing statements and executive orders occurred in defense policy relative to all others. Similarly, we saw that the plurality of objections to varying provisions of law also occurred in the defense policy area. Thus, we take a closer look at this area for two reasons. First, defense policy is often highly salient, consistently attracting high levels of attention from policymakers, scholars, and the public. Second, we want to reconsider the fact that in the preceding chapter objections in signing statements were attributed to the same policy area as the associated bill. Given that bills are often multidimensional, could signing statement objections be similarly multidimensional?

Recall from the preceding chapter that we collected every signing statement from 1997 to 2018 and connected each statement to its relevant statute. Each statement was also coded for unique objections, and those objections were simple counts.[1] In Chapter 4, objections within a signing statement were associated with the same policy area that the Policy Agendas Project assigned to the bill. In that chapter, we also found that defense policy generated most of the objections to provisions of law contained in presidential signing statements. In sum, the measures used in Chapter 4 were less refined than what we employ here.[2] Recall our central argument that bills often aggregate myriad issues. In this chapter, we explore the signing statement objections themselves to assess their policy area focus.

The defense-related bills we examine in this chapter often include provisions that affect a wide array of issues, reflecting the multidimensional aspect of legislation *and* signing statements. For this chapter, we assessed every signing statement objection, coding it as defense related or not. Accordingly, in this chapter, not all objections in signing statements tied to defense bills are related automatically to defense policy. This refined measure is important because it highlights the multidimensionality of legislation and the surgical attention to the implementation of policy. Just as signing statement objections are refined and narrowly focused, congressional pushback should be most closely tied to signing statement objections related to defense. Raw counts of objections (as in Chapter 4) are a good start, but here we bore more deeply into the targets of those objections. Therefore, our measure of policy-specific objections should be better in this chapter, and the congressional pushback should increase concomitantly.

In the next section, we review the underlying literature on defense policy and consider the different factors that drive relations between Congress and the president in this policy area. We then test the theoretical expectations derived in Chapter 3 using the defense policy subset of the data introduced in Chapter 4. In the final sections, we discuss our results and examine how legislators work to avoid blame and claim credit as they negotiate policy with the president and engage in ex-post evaluations of the implementation of policy.

Presidents, Congress, and Defense Policy

Many scholars view the interbranch conflict over defense policy as one in which the president has the upper hand (e.g., Canes-Wrone, Howell, and Lewis 2008; Wildavsky 1966). These scholars argue that there are two presidencies (one focused on domestic policy and the other on foreign policy) and that Congress has much more influence over domestic policy than over foreign policy (Canes-Wrone, Howell, and Lewis 2008; Wildavsky 1966). Canes-Wrone, Howell, and Lewis (2008) discover evidence that favors the "two presidencies" thesis, as presidents exercise significant influence when it comes to budgetary appropriations related to foreign and defense policy.[3] In their exploration of executive orders, Chiou and Rothenberg (2017) find that presidents have the freest rein with foreign affairs.

The incentive systems underpinning the two presidencies thesis are clear. Members of Congress seek to claim credit and avoid blame. Credit claiming for narrowly focused domestic policies is more credible than credit claiming on foreign policies. Blame avoidance also prescribes caution relative to involvement in foreign affairs. Given limited benefit and considerable downside for members of Congress, presidents operate more freely. Indeed, Fisher (2012) expressed concern that Congress has over-delegated to the executive branch with respect to national security policy to such an extent that it has endangered civil liberties.

Presidents also appear to become more powerful, relative to Congress, during wartime (see, e.g., Howell 2011). Presidents achieve more legislative victories and have more of their budget requests honored during military conflicts (Howell, Jackman, and Rogowski 2013). Howell, Jackman, and Rogowski (2013) and Howell and Jackman (2013) also find that support for the president during times of war pervades policy areas beyond foreign and defense policy. Indeed, when foreign and defense policies are highly salient to the public, presidents are more successful legislatively (Schorpp and Finocchiaro 2017).

A concurring line of research questions whether Congress is willing or capable of overseeing the executive branch regarding either foreign or defense policy. Auerswald and Campbell (2012, 5–6) state that Congress is frequently so preoccupied with domestic policy that it seldom intervenes in foreign policy arenas. Worse yet, Auerswald and Campbell (2012) and Art (1985) note that when Congress does become involved, it is more motivated by parochial interests like reelection than by national interest. In addition, Congress is frequently unwilling to engage with foreign or defense policy when the president comes from the same political party (Auerswald and Campbell 2012). Yet Auerswald and Campbell (2012) also argue that Congress is somewhat incapable of overseeing the presidency with respect to defense or foreign policy because of partisan differences within or across chambers, turf wars between committees (cf. King 1997), and supermajoritarian requirements.

Similarly, Oleszek and Oleszek (2012) argue that Congress has a difficult time keeping pace with the executive branch in defense policy because it crosses several discrete policy areas, ranging from cybersecurity to climate change. Fowler (2015) and Oleszek and Oleszek (2012) argue that Congress has been less willing to engage in oversight over defense policy than in domestic affairs. For instance, Representative Barney Frank (D-MA) lamented on the House floor on July 13, 2006, that:

> we have seen an overreaching by the President. . . . a seizing of power that should not have been seized. . . . But executive over-reaching could not have succeeded as much as it has without congressional dereliction of duty. (Oleszek and Oleszek 2012, 53)

Finally, Congress has a hard time overseeing defense policy because the presidency has taken on a larger role in these policy areas after September

11, 2001 (Oleszek and Oleszek 2012, 59). Thus, a Congress that is neither willing nor capable of effectively overseeing the executive branch concedes significant institutional power, the placement of highly salient policy, and an important democratic check on a "grave danger."

Congressional Responsiveness

Presidential dominance may not be absolute with respect to defense and foreign policy, however. Even in an era in which presidents often act unilaterally across policy areas, including defense, congressional preferences can meaningfully constrain executive action. Lindsay (1992–1993) argues that Congress matters in several respects with respect to influencing how presidents conduct defense and foreign policy. More specifically, Congress can influence policy indirectly through political grandstanding, anticipating reactions from individual members of Congress, and changing the ways that decisions get made within the executive branch (Lindsay 1992–1993, 609). Congress can change how decisions get made in the executive branch by employing legislative vetoes,[4] attaching conditions before the president can go forward with a policy, using reporting requirements for agencies, or adding new groups to the public policymaking process (Lindsay 1992–1993).

Blechman (1992), Fisher (2012), Kriner (2010), and Krutz and Peake (2009) suggest that Congress sometimes asserts itself with respect to defense policy, though with mixed success. Congress asserted itself during the 1970s by passing the War Powers Resolution, limiting funding for the Vietnam War, and requiring Congress to be kept aware of any foreign weapons sales (Blechman 1992). Congress has become more involved with respect to military appropriations since the Vietnam War (Blechman 1992; Carsey and Rundquist 1999), partly because subcommittees became more powerful following the 1974 congressional reforms (Smith and Deering 1997; Blechman 1992). Moreover, the Congressional Budget and Impoundment and Control Act placed new limits on the executive branch regarding spending decisions, effectively mandating that Congress consider revenues and expenditures across policy areas in ways that forced members to consider trade-offs between domestic and foreign policy (Blechman 1992).

During the 1980s, Congress, sensitive to wasteful spending, asserted itself in the appropriations process with increased oversight. In a speech at Central College on November 13, 1985, Senator Chuck Grassley (R-IA) commented:

You can learn a lot from watching pigs. They lie around and eat all you feed them, but the end result is good eating and an efficient use of food. Defense Department procurement officials are a lot like pigs. They eat all you feed them, but the end result is $700 toilet seats. Pigs will be pigs, whether they wear three-piece suits or mud. . . . Congress can and must change the eating habits of the Pentagon pig. When they find the courage to change that diet, the Pentagon pig will squeal loud and clear. All it takes, however, is a little courage. (Blechman 1992, 36)

Since that time, Congress has become more active with respect to defense and foreign policy appropriations. Carsey and Rundquist (1999) find that the distribution of military expenditures is consistent with the geographic distribution of members of Congress on committees that deal with defense policy. However, this distribution also occurs with a partisan overlay, as benefits are disproportionately distributed to members of the majority party (Carsey and Rundquist 1999; Evans 2004).

Caruson and Farrar-Myers (2007) and Krutz and Peake (2007) note the rise in the use of executive agreements in forming partnerships with other countries as opposed to treaties. To many, this change is significant because treaties go through the Senate for ratification, while executive agreements require no ratification (Krutz and Peake 2007). Thus, the president can negotiate and sign executive agreements without congressional input. Some may read this shift as yet another indicator among many that presidents make an increasing proportion of public policy unilaterally (see Crenson and Ginsburg 2007; Howell 2003; Mayer 2001; Rudalevige 2005).

Kriner (2010) finds that Congress uses oversight to constrain the president during wartime, especially when partisan control differs from the party occupying the White House. However, this is done somewhat strategically, as Congress waits for easy openings, lest it be accused of inadequately supporting American troops (Kriner 2010). Kriner (2010) goes beyond oversight and discovers that Congress constrains the executive in defense and foreign policy in other ways as well.

This discussion suggests that Congress is sometimes influential with respect to defense and foreign policy, even as the president acts unilaterally. Of course, congressional influence requires congressional awareness. Oversight is one means of maintaining awareness and exercising influence. Art (1985) notes that Congress has expanded opportunities to engage in policy oversight due to the increased influence of subcommittees and the overlap in committee jurisdictions (cf., King 1997). Art (1985) states that Congress has capitalized on these opportunities as it has become more active in managing defense appropriations. However, non-budgetary oversight of defense policy has taken a backseat because many members of Congress adhere to their party dictates and focus on electoral considerations (Art 1985). Owens (2009) finds that this trend held strongly after the September 11, 2011, attacks, as Congress largely deferred to the executive branch.

Fowler (2015) extends and corroborates Art's observations regarding defense policy: there are lower levels of oversight with respect to defense and foreign policy. In particular, Fowler (2015, 5) finds that the Senate Armed Services Committee shielded Republican presidents from public oversight related to policy implementation and crisis management, but that the Senate Foreign Relations Committee initiated broad inquiries during times of divided government. What is more, Fowler (2015) discovers that senators were more attuned to policy effects on particular constituencies than to the broader foreign policy decisions that garner most public attention.

To summarize the literature, presidents act unilaterally with respect to foreign and defense policy and, in that sense, are privileged in directing defense-related policy relative to Congress. Additionally, some evidence indicates that patterns in these defense-related policy areas differ from those observed in domestic policy areas (Canes-Wrone, Howell, and Lewis 2008). At times, unilateral actions received either implicit or explicit endorsement from Congress (e.g., Krutz and Peake 2007; Owens 2009), but the behavior is hardly universal. When Congress responds, it can be effective, especially on budget-related issues (Carsey and Rundquist 1999) and when wars begin (Kriner 2010). In the area of defense policy, congressional deference to presidential policy priorities appears to be the norm, especially during wartime. However, under some conditions, members of Congress are motivated to influence the shape of those policies. We expect that even in the context of this "harder case" of defense policy (as opposed to domestic affairs), where presidential unilateralism is common and congressional deference is the norm, Congress responds to unilateralism with heightened oversight activity.

Data and Methods

Linking the substance of unilateral actions (signing statements, executive orders, and memoranda) with that of oversight hearings is a nontrivial task. To do so, we gathered data on every oversight hearing on defense policy held each month from 1997 to 2018 using data from the Policy Agendas Project.[5] As in Chapter 4, we use a variant of McGrath's (2013) operationalization and filter the hearings data from the Policy Agendas Project using keywords related to oversight.[6, 7] The keyword search likely captures reauthorization hearings, but their inclusion is not guaranteed. Thus, we add reauthorization hearings to the mix because, by design, they review policy.[8]

Figure 5.1 displays defense oversight hearings from 1997 to 2018 for the House and Senate. Because our dependent variable is the month-by-month *change* in defense oversight hearings, the observations in our dataset may not be independent of each other. If there is serial correlation in a dependent variable, then using ordinary least squares (OLS) can produce results that appear to be statistically significant, while in reality they are not. Thus, we need to check for autocorrelation and stationarity to determine which estimation technique is most appropriate.

Although Figure 5.1 hints at nonstationarity, our dependent variable is the change in defense oversight hearings. The augmented Dickey-Fuller (ADF) and Phillips-Perron tests suggest stationarity in the change in defense oversight for both the House and Senate.[9] Similarly, the results of the Kwiatkowski, Phillips, Schmidt, Shin (KPSS) test, in which stationarity is the null hypothesis, rejects the null in all 15 lag orders for both House and Senate oversight. Consequently, we cannot conclusively eliminate the possibility that a unit root exists since the results of the KPSS test indicate some sensitivity to the lag-order specification.

Since the KPSS test does not eliminate the possibility of a unit root and the ADF test suggests that this might be present, a conservative estimation approach is to apply an error correction model (ECM). Consistent with De Boef and Keele (2008), we employ the modeling structure that is simultaneously the least restrictive in the assumptions that it places on the data and is the most appropriate for non-stationary data. Enns et al. (2016, 3–4) argue that an ECM can be used in a situation where the dependent variable is a bounded unit root, which exists in our work because the lower value of oversight is zero. More specifically, "[T]he GECM [generalized error correction model] performs no worse with bounded unit roots than it does with the integrated time series" (Enns et al. 2016, 3). The ECM estimates whether our independent variables have short-term effects or long-term, equilibrium-like effects or both.[10]

This approach also allows us to gain a degree of causal leverage (Hainmueller and Hangartner 2019), as our work meets some of the assumptions that underlie causal inference techniques. First, the process by which values of our primary independent variables (objections to provisions in

House

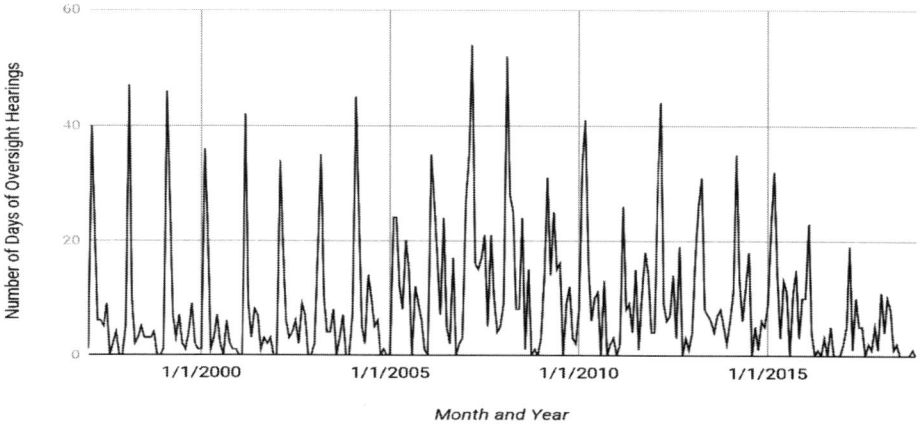

Month and Year

Senate

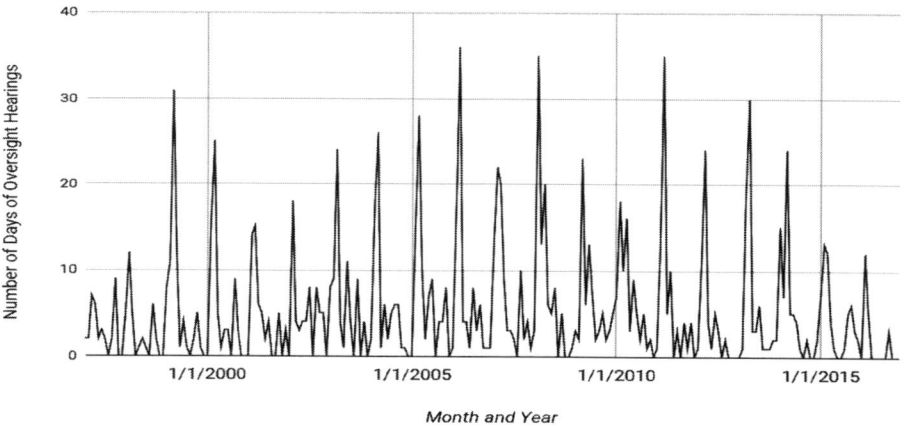

Month and Year

Figure 5.1. Oversight on Defense Policy by Month, 1997–2018

law in signing statements, executive order issuance, and policy memoranda issuance) are generated differs from the process by which our dependent variables (House and Senate oversight, respectively) are produced. Second, there is no self-selection, as Congress cannot "opt out" of presidents issuing objections to provisions of law in signing statements or having executive orders and policy memoranda issued.

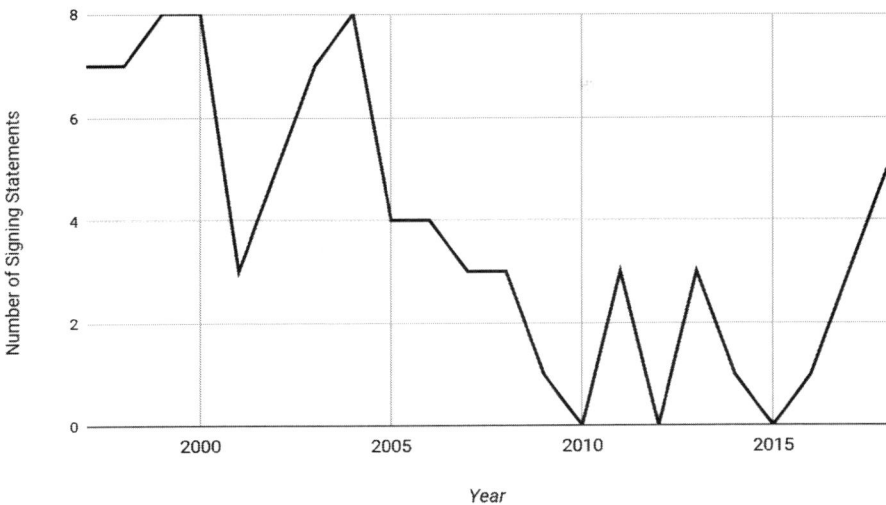

Figure 5.2. Annual Number of Signing Statements on Defense Bills, 1997–2018

Signing Statements, Executive Orders,
and Policy Memoranda

We collected all signing statements from 1997 to 2018.[11] Recall that we did not consider rhetorical signing statements, as those tend to thank specific members of Congress for their help on a bill or to criticize Congress for its work on a specific piece of legislation (Kelley 2007, 285). Figure 5.2 displays the number of signing statements placed on defense bills annually.[12] This figure indicates that the use of signing statements on defense bills peaked between 2000 and 2004, decreased thereafter, but had a notable resurgence during the Trump administration.

After we read each signing statement, we connected it to its relevant statute. We used bill categorization data from the Policy Agendas Project to connect public laws to the defense policy area. In addition to categorizing the policy area for the bill, we read the signing statements to record the number of objections to provisions of the law. Through 2018, there were 739 objections to varying provisions of law in defense bills, but not every objection addresses defense even though the signing statement itself is tied to a defense bill. As we have argued earlier, bills, including defense bills, are multidimensional. Of the 739 objections, 412 (or 55.75%) were defense-related objections. Overall, this works out to an average of slightly more than 35 objections per year on defense-related bills and a little less than 20 defense-related objections per year on these bills. When we analyze this data by president, Clinton averaged 1.5 objections per month (with an average of 0.75 defense-related objections per month). George W. Bush averaged nearly 5 objections per month (with an average of 3 defense-related objections). Obama averaged slightly less than one objection per month (with an average of slightly less than 0.3 defense-related objections per month). And Trump averaged almost 6 objections per month (with an average of 2 defense-related objections).

Figure 5.3 illustrates the categorization of signing statement *objections* by the policy areas designated in the Policy Agendas dataset. The vertical axis for this figure indicates the percent of objections in a particular policy area, while the horizontal axis corresponds to each policy area.

As one might imagine, a majority of objections directly relate to defense policy. Figure 3 indicates that 55.8% of objections on defense bills directly relate to defense policy. Although a majority of objections to defense bills are defense related, a substantial percentage (44.2%) are not. Of the non-defense objections, 26.9% relate to government operations. Only 7.2% of objections are categorized as dealing with international relations or foreign affairs, policy areas that might be considered "closest" to defense. The remainder occur in a roughly even distribution across the other policy areas. Thus, just as bills are multidimensional, signing statements are also multidimensional—as measured by the diversity of the policy areas in the objections.

We employ one-, two-, three-, four-, and five-month lags for the change in objections in signing statements. Distributed lags are appropriate because we have little temporal aggregation in our data, and there are severe institutional constraints that prevent immediate congressional responses to presidential actions. Given that Congress meets on average for fewer than 11 days per month, planning and scheduling committee hearings on short notice seems unlikely.[13] We expect the effect of objections in signing statements to occur within the few months after signing statements are issued. Figure 5.4 displays the number of objections by month and year to provisions of law in defense bills (top panel) and the number of defense-related objections by month and year on these bills (bottom visual). The vertical axes for both figures represent the number of objections, while the horizontal axis represents the month and year.

The patterns in these figures generally mirror the patterns found for signing statements. The number of objections on all bills generally peaks

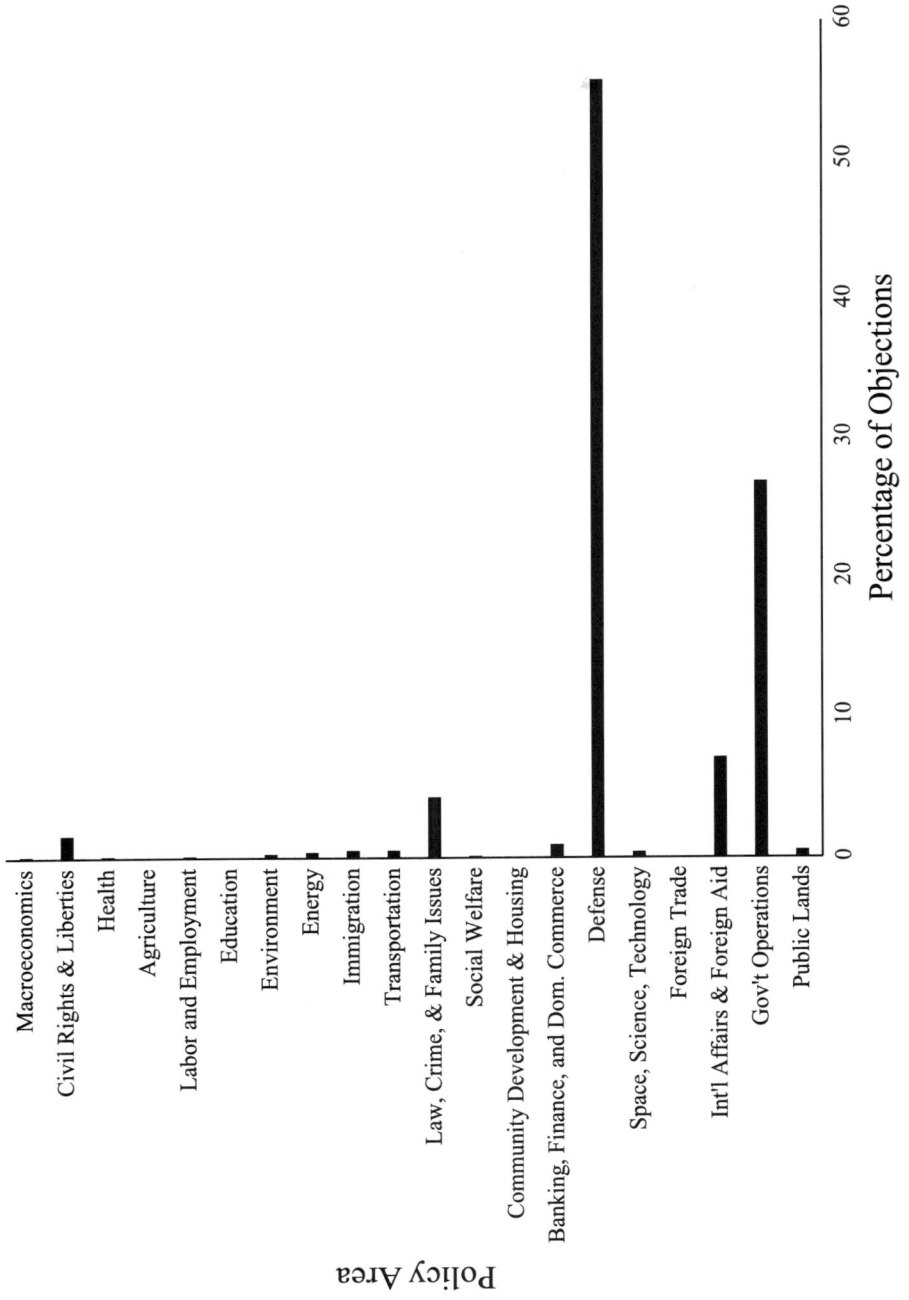

Figure 5.3. Signing Statement Objections on Defense Bills by Policy Area of Objection, 1997–2018

All Objections

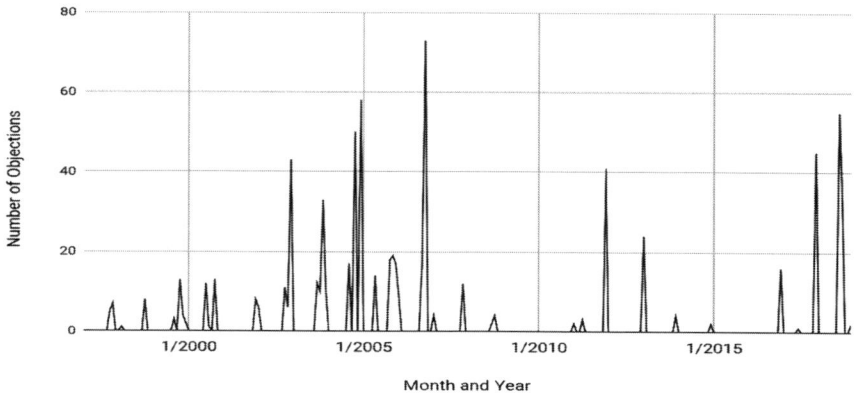

Defense-Related Objections

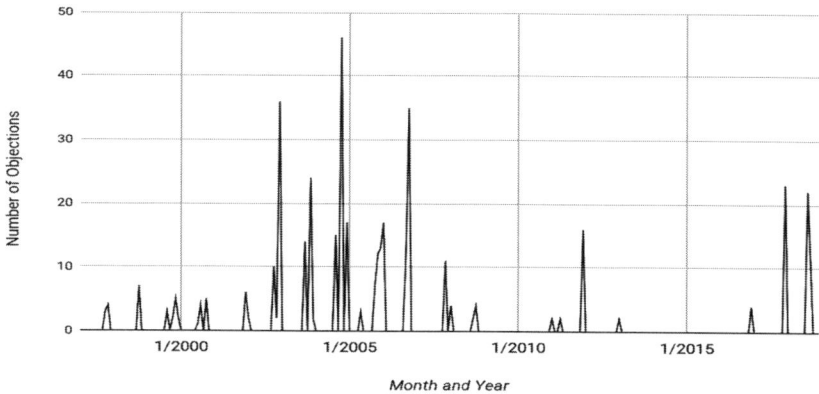

Figure 5.4. Number of Objections on Defense Bills by Month, 1997–2018

between 2004 and 2006, with secondary peaks during the Trump administration. The number of objections on defense bills generally peaks between 2002 and 2008, with additional peaks during the Trump administration. The number of objections on bills varies considerably by month and year, which one would expect given our narrower focus on just defense bills. We expect that the more focused, defense-related objections in the signing statements will spur greater defense oversight.

To examine the effects of executive orders on defense policy oversight, we identified all nonclassified executive orders related to defense policy that presidents have issued between 1997 and 2018. We recorded the num-

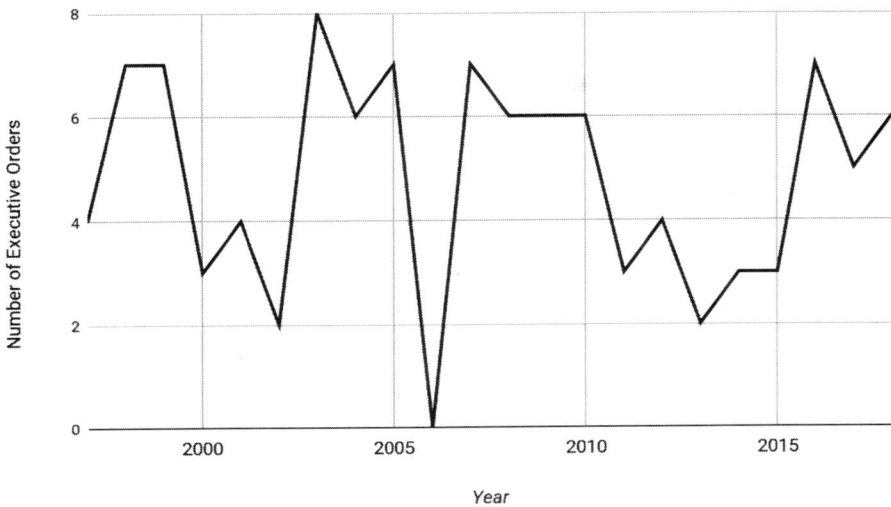

Figure 5.5. Number of Defense Policy-Related Executive Orders, 1997–2018

ber of defense-related executive orders by month and year and visualized the annual trend in the issuance of these documents in Figure 5.5.

There were 106 nonclassified executive orders on defense policy issued from 1997 to 2018–21 by Clinton, 40 by George W. Bush, 34 by Obama, and 11 by Trump. Figure 5.5 indicates some variance in the issuance of executive orders in this policy area between 1997 and 2010, a decline in the number of nonclassified orders between 2010 and 2016, and a resurgence under Trump. We predict that as the number of executive orders increases, congressional oversight of defense policy also increases.

Policy memoranda have also been used increasingly by presidents, especially during the Obama and Trump years (Lowande 2014). Lowande (2014) argues that policy memoranda may have supplanted executive orders as a device by which unilateral policymaking occurs. We narrow our focus in a manner similar to our streamlined focus on executive orders and objections. To examine the effects of policy memoranda on defense policy oversight, we identified all nonclassified policy memoranda related to defense policy that presidents have issued between 1997 and 2018 that either Lowande (2014) identified as such in the *Federal Register* or by us extending his dataset using his selection criteria from 2013 forward.

There were 122 nonclassified policy memoranda on defense policy issued from 1997 to 2018–13 by Clinton, 36 by George W. Bush, 51 by Obama, and 22 by Trump. Figure 5.6 illustrates the variance in the issuance of policy memoranda related to defense during this time span, with

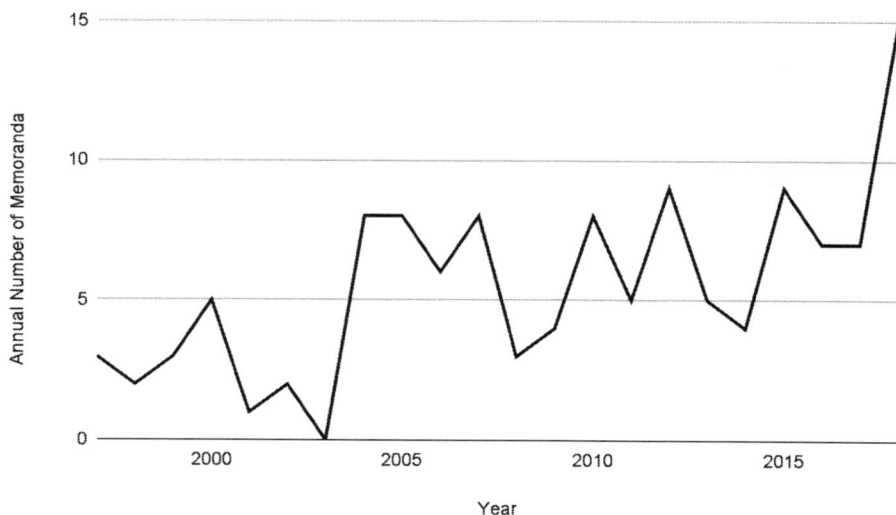

Figure 5.6. Number of Defense Policy-Related Memoranda, 1997–2018

more memoranda being issued in each year, with a substantial increase during George W. Bush's second term as president and continuing since, and with a notable rise in 2018 during Trump's presidency. As with executive orders, we expect that as the number of policy memoranda increase, congressional oversight of defense policy also rises.

Control Variables

Divided government remains one of the most commonly employed control variables whenever investigating a wide array of legislative activities, including congressional oversight (see, e.g., Aberbach 1990; Mayhew 2005).[14] Most scholars argue that Congress is more apt to give the executive branch broad discretionary authority when both actors hold similar policy preferences. Conversely, under divided government, Congress is less likely to delegate control (Epstein and O'Halloran 1999; Huber and Shipan 2002).

Signing statements complicate these claims. If the president and Congress share preferences, one might expect there would be less need for signing statements, but Kelley and Marshall (2010) have found that more signing statements are issued under unified government than under divided government because congressional reaction to presidential unilateralism under unified is less likely.[15] Bolton and Thrower's (2016) work demonstrates some of the nuances associated with this dynamic in the context of executive orders, finding that when legislative capacity is high and aligned with presidential preference, more executive orders are issued. However, under conditions of diminished legislative capacity, an ideologically divergent president can make policy gains by issuing executive orders (Bolton and Thrower 2016). We suggest that there might be another compatible explanation for the issuance of signing statements during unified control. Specifically, the multidimensionality of legislation generates supermajority support but invites presidential "improvement" on specific dimensions through signing statements. Congressional oversight along those specific dimensions could therefore be spurred by the expectation of congressional policy loss.

We operationalize the presidential approval hypothesis by using a one-month lag of the average percentage who approve of the president's job performance as measured by Gallup. We consider the effects of changes in defense spending by including the percentage of the federal budget that is spent on defense in the previous fiscal year. We acquired this data from the Office of Management and Budget.

We employ controls for ideology, partisan control, electoral cycles, and institutional time constraints. We consider the effects of ideology by examining the distance between the president and the median member of each chamber, using Bailey's (2013, 2021) ideal point data. We also interact the ideological distance measure with Republican control of the chamber.[16] We included the number of days that the House and Senate were in session, as legislators are less able to conduct oversight hearings as the number of days in session decreases.[17] Finally, we controlled for the second session of Congress, as incentives to engage in oversight might be affected by electoral cycles. Finally, we include a lagged dependent variable in the model, as is standard when using ECMs. A lagged dependent variable models the rate of decay with respect to the effects of the coefficients over time.

Results

We estimate two ECM models for the House and two for the Senate. In one set of models, we only measure the defense-related objections contained in the signing statements placed on defense bills. In the other set, we use the *total* number of objections, regardless of the policy focus of those objections, contained in signing statements placed on defense bills, with all other covariates being the same.[18] Table 5.1 shows the results for the two House models and the two Senate models.

Table 5.1. Objections to Provisions of Law and Oversight Hearings by Chamber for Defense Policy

	House of Representatives				Senate			
	Defense-Related Objections		All Objections		Defense-Related Objections		All Objections	
Independent Variable	Short-Term Effect	Long-Term Effect	Short-Term Effect	Long-Term Effect	Short-Term Effect	Long-Term Effect	Short-Term Effect	Long-Term Effect
Objections Variables								
⊗Objections$_{t-1}$	–	-.057 (.133)	–	-.022 (.073)	–	-.092 (.089)	–	-.054 (.048)
⊗Objections$_{t-2}$	–	.108 (.170)	–	.125 (.093)	–	-.027 (.114)	–	.012 (.061)
⊗Objections$_{t-3}$	–	.511** (.166)	–	.292** (.095)	–	.285* (.112)	–	.213** (.063)
⊗Objections$_{t-4}$	–	.461** (.169)	–	.241* (.095)	–	.272* (.114)	–	.165* (.063)
⊗Objections$_{t-5}$	–	.293* (.133)	–	.137 (.076)	–	.118 (.090)	–	.063 (.050)
Executive Orders								
⊗Executive Order Count$_{t-1}$	–	-1.231 (1.062)	–	-1.197 (1.064)	–	-.633 (.714)	–	-.423 (.703)
⊗Executive Order Count$_{t-2}$	–	.777 (1.080)	–	.655 (1.075)	–	-.087 (.727)	–	-.269 (.710)
⊗Executive Order Count$_{t-3}$	–	.154 (1.066)	–	-.086 (1.059)	–	.267 (.717)	–	.075 (.700)
ΔExecutive Order Count$_{t-4}$	–	.293 (1.049)	–	.238 (1.055)	–	.527 (.701)	–	.521 (.692)
ΔExecutive Order Count$_{t-5}$	–	-.533 (1.046)	–	-.323 (1.049)	–	.308 (.696)	–	.391 (.686)
Policy Memoranda								
⊗Memoranda Count$_{t-1}$	–	-.267 (.961)	–	-.392 (.988)	–	-.093 (.645)	–	-.373 (.650)
⊗Memoranda Count$_{t-2}$	–	-.607 (.963)	–	-.444 (.984)	–	-.099 (.649)	–	.006 (.652)
⊗Memoranda Count$_{t-3}$	–	-1.288 (.998)	–	-.913 (1.010)	–	-.989 (.673)	–	-.784 (.669)

	(1)	(2)	(3)	(4)	(5)	(6)	(7)	(8)
ΔMemoranda Count$_{t-4}$	—	-1.013 (1.012)	—	-.755 (1.019)	—	-.812 (.686)	—	-.637 (.678)
ΔMemoranda Count$_{t-5}$	—	-.119 (1.038)	—	.050 (1.047)	—	-.090 (.701)	—	.039 (.694)
Control Variables								
Presidential Approval	.235 (.194)	-.013 (.082)	.254 (.193)	.010 (.083)	.085 (.131)	-.006 (.059)	.097 (.128)	.005 (.058)
% Defense Spending	-1.661 (2.983)	.075 (.476)	-1.846 (2.991)	.119 (.478)	-.500 (2.011)	-.061 (.349)	-.608 (1.980)	-.009 (.346)
President-House Distance	4.582 (11.138)	-.880 (3.815)	5.860 (11.398)	-.051 (3.864)	—	—	—	—
Republican Control*President-House Distance	-3.269 (8.593)	.126 (2.419)	-4.785 (8.708)	-.232 (2.442)	—	—	—	—
President-Senate Distance	—	—	—	—	1.475 (5.121)	-.071 (1.675)	-.044 (5.137)	.239 (1.667)
Republican Control*President-Senate Distance	—	—	—	—	2.317 (5.774)	-.374 (1.894)	3.674 (5.732)	-.529 (1.874)
Days in Session	.723*** (.136)	.024 (.190)	.718*** (.136)	.017 (.189)	.292** (.093)	-.052 (.130)	.294** (.091)	-.029 (.127)
Second Year of Session	1.986 (2.550)	—	1.120 (2.493)	—	.545 (1.713)	—	.278 (1.645)	—
Lagged Dep Var⊗Oversight$_{t-1}$	-.195** (.059)		-.195** (.060)		-.280*** (.061)		-.291*** (.061)	
Constant	1.426 (11.629)		-1.318 (11.854)		3.027 (8.348)		1.030 (8.355)	
N	258		258		258		258	
F-Statistic	4.04		3.96		2.920		3.26	
Prob<F-Statistic	<.0001		<.0001		<.0001		<.0001	
R2	.322		.317		.255		.277	
Adjusted R2	.242		.237		.168		.192	
Mean Squared Error	10.993		11.030		7.406		7.297	

Notes: The dependent variable is the change in oversight activity for each month and year. The values in parentheses are standard errors. * denotes p<.05, ** denotes p<.01, and *** denotes p<.001, using one-tailed tests.

Control Variables

The results for the control variables are very similar across models and chambers. Monthly variations in a president's approval ratings have no demonstrable effect on congressional oversight of defense policy. The models demonstrate no evidence to indicate that the presidential approval ratings affect congressional oversight. There is also no clear connection between changes in the percentage of the budget spent on defense and defense-related oversight.[19] Defense spending can affect broad swaths of society, and the connections between defense spending and economic conditions are intricate. For instance, defense spending has been regularly connected to domestic economic conditions (e.g., Mueller and Atesoglu 1993; Heo 2010) and employment (e.g., Nincic and Kusack 1979). An analysis of the economic effects of sequestration on the U.S. economy prepared for the Aerospace Industry Association in 2012 stated that "the automatic spending cuts affecting DOD and non-DOD agencies' discretionary spending authorities beginning January 2, 2013 will [r]educe the nation's GDP by $215 billion . . . [and] . . . [c]ost the U.S. economy 2.14 million jobs" (Fuller 2012). Regardless of the potential economic and security-related impact, we found no evidence that changes in the percentage of defense spending have a positive effect on defense-related congressional oversight.

Our measures of ideological distance have no statistical significance in any of the four models we estimate. Conversely, the number of days in session has a short-term positive effect on defense oversight activity in each chamber. The impact of this time constraint is similarly significant whether we use defense-related objections or overall objections. In the House, each additional day in session yields approximately 0.7 days of increased oversight activity in the short term. In the Senate, an additional day in session yields roughly 0.3 days of increased oversight activity in the short term. There are no long-term effects of days in session on oversight.

Unilateral Actions and Oversight Activity

After considering a wide range of covariates, our key variables of interest show considerable statistical and substantive impact. Figure 5.7 displays a coefficient plot that shows the impact of objections on oversight in each chamber, with the dot denoting the coefficient and the line denoting the 95% confidence interval for that coefficient estimate. The solid line corresponds to defense-related objections, while the broken line considers all objections to provisions of law in signing statements.

Figure 5.7 illustrates that the impact of signing statements follows a similar temporal pattern, rising over the first three or four months and clearly dissipating in impact by the fifth month in each chamber. For both chambers, objections have a negative but not statistically significant impact in the first month, and do not exert a statistically significant effect during the second month. By the third and fourth months, changes in signing statement objections yield statistically and substantively significant increases in defense oversight. During the fifth month, changes in defense-related objections in signing statements are connected with increases in House oversight, but not in the Senate. For each chamber, the substantive impact is greater for the specific, defense-related objections than for the total number of objections by 75% (House, three months), 91% (House, four months), 34% (Senate, three months), and 65% (Senate, four months).

The significance of the long-term variable shows that there is a positive connection between the levels of objections in signing statements in months 3 and 4 and defense-related oversight, regardless of the chamber. The coefficient on the lagged dependent variable allows us to provide a more precise estimate of the nature of the relationship between oversight and signing statements. We calculate the impact of the long-run effects of statistically significant variables by dividing their coefficients for the long-run effect by the lagged dependent variable coefficient, assuming that the lagged dependent variable itself is equal to one (see, e.g., DeBoef and Keele 2008).

When the lagged dependent variable equals one, the long-run response is that each additional objection to provisions of law results in an increase in oversight by 1.5 days in the House and 0.73 days in the Senate starting at three months after the objections were lodged. At four months (and with a lagged dependent variable equal to one), each additional objection to provisions of law is associated with an increase in oversight by 1.24 days in the House and 0.57 days in the Senate. These total effects are distributed over future time periods with decays of 19.5% in the House and 29.1% in the Senate per additional month, based on the coefficient on the lagged days of oversight.

In each chamber, the effect of defense-specific objections is greater than the impact of total, unspecific objections. At three months, each additional objection to provisions of law is connected with increases in oversight of 2.62 days (House) and 1.02 days (Senate). At four months, each additional objection to provisions of law is connected with increases in oversight of 2.36 days (House) and 0.97 days (Senate). At five months, each additional objection to a provision of law is associated with an increase of 1.50 days

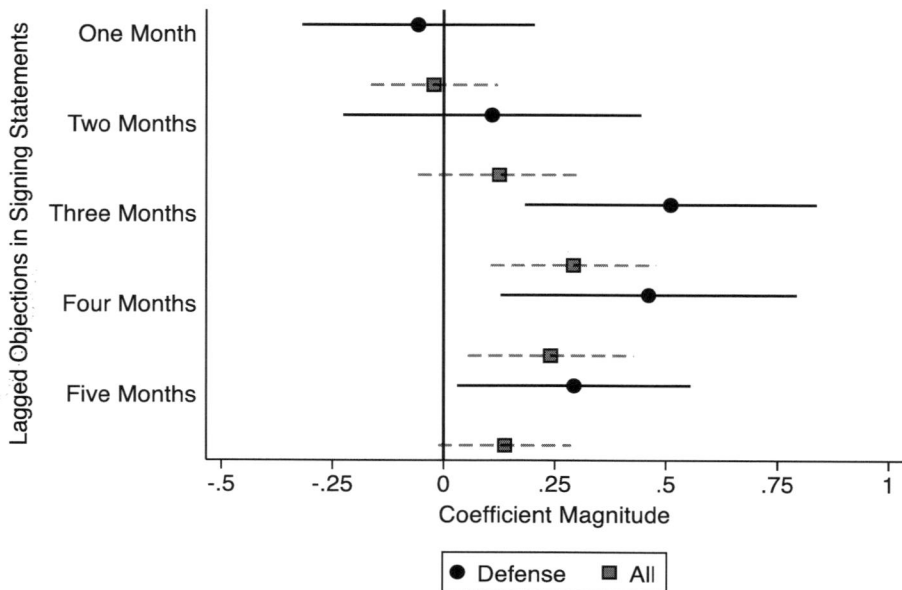

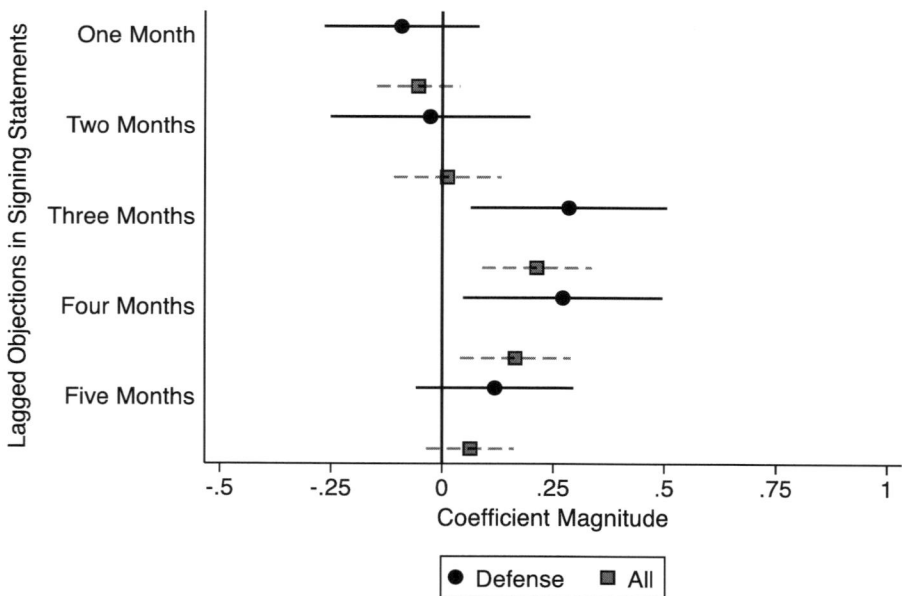

Figure 5.7. Effects of Objections on Congressional Oversight Activity

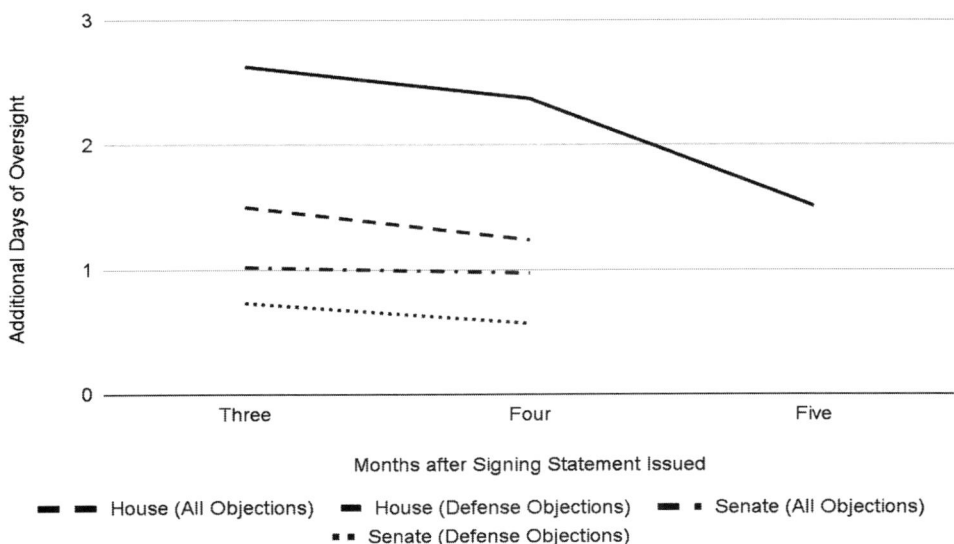

Figure 5.8. Signing Statement Objections and Changes in Oversight Activity

of additional oversight in the House.[20] These total effects are distributed over future time periods with decays of 19.5% in the House and 28% in the Senate per additional month, based on the coefficient on the lagged days of oversight. In this way, we find substantial support for our first hypothesis—issue-specific and concentrated losses tied to unilateral efforts lead to greater congressional oversight. There are higher levels of oversight when we focus on defense-related objections. We conclude that issue specificity matters in a multidimensional setting. These results are visualized in Figure 5.8.

In sum, we find evidence that Congress varies its oversight activity on defense policy in response to specific, *defense-related* objections in signing statements. Uncategorized objections create a similar temporal pattern in defense oversight but with lower levels of substantive impact. The results for the House exhibit more pronounced effects than the Senate. One interpretation of this distinction between the chambers' members is that senators are more likely to set their own agendas without regard to external forces. In addition, supermajoritarian requirements in the Senate ensure that many senators possess individual-level influence rather than influence tied to committee structures.

These findings are consistent with discussions of policy traceability (e.g., Arnold 1990). Members have electoral and policy-related incentives for taking an interest in specific policy outcomes of multidimensional policy, even in defense. Congressional oversight of defense policy follows concentrated efforts to use signing statements to alter defense policy. We demonstrated a direct link between the contents of a unilateral policy instrument and congressional responsiveness to that content. Second, we found similar results across the chambers for the time constraints that days in session create. Third, ideology and presidential approval matter little when compared to issue-specific objections in signing statements and institutional constraints as measured by days in session.

Possible Limitations

Two empirical issues may arise from the analysis.[21] First, it is possible that oversight causes higher levels of objections to provisions of law in signing statements or increased numbers of executive orders or policy memoranda. To examine whether evidence of reverse causality exists, we used each of our unilateral policy instruments as dependent variables in place of oversight while retaining the lag structures of all remaining independent variables in Table 5.1. In 55 of 60 estimations (91.67%) where reverse causality could occur, there is no evidence that it happens, as oversight is not statistically significant. When we examine the remaining five instances, the signs on the variables of interest are negative two times and positive three times, indicating no clear underlying relationship. Thus, reverse causality is not an issue.

Second, specifying our models by month and year in Table 5.1 might drive the results that we obtained (see Ho et al. 2007; Head et al. 2015). To systematically examine whether this occurs, we removed one year at a time, one month at a time, and one control variable at a time from each of the models. Then we re-ran the models with the remaining covariates. When we examine these models, 83.97% (131/156) of the estimations contain results that mirror those presented. Most of the remaining cases involve one or two variables having signs or significance patterns with little systematic patterning to indicate a broad divergence from the results.[22] Thus, we have little reason to believe that there is a common, systematic set of specifications that drive the results.

Conclusion

Defense-related legislation and defense policy share certain features with other policy areas while also exhibiting unique qualities. Multidimensionality is a feature shared across numerous policy areas. Defense legislation and policy are in fact multidimensional.[23] In addition, the signing statements tied to defense legislation are themselves multidimensional. Recall that in the signing statements tied to defense legislation we recorded objections to a wide range of policies unrelated to defense. Whereas in Chapter 4 we used raw counts of objections in signing statements, here we paid closer attention to the focus of the objections. In our empirical analyses, we found that a greater incidence of defense-related objections led to higher levels of defense-related oversight. Once again, legislators respond strategically to a president's unilateral actions.

For a unique quality, consider that defense policy dominates presidents' unilateral efforts. Defense is by far the most common issue area to generate both signing statements and objections from presidents. Defense policy dominates the focus of policy memoranda (Chapter 4, Figure 4.11), and it is a prominent focus for executive orders (Chapter 4, Figure 4.9). Studying presidents' unilateral actions without carefully considering the policy area in which presidents are most apt to operate unilaterally risks misidentifying congressional responsiveness.

Another quality unique to defense policy has been long recognized. Defense policy is an issue area, like foreign affairs, in which Congress traditionally gives the president substantial discretion. As such, we studied congressional reaction to unilateralism in a policy area in which the president is expected to dominate. In this "difficult case," we find that Congress *still* responds with increased oversight to the president's disaggregation of policy through signing statements. Congressional responsiveness, as measured by defense policy oversight, is greatest in reaction to defense-related unilateral efforts. We also showed how presidents hint at their disaggregation of policy with issue-specific objections in signing statements. As in Chapter 4, when legislators push back on presidential unilateralism, they are less concerned with general presidential overreach and more concerned with specific policy adjustments. By responding to policy-specific overreach, legislators get to claim credit for general policy gains as well as for pushing back in specific areas where policy losses occurred. As such, legislators reassert themselves in the politics of structure, fighting the "imperial executive" in an issue-specific manner.

Handwringing over presidential imperialism is tempered by recognizing that members are not typically focused on a desire to protect their institutional powers (see, e.g., Levinson and Pildes 2006; cf. Matthews 1960). For legislators, electoral concerns remain prominent, whereas for presidents, concerns about institutional prerogatives remain prominent. Moe (1989, 448) writes that "presidents care intensely about securing changes that promote their institutional power, while legislators typically do not. They are unlikely to oppose incremental increases in the relative power of presidents unless the issue in question directly harms the special interests of their constituents" (quoted in Howell 2003, 111). We saw greater evidence of policy-specific pushback than evidence of concerns about institutional power, democratic principle, or broad unilateral efforts. Legislators' protestations, lamenting presidential overreach and decaying constitutional limits, are distracting. Legislators' behaviors indicate that the instruments of unilateralism are less problematic for them than the associated policy losses.

The canonical view in the literature on unilateral actions suggests that the signing statement is an effective device for presidents to rein in bureaucratic drift, move policy closer to presidential preferences, influence future judicial decisions, and ultimately assert presidential power in the coordinate construction of the constitution (cf. Halstead 2008 and Ostrander and Seivert 2013). We suggest that there might be more nuance to the story. As a president acts unilaterally to capture policy gains, legislators can respond to specific policy losses tied to that presidential unilateralism.

SIX

Conclusion

Modern presidents are expected to lead Congress. This expectation, with all of its ambiguities, is as widespread on Capitol Hill as anywhere. . . . If . . . senators expressed opposition to presidential leadership . . . if they objected at all, it was to the [policy] direction.

—Matthews 1960, 140–141

Lacking either statutory or constitutional authority, presidents can muster only a rough facsimile of what is actually needed.

—Howell and Moe 2016, 151

We return to three core insights of our work: (i) There are times when members of Congress have incentives not to legislate. Concerns about blame avoidance and vote explanation, which remain prominent for most members and senators, act as a brake on demonstrative legislative efforts. (ii) Presidents can lead by acting unilaterally whether or not Congress has recently legislated in the affected policy area, as presidents have used orders to preempt legislative efforts (e.g., Belco and Rottinghaus 2017) and used the absence of legislative action as an opportunity to act unilaterally. (iii) As presidents act unilaterally, Congress can respond. Two questions immediately arise: What do we mean by unilateral action? And how does Congress react to unilateral actions?

Unilateral actions have three key features. First, presidents possess residual decision-making powers (Moe and Wilson 1994) that allow those in the office "to take unilateral action at [the president's] own discretion when the formal agreement is ambiguous or silent about precisely what behaviors are required" (Moe and Wilson 1994, 14). Residual decision-making rights secure the ability to make significant decisions after an initial agreement has been reached. Executive orders and policy memoranda are examples of the exercise of residual decision-making powers. Orders and memoranda are unilateral actions that are linked to either legislative or constitutional authority, but they follow the formal delegation of authority to the executive branch. Frustration among legislators can occur when presidents interpret legislative acts so broadly as to allow orders and memoranda that implement policy in ways that legislators do not approve. Even under a strictly contractual interpretation of laws, presidents retain residual decision-making authority as the final implementers or executors of law because specifying a complicated contract with an eye toward all possible states of the world and exigencies is virtually impossible.

For an analogy, consider two people who split shopping and cooking duties. Choosing all of the ingredients for a wonderful meal is not the same as actually creating (or implementing) the meal. The ingredients can limit the implementation, but the ingredients do not dictate the meal, especially in the hands of a skillful chef. A fish could be presented head-on, nicely fileted, or cut into steaks. The fish could then be smoked, poached, grilled, brined, broiled, baked, or used for sushi. Baking might seem straightforward, but an experienced chef might bake the fish in a sauce, with a few herbs and wrapped in paper, or encrusted in salted egg whites. The variations are unbounded. The legislative body (purchasing the ingredients in this analogy) might prefer certain preparations over others, but without expertise that rivals the chef's it would be hard to stipulate the exact nature of the meal prepared. Even in the face of constraints, presidents (and chefs) have considerable expertise (within the agencies) and residual authority to affect policy.

In Chapter 3, we demonstrated how residual decision-making authority residing in one individual can yield Pareto improvements for all actors. Of course, a Pareto improvement might entail making trade-offs across multiple dimensions. Those trade-offs mean that losses can occur for some legislators along specific policy dimensions despite overall policy gains. Members of Congress might appreciate the overall policy gains even as they investigate policy losses along specific dimensions. After all, constituents often demand that members and senators respond to the specific items or dimensions of large, multidimensional policy efforts.

A second feature of unilateral tools is that they reveal presidential policy preferences. Presidents are typically transparent with respect to their policy motives when interacting with agencies, Congress, the courts, and the public. Presidents, members of Congress, other government officials, and the public strategically engage with one another. In some strategic interactions, actors might choose not to reveal their true intentions. However, whenever an actor has last-mover status (or residual decision-making authority), there are no longer any incentives to hide intentions. One example of this occurs in signing statements, as presidents have consistently stated that they will implement statutes in ways consistent with their own policy preferences. For instance, in the signing statement that accompanied the CARES Act on March 27, 2020, President Trump stated that he would implement one provision of the law as "hortatory, but not mandatory" and other provisions as "advisory and non-binding" (Trump 2020b). When presidents "tip their hand" by revealing their preferences, congressional uncertainty about the placement of a particular policy upon its implementation is reduced.

Third, unilateral tools do not need to create new law, but they do *perfect* it. Executive orders and policy memoranda have the force of law behind them, and they perfect the law by indicating what statutes get implemented and how. Signing statements do not have the force of law, but they elaborate a president's policy preferences regarding how a law is executed and implemented. Thus, signing statements also perfect law. As presidents deploy unilateral tools to modify policy, policymakers in Congress are aware of the direction of those modifications and can respond to avoid policy loss on particular dimensions.

Throughout this work, we focused on three key instruments of unilateralism: policy memoranda, executive orders, and signing statements. In Chapters 4 and 5, we found that when presidents objected to provisions of law through signing statements, committees in each chamber of Congress responded with higher levels of oversight three, four, and five months later. These committee-level responses occur in all policy areas, even with respect to defense policy, an area where presidents frequently act unilaterally and are typically afforded a higher degree of discretion. Emphasizing committee responses via oversight is important because the chambers are hindered with tremendous collective action problems. Operations at the committee level are much easier to conduct.

We found similar results for executive orders and memoranda. Congressional committees responded with higher levels of oversight across all policy areas when the president issues executive orders and policy memoranda. For different unilateral tools and for different policy areas, the length of time it takes Congress to respond varies, but the congressional committees nonetheless respond. As such, Congress might not always respond as an institution to unilateral actions, but members and senators acting through committees do muster responses.

Unilateralism under Trump and Biden

A limitation to the analyses in Chapters 4 and 5 is that they extend only to 2018 due to data availability on key variables. Naturally, one would be curious about the most recent presidencies. We can examine aspects of unilateral activity under Trump (2017–2021) and during the first year of Biden's presidency (2021) to see how it compares with prior presidents in our analyses (Clinton's second term, George W. Bush, and Barack Obama), but we cannot employ the same models as we did in Chapters 4 and 5. Nonetheless, basic comparisons will provide some insights with respect to the ways in which unilateral policy instruments are used.

Unilateral Policymaking during the Trump Presidency

We begin by comparing President Trump to his three immediate predecessors. The horizontal axes in Figures 6.1 through 6.3 identify policy areas, as coded in the Comparative Agendas Project, while the vertical axes in those figures indicate the percentage difference between Trump and his predecessors across each of those policy areas. We calculated the percentage difference by computing the percentage in each policy area for Trump and his predecessors. Then we generated the difference in percentage for Trump from that of his predecessors. A positive sign denotes that Trump was proportionally more involved in a particular policy area as it relates to that unilateral policy instrument relative to his predecessors.

Figure 6.1 displays differences between Trump and his immediate predecessors (Clinton, George W. Bush, and Obama) on signing statement objections, Figure 6.2 displays these differences on executive orders, and Figure 6.3 visualizes these differences for policy memoranda. Figure 6.1 shows that Trump issued 8.61% more objections on healthcare bills and 23.05% more objections to provisions of law on bills related to government operations. On the other hand, Trump issued 4.48% fewer objections to provisions on law on agriculture bills, and 7.95% fewer objections on foreign trade bills. Figure 6.2 shows that Trump issued 5.1% more executive orders on health care, and 4.82% more of these documents on law, crime, and family issues compared to his predecessors. However, Trump issued

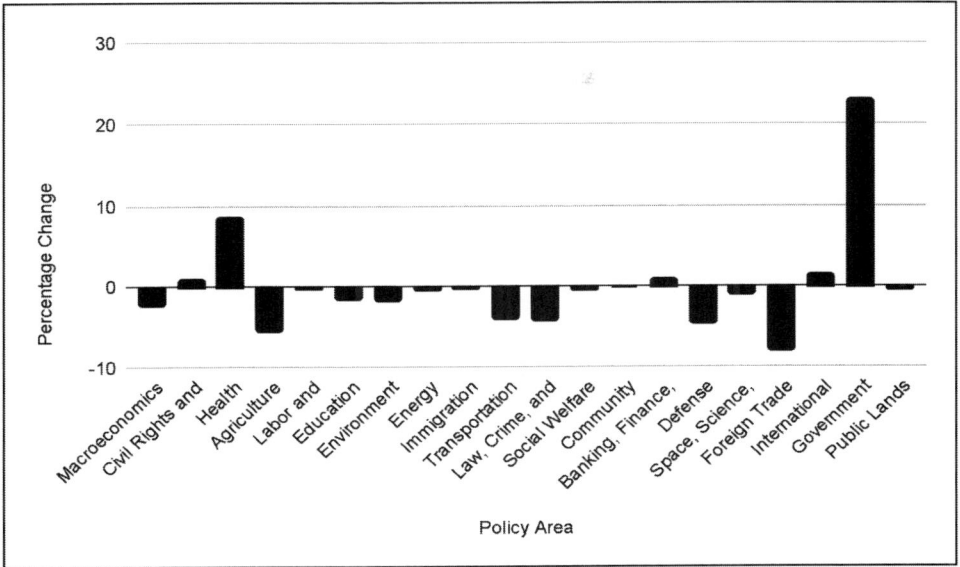

Figure 6.1. Pre-Trump and Trump Differences in Signing Statement Objections

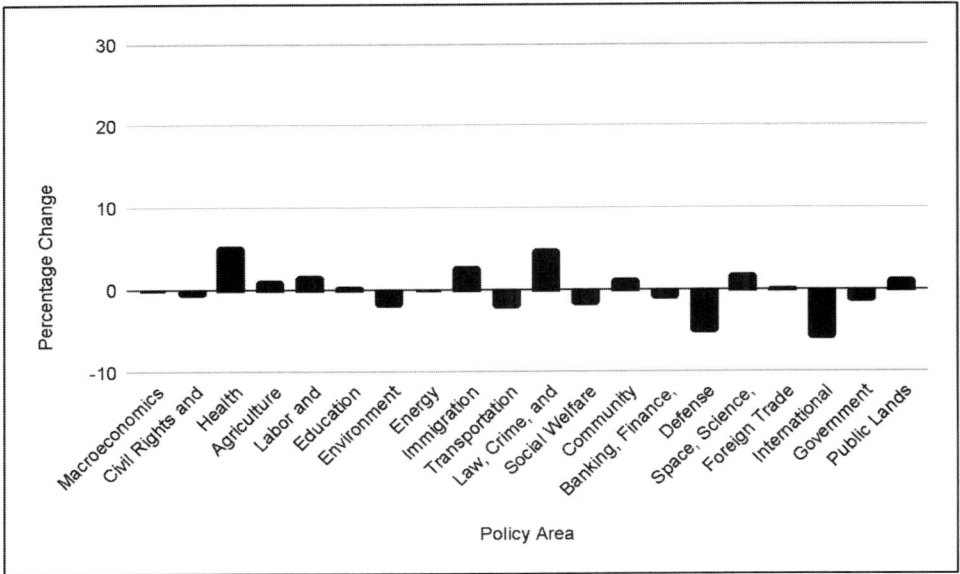

Figure 6.2. Pre-Trump and Trump Differences in Executive Orders

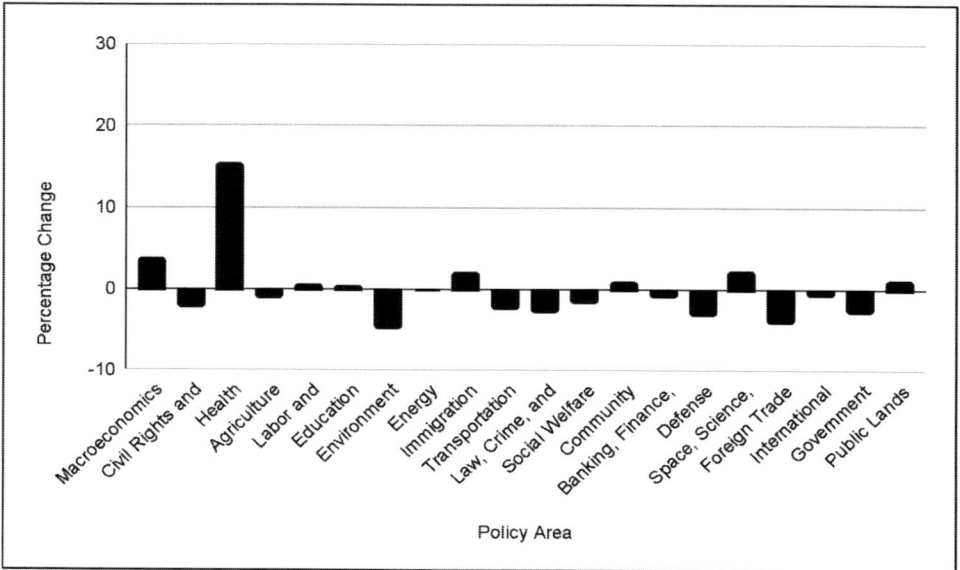

Figure 6.3. Pre-Trump and Trump Differences in Policy Memoranda

5.1% fewer executive orders on defense, and 5.94% fewer on international affairs and foreign aid. Figure 6.3 demonstrates that Trump issued 15.35% more policy memoranda than his predecessors on health care, while he issued 4.73% fewer memoranda on the environment.

The differences between Trump and his predecessors consistently indicate one clear trend: Trump prioritized healthcare policy when utilizing unilateral policy instruments.[1] This is unsurprising, since a major cornerstone of Trump's 2016 run for president centered around repealing the Affordable Care Act. Immediately before his election in 2016, Trump stated in a speech in Valley Forge, Pennsylvania that Obamacare, was a "catastrophe" and that he was going to "ask Congress to convene a special session so that we can repeal and replace" (Trump 2016). While Trump was eventually successful in working with Congress to repeal the financial penalty associated with the individual mandate for health insurance, he did little else on health care legislatively. However, he was actively developing objections in signing statements to provisions of law and using executive orders and, particularly, policy memoranda.

There are other trends too. For instance, Trump focused less unilateral attention on environmental policy areas. Regardless of the tool, Trump employed fewer unilateral actions aimed at environmental policy than his predecessors. De-emphasizing environmental policy is perhaps unsurprising, but Trump was also less active when it came to defense policy regardless of the unilateral tool. With foreign trade and international relations, there is variation across policy tools; but Trump seemed to bypass unilateral tools in those areas as well. Notwithstanding his America First mantra and aside from immigration, Trump's employment of unilateral tools focused in policy areas less closely tied to America First.

Unilateral Policymaking during the Biden Presidency

The second comparison we make is between the Trump presidency with the first year of Biden's presidency. We first note that Biden only issued four signing statements during his first year as president, and each of those was on a defense bill. This is a particularly low level of signing statement activity. Given the presence of more data, we perform tabular analyses of Trump and Biden's usages of executive orders and policy memoranda. As in the earlier figures, the horizontal axes in Figures 6.4 through 6.5 reflect policy areas, as coded in the Comparative Agendas Project. The vertical axes in these figures display the percentage difference between Biden and Trump across each of the policy areas. We computed the percentage difference by first computing the percentage of activity in each policy area for Biden and Trump and then generated the differences in those percentages between Biden and Trump. A positive sign denotes that Biden did more proportionally in a particular policy area as it relates to that unilateral policy instrument than Trump.

Figure 6.4 displays differences between Biden and Trump with respect to executive orders, and Figure 6.5 illustrates these differences related to policy memoranda. Figure 6.4 indicates that Biden issued 6.81% more executive orders on education, while he issued 4.78% fewer of these documents on law, crime, and family issues, and 4.56% fewer on public lands. Figure 6.5 shows that Biden issued 7.41% more policy memoranda on civil rights and liberties, 7.24% more on immigration, and 4.22% more on international affairs and foreign aid. Conversely, he issued 9.04% fewer policy memoranda on defense policy than Trump.

These visuals provide three takeaways. First, in terms of unilateral policymaking, Biden prioritized education more than Trump. One reason for this is that Biden campaigned in 2020 on managing the COVID-19 pandemic to get children back into schools safely as soon as possible. Thus, many of the executive orders that were issued on education related to the pandemic. For example, Executive Order 14000 directed various agencies

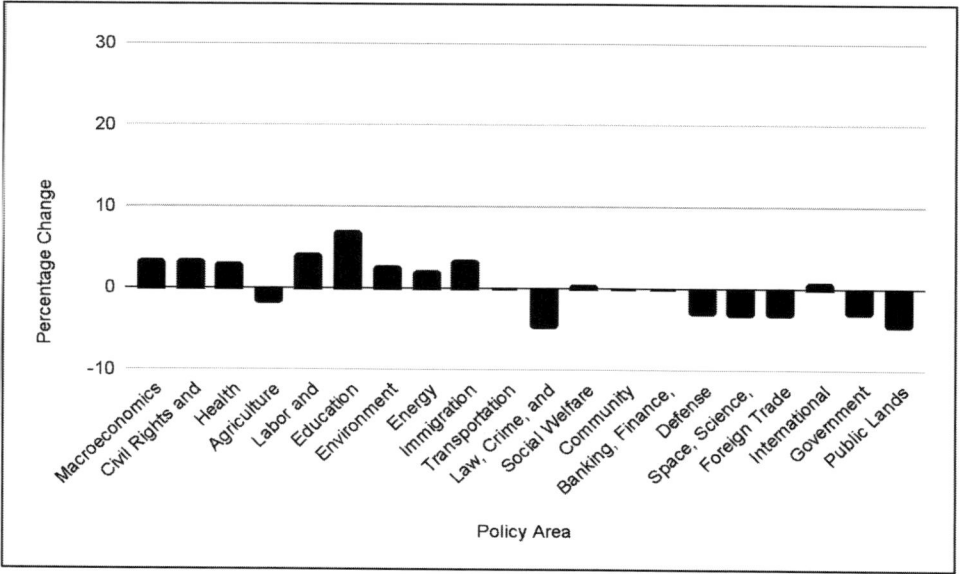

Figure 6.4. Differences between Biden's First Year and Trump's Presidency on Executive Orders

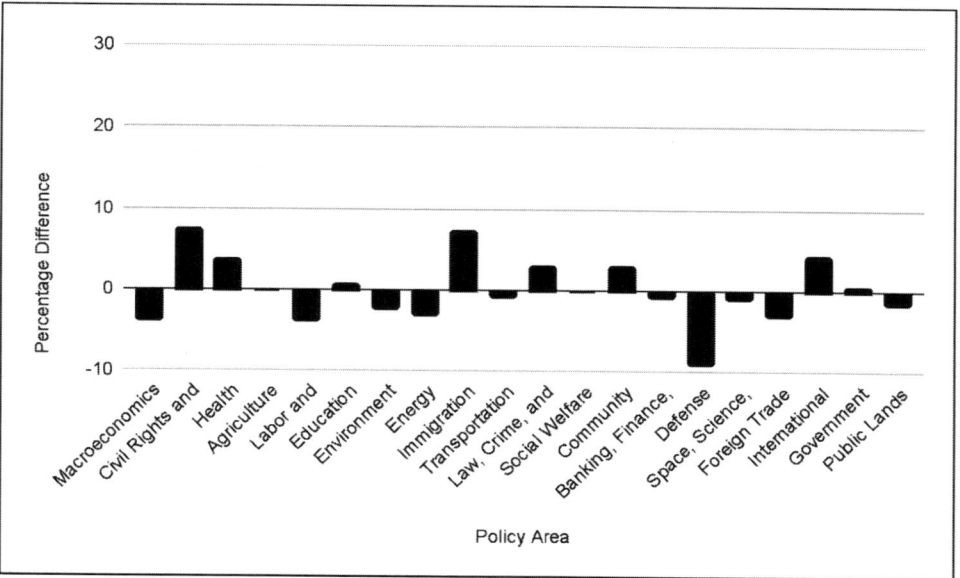

Figure 6.5. Differences between Biden's First Year and Trump's Presidency on Policy Memoranda

in the federal government to help K-12 schools reopen safely and to provide the resources by which this could occur (Biden 2021).

Second, in the defense policy area, Trump used unilateral tools less often than his predecessors. Biden, however, employed unilateral tools even less frequently than Trump in the defense policy area. A closer, follow-up look at the defense area might indicate whether there are fundamental changes afoot. Perhaps world events have allowed Trump and Biden to focus their energies elsewhere.

Third, via policy memoranda, Biden prioritized civil rights and immigration more than Trump. A plank of Biden's campaign considered racial justice and equity in response to protests and police killings in 2020. Consequently, Biden issued several memoranda with respect to addressing housing discrimination, combating racism against Asian Americans, and advancing human rights of LGBTQIA individuals. In addition, Biden campaigned on making DACA permanent, and liberalizing U.S. immigration policy. Toward those ends, the Biden administration issued one policy memorandum on his first day in office to make DACA permanent, and subsequent policy memoranda to allow for those who helped the United States in Afghanistan to emigrate to the United States.

Unilateral actions can also reflect electoral commitments and address crises of the moment. Presidents are expected to provide public leadership, particularly during times of crisis (see, e.g., Kernell 2006; Light 1998; Neustadt 1990). For instance, Trump used many unilateral actions related to healthcare policy to enact his desire to reduce or eliminate the Affordable Care Act. Simultaneously the COVID-19 pandemic began while Trump was president, and the public expected governmental responses whatever the means (see, e.g., Lowande and Rogowski 2021). Biden, then, took over management of the COVID-19 pandemic on the federal level when he became president. He substantially focused his efforts on K-12 education policy to get school-age children back into school in person.

Unilateral actions are also a product of the president's policy goals when Congress is gridlocked (Howell 2005). During Biden's and Trump's presidencies, congressional gridlock and inaction had been a major theme (Smith 2021), even during periods of unified government. For example, Biden may have issued a higher proportion of policy memoranda on civil rights and liberties in the aftermath of Congress's inability to pass policing reforms after George Floyd was murdered in 2020 even though Democrats controlled both chambers of Congress.[2]

Directions for Future Work

Our work suggests several directions that other researchers can take to build upon our theoretical model and empirical results. First, we did not examine the role that the federal courts play with respect to unilateral action. Our model in Chapter 3 provides some indirect clues on how this could occur, particularly with respect to when federal courts decide cases that involve unilateral action by the president. Just as presidential unilateralism signals to Congress the possibility of policy drift, court decisions may operate in a similar fashion, but with perhaps even less uncertainty. Courts can also play a role in the disaggregation of issues brought together in an order or memorandum. Generally, constitutional courts follow the doctrine of severability (see, e.g., Vande Kamp 2022). Severability allows courts to disaggregate statutes, executive orders, and memoranda to preserve whatever is constitutional while overturning whatever is unconstitutional. Thus, courts have their own role in disaggregating issues. Our model and empirical approach is easily extendable to cover the courts, as rulings from the judiciary provide a powerful counterbalance to Congress, the president, and the executive branch.

Second, we examined some types of unilateralism (signing statement objections, executive orders, and policy memoranda) but not others. Presidents have many other tools by which to act unilaterally, including pardons (Crouch 2008), executive agreements in favor of treaties (Krutz and Peake 2009), the appointment of policy czars (Vaughn and Villalobos 2015), disaster declarations (Reeves 2011; Kriner and Reeves 2015), and recess, emergency, or interim appointments (Black et al. 2007; Black et al. 2011; Kinane 2021; Ostrander 2015). One logical extension of our approach would be to examine other ways in which presidents act unilaterally to see whether they function as triggers for congressional response. Individual members of Congress and committees have occasionally expressed concern about these tools. One or more of these are likely to act as triggers for congressional responsiveness. One might also consider more carefully the manners in which unilateral tools might complement one another.

Third, we did not investigate the role that state governments can have with respect to responding to unilateral action by the president. Although state sovereignty is limited by the supremacy clause of the Constitution, federalism remains a cornerstone of the U.S. government. State governments can push back against unilateralism in numerous ways, including by implementing programs in ways that the president does not prefer

(Kousser 2014), passing laws that undercut those programs or initiatives (Reich 2018), not cooperating with the federal government on policy initiatives (Blizzard and Johnston 2021), instituting interstate compacts (Merriman 2019), or filing lawsuits to block federal programs from operating (Farhang 2010; Lin 2017). Scholars can and should investigate the ways in which state governments can respond to unilateral action by the president.

Fourth, we do not examine the ways in which the public might act as a constraint on the unilateral presidency. Many scholars have noted the rise of the unilateral presidency and have explored how acting alone can be a best response given the preferences of other institutional actors (see, e.g., Howell 2003; Kernell 2006; Lowande 2014; Mayer 2001; Moe 1993). In fact, a defining feature of the modern presidency is unilateral action—as Americans have come to expect the president to act unilaterally to aggressively confront pressing public policy problems (Howell 2003; Moe and Howell 1999; Kernell 2006; Rutledge and Larsen Price 2014; Lowande and Rogowski 2021). Some work reveals that expectation is tempered, however, by too-frequent exercises of unilateralism (Lowande and Rogowski 2015). Moreover, Christenson and Kriner (2020) discover that public opinion constrains a unilateral president, provided that such a president is concerned about public opinion. Nonetheless, Lowande and Rogowski (2021) find that the public wants major crises resolved and is largely agnostic regarding the mechanism by which that happens.

Fifth, we study *post-enactment* tools of unilateralism such as signing statements, executive orders, and policy memoranda. However, there is some evidence that tools deployed prior to passage also affect congressional response to unilateral action (see, e.g., Ainsworth et al. 2014; Belco and Rottinghaus 2017; Kernell and Rice 2005) as when statements of administration policy are issued on legislation prior to any final passage vote or when executive orders preempt or guide congressional legislative efforts.

Finally, we did not investigate the many ways in which Congress can respond to unilateralism beyond oversight. Congress has an array of policy tools that it can use against the executive branch, including its check on presidential appointments (emergency, recess, or interim appointments notwithstanding) and *ex ante* controls such as delegating narrow bounds of discretion to counter unilateral action, limitation riders, budgetary control, deck-stacking, and more. Scholars should explore the ways in which these tools can be used as well as their effectiveness when it comes to countering unilateral activity by the president.

Implications of Our Research

We detail five implications of our research. The first four focus on Congress and its members. First, *Congress is not as weak as many perceive it to be, even in the unilateral presidency era; but the resilience of members and senators is tempered by their policy focus.* Following the path of the presidency scholar Arthur Schlesinger (1973), many have written about the dangers of an imperial presidency that runs roughshod over Congress. More recently, concerns arose after George W. Bush's use of the signing statement in the Detainee Treatment Act of 2005 as brought to light by Charlie Savage (2006b).[3] Broader discussions of the propriety of the unitary executive theory have also gained prominence as officials like Bush's deputy attorney general John Yoo, U.S. Supreme Court justices Alito and Scalia, and Trump's attorney general Bill Barr articulated their view that the presidency has plenary authority to execute law without regard for concerns from the other branches.

Unitary executive theory surely emboldens presidents to take unilateral actions, heightening the "grave dangers" associated with presidential powers. If reelected, Trump will surely pursue policies in a manner consistent with the unitary executive theory. As noted earlier, Trump opined, 'Article II says I can do anything I want.' These dangers are real. However, in Chapters 4 and 5 we found that members of Congress push back against a president who acts unilaterally.[4] That pushback, however, is in regard to the policy focus of unilateral action. Mundane policy losses created by unilateral presidential actions capture the attention of members and senators. The aggrandizement of the presidency and the usurpation of congressional control are not protested, but ordinary policy losses are. For members and senators, presidential overreach is fine as long as the policy wins keep occurring.

A comparison to views from some Wall Street executives and analysts might highlight what is at stake when congressional pushback to a president's unilateral actions is so narrowly oriented. Numerous donors from Wall Street pulled away from Trump after the 2020 election denialism and even more after the January 6 insurrection. When asked why so many folks on Wall Street in 2024 were once again supporting Trump, a Wall Street analyst Komal Sri-Kumar stated, "People in business will fall into line with whoever is the next president. . . . If you're responsible to shareholders and your shareholders judge you on your profitability, *that can come from a more or less democratic administration*" (Stein 2024, emphasis added). Just as profits might not depend on democracy, policy gains and congressional reelection might not require a president who abides by long-established democratic norms.

Second, *Congress has fundamentally changed*. Many researchers have documented the enhanced role that political parties have played in Congress since 1975 (see, e.g., Binder 1997; Cox and McCubbins 1993, 2005; Dion 1997; Evans 2004; McCarty, Poole, and Rosenthal 2016; Rohde 1991; Sinclair 2016). Jacobson (2015) notes that one side effect is that the incumbency advantage has declined while congressional elections have become more nationalized. In addition, Lewallen (2020) notes that lawmaking in Congress has declined because party leaders have more control over the legislative agenda. As a consequence, congressional committees have shifted toward more policy oversight because many members are sidelined from the policymaking process in the face of increased leadership control (Lewallen 2020).

A fundamentally changed Congress carries implications for the separation of powers in American politics. If Congress partially abdicates lawmaking, even as it is increasing time spent on oversight, then it brings a different mix of activity relative to the executive branch. MacDonald and McGrath (2016) note that oversight is frequently used to persuade a more friendly president to revisit existing policy made under a previous, opposing president. Also, McGrath (2013) argues that oversight hearings are conducted as a response to agencies whose policy preferences differ from those that House and Senate committees hold. Similarly, Lowande and Potter (2021) find that agencies that advance proposals that are more ideologically distant from Congress are more likely to receive requests for documents and have more oversight hearings.

These authors point toward a common theme: *more* congressional involvement in the administrative state. Ritchie (2023), for example, examines the degree to which members of Congress make policy gains through pressuring agencies to craft favorable regulations that would not otherwise pass Congress.[5] Potter (2019) argues that Congress involves itself in the bureaucratic rulemaking process, but that bureaucrats use procedures to resist the influence of other branches at each stage of the process. In addition, Potter and Shipan (2019) find that government agencies adjust their rules output in response to separation of powers oversight. Further, Potter (2017) finds that agencies modulate the pace at which they make rules in an effort to undermine congressional oversight, as well as policy challenges from the president and courts.

In addition, the Supreme Court has invited increased congressional control over the administrative state, as it substantially limited the Environmental Protection Agency's ability to regulate carbon dioxide emissions in *West Virginia v. Environmental Protection Agency* (2022). One rationale that the Court cited was that this level of regulation was predominantly Congress's responsibility and not that of bureaucratic agencies. In policy areas of "vast economic and political significance," the Court reasoned that the discretion typically afforded agencies in interpreting statutes would be limited. Thus, through the so-called major questions doctrine, the Court has invited Congress to enhance its role in the legislative and public policymaking processes (see also, e.g., *Biden v. Nebraska*, 2023).

Our formal model in Chapter 3 suggests that members of Congress have selective incentives to avoid full engagement with lawmaking, so as to preserve abilities to avoid blame. Credit claiming for legislators occurs when they engage in subsequent oversight. As members anticipate policy loss through presidential actions on particular dimensions of multidimensional bills, oversight becomes an *ex post* means of limiting that policy loss. Since the *Chevron* doctrine has been abandoned by courts in *Loper Bright v Raimondo* (2024), and Congress has been admonished to limit delegations of broad discretionary authority to agents, we might expect to see the dynamic of congressional responsiveness shift once again (eg., Chiou and Rothenberg 2017; Rottinghaus 2019).

Third, the degree to which Congress is motivated to constrain presidential unilateralism *hinges on individual policy loss, not regime-level threat; but under some conditions policy losses might still fail to prompt Congress to act.* Recall the thesis we explored in the first chapter: the constitutional order is conditioned by political struggle (Whittington 2009). The particular form that order takes, what guardrails remain and which do not, is shaped by the political context. That is, the "force" of constitutionalism and the attendant habits, conventions, and rules of the political community depend upon the willingness of political authority to exercise those constraints. However, individual members of Congress cannot regularly overcome collective action challenges posed by bicameralism, polarization, and supermajoritarian requirements to effectively constrain "regime level" threats to constitutionalism posed by presidents. Nonetheless, we have discovered that members of Congress strategically respond to particular policy loss at the hands of presidential unilateralism. The powerful finding of this strategic responsiveness may incline those who fear executive overreach to find solace in the ordinary push and pull of policy struggle. Though we may not observe grand congressional challenges to presidential power, meaningful policy level responsiveness can limit executive control.

This key finding reveals how profoundly important policy-level disputes are in the politics of maintaining a particular constitutional order. However, if those policy-level disputes and policy losses felt by individual members of Congress are the principal means of constraining executives, the salience of those policy losses to members matters a great deal. Deep concerns arise if members are no longer attentive to the particular. As our politics become more and more nationalized (Hopkins 2018; Carson, Seivert, and Williamson 2023; Jacobson 2015), individualized policy loss may not be sufficient to invigorate congressional pushback to executive authority. A majority party that prioritizes unity with a sitting president, for example, may not be inclined to constrain that president, even as individual members face significant policy loss on issue dimensions that are critical to their districts. As nationalization takes hold, even farmers might subordinate a farm bill to concerns about national themes or to deference to political figures who are unfettered by strong institutions and norms. And that matters a great deal for our constitutional system. As members of Congress see their electoral futures tied to larger frames featuring national themes, national parties, and national leaders, the "engine" of congressional constraint on presidential power grinds to a halt.

Fourth, *congressional responsiveness to unilateral action differs by policy area.* Policy areas have varying salience to differerent members of Congress, and this variance is tied to members' electoral interests (see, e.g., Hall 1996; Harward and Moffett 2010; Jacobson and Carson 2019; Minta 2011, 2021; Sulkin 2005; Swers 2002, 2013). We found that Congress responds in all policy areas, but has a more particular response when it comes to objections in signing statements on defense-related bills. Also, Congress is especially sensitive to defense-related objections tied to defense bills as it is much more triggered to engage in oversight activity. Of course, defense bills are multidimensional, encompassing a range of policy areas. When objections on defense bills focus on policies beyond defense, they generate less oversight response from the defense committees in Congress.

Fifth, *the politics of separated powers are multidimensional.* Numerous scholars have argued that politics fundamentally involves the aggregation of individuals' preferences into some sort of group choice (see, e.g., Riker 1982). The policymaking process, as we argued in Chapters 1 and 3, is fundamentally about the aggregation and disaggregation of issues. Political entrepreneurs seek to combine issues along separate dimensions to garner sufficient support to move proposals toward adoption.[6] In Chapter 3, we noted that the issues that members of Congress aggregated can be subsequently disaggregated by a president's deployment of unilateral tools. The enhanced oversight explored in Chapters 4 and 5 occurs in response to specific policy losses. When legislators push back on unilateral actions, they are not focused on preserving the institutional sanctity of Congress. Rather, they are concerned about more immediate policy losses along specific issue dimensions. Indeed, we believe that individualized policy losses are critical elements of the politics that shape the constitutional order.[7]

Concluding Thoughts

Broadly speaking, Article II of the U.S. Constitution vests the president with "the executive power" to "take care that the laws be faithfully executed." Those constitutional provisions are imprecisely defined, and that ambiguity gives rise to many interpretations (see, e.g., Howell 2005). Recent presidents, including Obama, Trump, and Biden, have cited these provisions as bases for acting unilaterally, independent of Congress. This phenomenon has become so regularized that political scientists understand the ability of presidents to act unilaterally as a defining feature of the contemporary American presidency.

In this era of high political polarization and small partisan majorities in Congress, the likelihood of congressional inaction on any particular policy issue is high, and opportunities for the passage of sweeping congressional reaction to presidential unilateralism is low. Ideological polarization and small partisan majorities in Congress, then, invite presidents to extend executive power through unilateral actions where possible rather than to bargain with Congress to find solutions to policy disputes. Thus, the polarized character of our contemporary politics expands the set of possible actions of presidents that are resistant to constraints.

Throughout this book, we have argued that limitations on the executive are conditioned by politics. In the empirically oriented chapters, we identified those politics more specifically. We found that individualized policy losses incentivize legislators to resist the expansion of executive authority. If the nature of that politics changes, such that members are no longer sensitive to individualized losses, then a principal means by which Congress can constrain executives and maintain the constitutional order is lost. Unilateral tools are here to stay, but the norms and practices on which a strong, independent Congress relies change. We fully expect stability in unilateral tools, but we are less certain of the continuation of a strong, independent Congress with members willing to resist them.

One could hope for presidents with cooperative temperaments obviating the need for an attentive Congress; but Skowronek (1997) sees an inherent paradox in our constitutional structures. Presidents are expected to act and to "create order," but the power to create order "hangs on the authority to repudiate it" (1997, 27). One of the key challenges we face, then, is to find ways to invigorate congressional resilience in the face of presidential power. Shared powers in our system of government do not preclude unilateral actions; and unilateral actions do not eliminate shared powers and responsibilities. Preserving shared powers relies on the reactions of others to unilateral acts. Congress may or may not muster enough collective will to provide "the kind of sweeping, coordinated, and holistic change that many challenges demand" (Howell and Moe 2016, 151). But presidents will certainly press the vague boundaries of Article II in an effort to "impose coherent order, and make coherent policy, in a nation where separation of powers and Congress make those goals almost impossible to achieve" (Howell and Moe 2016, 150). Congressional response to the president's deployment of unilateral policymaking is central to analyses of separated powers. There is very little reason to expect Congress to act collectively to protect institutional prerogatives unless individual members of Congress have particularized incentives to do so. We find that presidential unilateralism—executive orders, signing statements, and policy memoranda—on specific policy dimensions creates individualized policy losses that motivate members to reassert congressional prerogatives in policymaking through increased oversight. With respect to the balance of power in our democratic order, much hinges on the degree to which they are motivated to do so.

Postscript

The themes developed in this book continue to resonate. There are contemporary challenges and opportunities for strategic congressional responsiveness to expressions of presidential unilateral power. For instance, in 2023, former president Trump faced multiple criminal indictments for state and federal violations. The special counsel, appointed by Attorney General Merrick Garland, spearheaded two separate federal investigations: one for violating national security by unlawfully taking secret documents and refusing to turn them over to government officials; the other for his efforts to subvert democracy and unlawfully conspire to overturn the results of the 2020 election, which he lost. The special counsel, Jack Smith, brought indictments in both investigations in the summer of 2023. In response, many Republicans criticized the Biden administration for "weaponizing" the Department of Justice (DOJ) in the interest of targeting a likely political opponent in the 2024 election. (Trump was the Republican nominee for the general presidential election of 2024.)

Although there is little formal authority that commands the political independence of the DOJ, it has been the conviction of most attorneys general to strive to limit political interference in any investigations. Since the attorney general is a political appointee, of course, those barriers are perhaps more porous than we might think. Curiously, a Republican critique of the Biden DOJ and special counsel Smith's investigations is that there is not sufficient political independence. However, in anticipation of a second Trump administration, likely Trump appointees to the DOJ have drafted proposals to remove *all* political independence of the DOJ (Stanley-Becker 2023). An explicitly politicized DOJ would then serve in the interest of the unitary executive (and further enforce the unitary executive theory as discussed in Chapter 2). Should such a proposal succeed, the conventional political independence of the department would disappear, concentrating law enforcement and investigatory authority within the executive branch.

The history of efforts by Congress to limit political influence over the DOJ suggests that Congress would not be very successful in preventing such a move. Indeed, during the Watergate era, a less-polarized Congress was unable to pass such restrictions, ultimately settling on the Ethics in Government Act of 1978. Congressional oversight, budgetary authorizations, and investigations over discrete exercise of DOJ authority would likely be the means by which members of Congress might limit the appointees' discretion at DOJ.

Other examples of the contemporary relevance of our work come from recent U.S. Supreme Court rulings regarding the so-called major questions doctrine, the demise of *Chevron* deference, and the Court's turn toward a preference for nondelegation generally. In sum, each obligates Congress to take a more central role in structuring policy by offering exacting detail to cover myriad potential circumstances and possible states of the world rather than delegating broadly. And Congress must do so without a concomitant increase in information or expertise.

The *Loper Bright* (2024) decision explicitly overturned *Chevron*, but also signaled the importance of respecting agency expertise in implementing statutes. Justice Roberts wrote for the Court:

> Courts must exercise their independent judgment in deciding whether an agency has acted within its statutory authority, as the APA requires. Careful attention to the judgment of the Executive

Branch may help inform that inquiry. And when a particular statute delegates authority to an agency consistent with constitutional
limits, courts must respect the delegation, while ensuring that the
agency acts within it. But courts need not and under the APA may
not defer to an agency interpretation of the law simply because a
statute is ambiguous. (*Loper Bright v Raimondo* (2024)

This suggests that, while striking *Chevron* deference, the majority
endorsed the respect afforded agency interpretations under *Skidmore*.
Though the *Skidmore* doctrine does not obligate courts to defer to agency
interpretations, when those agencies provide persuasive reasoning and
demonstrate consistency in their interpretation, courts should respect
those interpretations. It is therefore likely that the possibility of drift
remains, even if courts have abandoned *Chevron* deference. Indeed, in her
dissent, Justice Kagan notes the challenge courts will likely face in determining when deference is warranted:

> The majority makes clear that what is usually called Skidmore defer-
> ence continues to apply. Under that decision, agency interpretations
> "constitute a body of experience and informed judgment" that may
> be "entitled to respect." *Skidmore v. Swift & Co.*, 323 U. S. 134, 140
> (1944). If the majority thinks that the same judges who argue today
> about where "ambiguity" resides are not going to argue tomorrow
> about what "respect" requires, I fear it will be gravely disappointed.
> (*Loper Bright v Raimondo* (2024)

Congress will surely be sensitive to the shift away from *Chevron*,
even with the difficulties courts will face in determining "where ambiguity resides" and "what respect requires." We speculate that as broad delegations diminish, so too will the opportunities for unilateral action by
presidents and the subsequent congressional responsiveness. For instance,
as a result of the ruling in *Biden v. Nebraska* (2023), that the president is
unable to unilaterally forgive $430 billion in student loan debt because of
the major questions doctrine, similar actions that have such vast political
and economic significance would be limited. As those exertions of unilateral power diminish, opportunities for congressional strategic responsiveness also diminish. But even as broad delegations might decline in areas
untouched by the major questions doctrine, Congress could still aggregate
policies and presidents could still disaggregate them, so policy loss could
still be anticipated. If opportunities for significant legislative policymak-

ing do decline, the congressional role in structuring agencies' regulatory behavior may only increase (Ritchie 2023).

Broad, general concerns regarding presidential power remain relevant and surprisingly unsettled. Indeed, on the last day of oral arguments of the 2023–2024 term, the Supreme Court considered a broad claim of presidential immunity from criminal prosecution presented in *Trump v. United States* (2024).[8] Having been charged with attempting to overturn a valid election in violation of 18 U.S.C. § 371, former president Trump asserted absolute immunity for all actions taken while in office. While rejecting the absolute immunity argument, the Court made a distinction between official conduct (which would be immunized) and unofficial acts, which would not. In its decision, the Court remanded to the lower federal court to distinguish those actions taken by a president that are "official" rather than "unofficial, or private actions." Several members of the Court expressed concern that without immunity from criminal liability in their official capacities, future presidents would be subjected to opportunistic prosecutions by political rivals. Accordingly, they suggested that presidential immunity would attach to official conduct by the president, but not to private conduct. Others, like Justice Jackson, suggested the challenges of drawing a line between official and unofficial conduct could be eliminated by obligating all actions of the president—official and unofficial—to be bound by the law. Without the threat of criminal liability, she reasoned, future presidents could "turn the Oval Office into the seat of criminal activity in this country . . . and be emboldened to commit crimes with abandon while in office" (J. Jackson, oral arguments in *Trump v. U.S.* 2024).

It is hard to conclude a book about the ways in which Congress might counter executive power when the position of the presidency is being fundamentally changed by the Court. Surely, the private actions of former president Trump at issue in this case are unlikely to be completely immunized, but expanding the bounds of presidential immunity could fundamentally alter the dynamics of the separation of powers. In the face of broad immunity, impeachment itself might lose any force as a powerful constraint on executive action. The full scope of presidential power would expand anew in the absence of significant guardrails such as criminal liability. In some respects, such a shift would make the strategic responsiveness of Congress all the more important. But at the same time, if policy losses on particular dimensions of multidimensional policies are not keenly felt by members and senators, the motivation to constrain is gone.

Aside from his most hyperbolic claims, Trump's expansive view of presidential power is not unique to him; all modern presidents act unilaterally even as few adhere to the unitary executive view of presidential power. Presidents from Clinton through Biden have all taken unilateral actions placing policy or attempting to influence implementation in ways that "perfected law" on specific policy dimensions. Sometimes members of Congress benefited from blame avoidance and credit claiming on those dimensions, and sometimes they anticipated policy loss. In many ways, the strategic response from committees exercising oversight shaped the political context in which those unilateral actions were (or were not) able to penetrate. A Congress insufficiently attentive to specific policy loss invites presidential unilateralism, expanding the set of presidential actions that are accommodated by the constitutional order. While critics of the imperial presidency may bemoan the rise of unitary executive theory and its expressions, unilateral presidents coupled with an insufficiently attentive Congress generate a similar result. Many members and senators have shown a general willingness to accept highly problematic private and public behaviors as long as their own electoral circumstances and policy benefits are protected. As Justice Robert H. Jackson observed, executive power is contingent: "[O]nly Congress itself can prevent power from slipping through its fingers" (Robert H. Jackson concurring, *Youngstown Sheet & Tube Co. v. Sawyer*, 1952). Limits to executive authority are affected by the particular expression of presidential power, the preferences of relevant political actors, and the policies immediately at play. Political actors disagree about where the constitutional limits are and struggle to constrain the exercise of those powers that push the boundaries of the constitutional order. But on the discrete policy level, Congress can limit executive action in key ways. Oversight of the implementation of particular policies is a powerful tool that Congress can use to police the constitutional order, so long as they are incentivized to act.

Notes

Chapter One

1. Rao (2015) makes a similar claim regarding oversight, but she quickly veers into interpretations far removed from this book.

2. Too much explanation is typically a losing proposition for legislators (e.g., Bianco 1994), and simple explanations trump complex ones.

3. Since the post–World War II era, the rate of omnibus legislation has substantially increased. Since the 1990s, separate, independent spending bills have been supplanted by short-term continuing resolutions followed by omnibus packages. That said, if only two factions comprised the winning coalition, a similar result obtains.

4. Insecure majorities can also affect the willingness to compromise (Lee 2016).

5. Reeves has written extensively on public reactions to unilateralism (see, e.g., Reeves and Rogowski 2011, 2015, 2016a, 2016b).

6. Prior to the Great Compromise at the Constitutional Convention of 1787, there was some discussion among the delegates of a plural executive. Any support for a plural executive waned as the structure of the legislative branch became more firmly established.

7. In place of unitary executive theory, one might see references to departmentalism or the coordinate construction of the Constitution.

8. In earlier periods, this distinction might not have been necessary. Recess appointments were originally used more as a matter of convenience, but their use has increased since the 1980s (Black et al. 2007). Federal legislation affecting appointments has been interpreted varyingly as increasing efficiency, limiting Senate authority, and limiting presidential authority. The Federal Vacancies Reform Act of 1998 (5 U.S.C.§ 3347(a)) specifies those circumstances allowing the use of temporary appointees. The 2011 Presidential Appointment Streamlining and Effi-

ciency Act (P.L. 112-166) allows direct presidential appointment to hundreds of positions, eliminating the Senate's role from the process.

9. A game theorist would note that it is not sequentially rational for presidents to hide their policy motives from agencies or courts.

10. We exclude analyses of vetoes and veto threats. Vetoes might be most effective at fine-tuning a statute as it is being legislated in the shadow of a veto threat (e.g., Cameron 2000). If a veto is employed, there is neither refinement nor perfection of law through implementation regardless of whether the veto is upheld.

We also exclude national security directives (NSDs), proclamations, pardons, disaster declarations, and executive agreements. NSDs are hard to assess empirically because they are not always publicly available. Proclamations create a different empirical challenge. Few proclamations perfect law, so there is little empirical variation to investigate. Pardons and disaster declarations do not perfect law. Executive agreements are understandings with foreign nations, creating different dynamics with Congress (Caruson and Farrar-Myers 2007).

11. We leave the analysis of recess appointments and czars to other work. Recess or interim appointments are blunt instruments that can be used as an end run around the Senate's refusal to confirm (Kinane 2021). However, the pool of potential appointees is often limited, and presidents cannot calibrate any chosen recess appointee. Appointees come in whole units, as a president cannot build an appointee in the garage, customizing the appointee's views and consequent actions on specific policy dimensions.

Definitions of czars vary, but generally they are individuals in the executive branch who hold positions that have no clear statutory authority even as they are involved in directing and implementing policy. Presidents, acting alone, designate czars. Presidents have always had close, personal advisers, but when personal presidential advisers directly affect agency actions and guide policy, constitutional concerns arise (Sollenberger and Rozell 2012; Vaughn and Villalobos 2015). Like appointees, czars come in whole units and are not customizable.

Czar and recess appointments do not directly create or perfect law the way unilateral actions do. Additionally, executive orders, memoranda, and signing statements are fully customizable by the language employed.

12. Fowler (2015) focuses exclusively on foreign policy, finding that Congress has become less likely to hold the president accountable for the conduct of foreign policy due to growing disinterest on the Senate's part (cf. Howell, Jackman, and Rogowski 2013; Howell and Pevehouse 2011). Even with a more narrow policy focus, bills embody multiple issues with separate dimensions.

Chapter Two

1. Reliance on courts as a bulwark against presidential encroachment is similarly limited due to justiciability standards, limited enforcement authority, and the president's role in nominating jurists to the federal bench. For an exploration of the Supreme Court's role in rebalancing unilateral powers, see Thrower (2019).

2. *The Prize Cases* 67 U.S. 635 (1863); *Ex Parte Quirin* 317 U.S. 1 (1942). The *Prize Cases* addressed President Lincoln's blockade of southern ports. Blockades are considered an act of war, yet Congress had not at that time declared war. Some Lincoln supporters were opposed to a formal declaration because it might imply a

formal recognition of the independence of the Confederacy. The Supreme Court's majority decision argued that *the actions* of the Southern states meant that the nation was indeed at war and that a congressional declaration could only offer an official name for what was already under way. *Ex Parte Quirin*, the Nazi saboteurs case, dealt with the president's authority to prosecute foreign enemy combatants through military tribunals rather than civilian courts.

3. The *Korematsu v. U.S.* 323 U.S. 214 (1944) decision allowed the continuation of Japanese internment camps during World War II, thereby legitimizing the president's authority to impose by executive order extreme limitations on personal freedoms for Japanese American citizens in the interest of national security.

4. Fett (1994) found that President Carter's priorities moved cross-pressured legislators away from support. President Reagan's stated priorities, in contrast, were able to move cross-pressured legislators to support the White House.

5. See, for instance, Epstein and O'Halloran (1994, 1999), Huber and Shipan (2000, 2002), Ainsworth and Harward (2009), among others.

6. The OMB was developed in 1970. By the mid-1980s, it played an increasingly prominent role in overseeing rulemaking. As the OMB was strengthened and given greater jurisdiction, decision-making became more centralized within the executive branch, granting the president more power to manage the struggles inherent in policymaking.

7. See Skowronek (1997) for a more complete discussion of the Antiquities Act.

8. The array of executive branch agencies is vast, covering every aspect of policies related to banking, communication, social policy, economic policy, health, defense, and more.

9. See Hall (2004) and Adler and Wilkerson (2013) for more information on authorizations and reauthorizations.

10. McCubbins and Schwartz (1984) used a fire alarm analogy to describe the triggers for congressional oversight. With fire alarms, the monitoring costs effectively shift from members of Congress to those individuals who are most directly affected by agency actions.

11. Judicial review and statutory interpretation, for instance, are also often overlooked; but see work by Thrower (2019) for a model of courts and unilateral actions.

Chapter Three

1. Some of the work in this chapter is drawn from Ainsworth, Harward, and Moffett (2023, 2024).

2. The literature in this area is voluminous, encompassing much of the literature in social choice theory and most of the literature on spatial models of institutions. Foundational references in social choice theory include Arrow (1951), McKelvey (1976, 1979), and Schofield (1978, 1984). For applications of the spatial model to institutional settings, foundational work includes, for example, Black (1958), Shepsle (1979), Shepsle and Weingast (1981), and Krehbiel (1998).

3. Koopmans (1962) develops a utility-based model of decision-making in which actors face a series of sets of alternatives. Choices from an early set of alternatives can affect the range of alternatives available in subsequent sets. A decision-

maker must make a choice at each set. In Koopman's model, optimal early choices are designed to retain flexibility for subsequent choices.

4. An extreme policy in this setting indicates an alternative that is further to the left than the most leftward legislator or a policy alternative that is further to the right than the most rightward legislator.

5. Mershon and Shvetsova (2019) are critical of attempts to apply the same basic models repeatedly in different settings. It is better, they argue, to develop models from the ground up.

6. A stronger definition of rationality is not necessarily a better definition of rationality. Stronger, in this instance, means more restrictive. In the latter parts of this chapter and in the appendix, we explore the advantages and disadvantages of stronger and weaker definitions of rationality.

7. Insecure majorities can also affect the willingness to compromise (Lee 2016).

8. Each of the points in $NRZ_i(\mathbf{x})$ vector dominates $\mathbf{x}$.

9. Samuelson and Zeckhauser (1988), Kahneman (1994), and Kahneman and Thaler (2006) review experiments documenting the status quo bias and the related endowment effect. Rabin (1998) provides a nice review of loss aversion and the status quo bias.

10. To be certain, many scholars have noted the braking effect of veto players on social choices, but Herzberg and Tsebelis made more direct connections between veto players and policy change.

11. Presidential preferences are also conveyed to Congress by statements of administration policy, veto threats, and public pronouncements. However, one unilateral action, the signing statement, remains the most proximate to congressional action and the most directly responsive to what Congress *actually* passed—rather than what was being deliberated. Unlike statements of administration policy, veto threats, or public pronouncements, signing statements have been considered part of the formal legislative history since 1986.

12. Also see Howell and Kriner (2007). f

13. A relation, whether R or NR, is irreflexive if for all x in X, ~(xNRx). Asymmetry holds if for all x and y in X, xNRy implies ~(yNRx).

14. Value conflict is a shorthand expression used by Sen (2004) and others to indicate that an alternative is good in some respects but not so good in other respects.

Chapter Four

1. We thank Ian Ostrander for bringing this letter to our attention.

2. See Kane (2014) for a more complete discussion of this point.

3. Legislative vetoes are commonly studied in the congressional dominance literature (see, e.g., Fisher 1993).

4. Howell and Kriner (2007) focus more narrowly on congressional reaction—short of new legislation—to unilateral actions by then-President George W. Bush.

5. Lettermarks are missives sent by legislators to administrative agencies, asking that agency funds be used in particular manners. Ostensibly, legislators' lettermarks are used to bolster their own constituencies, and lettermarks have grown in popularity since the banning of earmarks in 2011.

6. The online appendix is available at https://kenmoffett.net/research/.

7. Following McGrath (2013), we defined a hearing as related to oversight if it included one or more of the following keywords: administration, budget request, consultation, contract, control, examination, explanation, impact, information, investigation, oversight, president, report, request, or review.

8. We did not consider rhetorical signing statements, as these tend to do things like thank specific members of Congress for their help on a bill or commend Congress for its work on a specific piece of legislation (Kelley 2007, 285). We have no reason to believe that congressional committees are induced to engage in oversight activity by rhetorical signing statements.

9. Institutional constraints revolve around planning and scheduling hearings when Congress meets for fewer than 11 days a month on average.

10. We validated our extension technique by applying it to a couple of years of Lowande's data and generating an identical list.

11. We did this with one caveat: if the policy area of the specific action lied in government operations or affected a cross section of policy areas without a clear, specific tie to one, then we coded the memorandum as government operations.

12. In Appendix B in the online appendixes, we examine whether divided government affects oversight. To do so, we replace our ideological distance variables for the House and Senate with a binary for divided government. When we do so, divided government is not statistically significant. Additionally, the signs and significance patterns for the remaining variables are unaffected.

13. These procedures are similar to centering variables (Lebo and Weber 2015). If we were to center oversight activity, we would contrast oversight in a particular month and year with the average oversight within that labeled month across all years. Indeed, we ran various models after centering our variables and secured results very close to those reported herein.

14. See Gelman and Hill (2007) for a more thorough treatment of multilevel or hierarchical modeling.

15. A result is considered to be helpful to the argument for policy memoranda *t* if it has a positive sign in the robustness check (consistent with theoretical expectations) but was not statistically significant in Table 4.1.

16. The models in this paragraph are available in Appendix D in the online appendixes for this chapter.

17. The models in this paragraph are available in Appendix B in the online appendixes.

18. We recognize that this is a somewhat rudimentary measure of this concept because policy importance cycles can change rapidly as policy windows open and close (see, e.g., Kingdon 1984). That said, the Comparative Agendas Project aggregates these data by year, which does not capture variation in an ideal manner.

19. This model is available in Appendix E of the online appendixes.

Chapter Five

1. Rhetorical signing statements, often used to thank key members or senators, are not included in our analyses.

2. Through 2018, defense policy generated 747 objections to provisions of law, while government operations, the second most common policy area, generated 277.

3. However, Schraufnagel and Snellman (2001) find no evidence that supports the two-presidencies hypothesis when analyzing roll-call votes in Congress.

4. Though the legislative veto was declared unconstitutional in *INS v. Chadha*, members of Congress regularly circumvent this prohibition.

5. Thus, our unit of analysis is each month and year during this time span and is analyzed as a time series, not as panel data. Consequently, Nickell (1981) bias is not a concern for this analysis.

6. As in Chapter 4, we defined a hearing as related to oversight if it included one or more of the following keywords: administration, budget request, consult, consultation, contract, control, examine, examination, explanation, explain, impact, information, investigate, investigation, oversight, president, reauthorize, reauthorization, report, request, or review.

7. There are broader definitions of oversight. Smith (2003) argues that any hearing not about new legislation or a new program or agency is focused on oversight. McGrath's (2013, 358) narrower definition of an oversight hearing is more likely to exclude hearings that do not focus on the "review or control of policy implementation" (Dodd and Schott 1979, 156).

8. See Oleszek (1995) for justification of the inclusion of reauthorization hearings.

9. For Senate oversight, the ADF test value was -11.465 ($p < .001$) and the Phillips-Perron test value was -11.282 ($p < .001$). For House oversight, the ADF test value was -11.421 ($p < .001$) and the Phillips-Perron test value was -11.259 ($p < .001$). Further, the Durbin-Watson tests for each model (2.227, 2.218, 2.218, and 2.192, respectively) indicate relatively little autocorrelation in the model.

10. Short-term effects occur if a change in the value of an independent variable results in an immediate change in oversight activity. Alternatively, long-term effects furnish evidence of a long-run equilibrium relationship between the dependent and independent variables.

11. Summary statistics are available in the online appendixes.

12. There were 85 defense bills during this time span on which a signing statement was issued. By comparison, there were a total of 7,274 bills introduced that related to defense policy. Thus, 1.17% of bills introduced had a signing statement placed on them.

13. The minimum and maximum values for days in session are 0 and 23.

14. We investigate whether this occurs by replacing the distance between the president and each of the two houses of Congress and the interactive terms with ideological distance in the models with divided government. When we do so, divided government in either the short or long term is not statistically significant. The remaining variables retain their signs and significance patterns, consistent with those contained in Table 5.1. This estimation is available in the online appendixes.

15. See Howell (2003) for related results with executive orders. Also see Mayer (2001).

16. The Republican control variable is consistent with literature in this area (e.g., McGrath 2013).

17. We acquired session data from the House Clerk.

18. A model in which defense objections to provisions of law in signing statements is compared with all objections, including defense, is suboptimal. A model

that contrasts defense objections to non-defense objections, as opposed to all objections, would be optimal. We address this concern by performing this comparison by running an additional model for exclusively non-defense objections. When we do so, we discover that non-defense objections are positive and significant for three months in the House and at three and four months in the Senate. The results from this set of estimations are available from the authors.

We assess whether the results from the aforementioned model illustrate a statistically significant difference from objections in defense bills that are related to defense. Clogg, Petkova, and Haritou (1995) provide a calculation indicating whether statistically significant differences exist across the defense and non-defense models. The z-statistics are .674 (p = .500, for signing statements for House oversight at three months), −.392 (p = .695, for signing statements for Senate oversight at three months), and .196 (p = .845, for signing statements for Senate oversight at four months). None of the z-scores attain statistical significance. Consequently, we retain the models in Table 5.1, as there may be a conceptual difference between defense- and non-defense-related objections, but that conceptual difference does not manifest itself empirically.

19. One can imagine high-profile oversight hearings being affected by presidential popularity; but for the set of oversight hearings tied to all defense-related legislation, there is no statistically significant connection.

20. As with the calculations in the previous paragraph, we presume that the lagged dependent variable is equal to one for these calculations.

21. The estimations in this section are contained in the online appendixes.

22. When we omit the month of April, a deviation does occur. The results demonstrate more overall variability, with the baseline findings still holding to a lesser extent for the House, but not for the Senate. We do not speculate what about April yields such a finding. Omitting the months around April (February, March, May, or June) while leaving April in the model does not change the findings that we report.

23. Although it is beyond the scope of our present work, one could consider Senator Tuberville's (R-AL) objections to military promotions as being more related to abortion policy than to military policy.

Chapter Six

1. Data on the extensiveness of orders and memoranda would qualify this finding.

2. Of course, the Democrats' control of the Senate was particularly fragile due to a handful of moderate Democratic senators and the presence of the filibuster.

3. Savage's coverage for the *Boston Globe* of the debates swirling around enhanced interrogation and torture likely introduced signing statements for the first time to the broader public.

4. Crouch, Rozell, and Sollenberger (2020) offer a less sanguine view.

5. Rao (2015) explores a similar theme from a less empirical angle.

6. One of the reasons agenda control is so vital to the policymaking process is that it affects the emergence of issues. The dynamics in work by Jeong, Miller, and Sened (2009) are close to what we envision.

7. Additional implications from the model in Chapter 3 are presented in the appendix to Chapter 3. Those implications are focused, among other things, on the

stability of social choices when members adhere to blame avoidance and vote explanation. They are less immediately tied to presidential unilateralism or Congress's strategic responsiveness.

8. In a split decision, the Supreme Court found that presidents have immunity from civil suits for their actions during the course of their tenure in office (*Nixon v. Fitzgerald*, 1982).

Works Cited

Abadie, Alberto and Guido Imbens. 2006. "Large Sample Properties of Matching Estimators for Average Treatment Effects." *Econometrica* 74(1): 235–267.

Abadie, Alberto and Guido Imbens. 2011. "Bias-Corrected Matching Estimators for Average Treatment Effects." *Journal of Business and Economic Statistics* 29(1): 1–11.

Abadie, Alberto and Guido Imbens. 2016. "Matching on the Estimated Propensity Score." *Econometrica* 84(2): 781–807.

ABC News / Washington Post. 2017. "Americans Back DACA by a Huge Margin." https://www.langerresearch.com/wp-content/uploads/1191a4DACAandImmigration.pdf. Accessed April 1, 2022.

Aberbach, Joel. 1990. *Keeping a Watchful Eye: The Politics of Congressional Oversight.* Washington, DC: Brookings Institution Press.

Achen, Christopher H. and Larry Bartels. 2016. *Democracy for Realists: Why Elections Do Not Produce Responsive Government.* Princeton, NJ: Princeton University Press.

Adler, E. Scott and John Wilkerson. 2013. *Congress and the Politics of Problem Solving.* New York: Cambridge University Press.

Ainsworth, Scott H. and Thad Hall. 2010. *Abortion Politics in Congress: Strategic Incrementalism and Policy Change.* New York: Cambridge University Press.

Ainsworth, Scott H. and Brian M. Harward. 2009. "Delegation and Discretion in Anticipation of Coalitional Drift." *American Politics Research* 37(6): 983–1002.

Ainsworth, Scott H., Brian M. Harward, and Kenneth W. Moffett. 2012. "Congressional Response to Presidential Signing Statements." *American Politics Research* 40(6): 1067–1091.

Ainsworth, Scott H., Brian M. Harward, and Kenneth W. Moffett. 2023. "Taking Blame Avoidance and Vote Explanation Seriously." Presented at the Annual Meeting of the American Political Science Association in Los Angeles, CA.

Ainsworth, Scott H., Brian M. Harward, and Kenneth W. Moffett. 2024. "The Multiple Dimensions of Blame Avoidance." Presented at the annual meeting of the Midwest Political Science Association in Chicago, IL.

Ainsworth, Scott H., Brian M. Harward, Kenneth W. Moffett, and Laurie L. Rice. 2014. "Congressional Response to Statements of Administration Policy and Presidential Signing Statements." *Congress and the Presidency* 41(3): 312–334.

Alesina, Alberto and Francesco Passarelli. 2019. "Loss Aversion in Politics." *American Journal of Political Science* 63(4): 936–947.

Alito, Samuel A., Jr. 1986. Memorandum, Deputy Assistant Attorney General, Office of Legal Counsel to the Litigation Strategy Working Group 1 (Feb. 5, 1986). https://www.archives.gov/files/news/samuel-alito/accession-060-89-269/Acc060-89-269-box6-SG-LSWG-AlitotoLSWG-Feb1986.pdf. Accessed August 3, 2023.

American Bar Association. 2006. *Task Force Report on Signing Statements.* https://www.americanbar.org/content/dam/aba/publishing/abanews/1273179616signstatereport.authcheckdam.pdf. Accessed June 6, 2019.

American Presidency Project. 2013. Papers and Historical Documents on the American Presidency. http://www.presidency.ucsb.edu. Accessed various dates.

Anderson, Sarah E., Daniel M. Butler, and Laurel Harbridge-Yong. 2020. *Rejecting Compromise: Legislators' Fear of Primary Voters.* New York: Cambridge University Press.

Antiquities Act. 1906. *Statutes at Large.* 16 United States Code 431–433.

Arnold, R. Douglas. 1990. *The Logic of Congressional Action.* New Haven, CT: Yale University Press.

Arrow, Kenneth J. 1951. *Social Choice and Individual Values.* New York: John Wiley & Sons.

Art, Robert J. 1985. "Congress and the Defense Budget: Enhancing Policy Oversight." *Political Science Quarterly* 100(2): 227–248.

Auerswald, David P. and Colton C. Campbell. 2012. *Congress and the Politics of National Security.* New York: Cambridge University Press.

Bailey, Jeremy and Brandon Rottinghaus. 2014. "Reexamining the Unilateral Politics Model: Source of Authority and the Power to Act Alone." *American Politics Research* 42(3): 472–502.

Bailey, Michael A. 2013. "Is Today's Court the Most Conservative in Sixty Years? Challenges and Opportunities in Measuring Judicial Preferences." *Journal of Politics* 75(3): 821–834.

Bailey, Michael A. 2021. Bridge Ideal Points. https://michaelbailey.georgetown.domains/data/. Accessed January 21, 2022.

Balla, Steven J. 1998. "Administrative Procedures and Political Control of the Bureaucracy." *American Political Science Review* 92(3): 663–673.

Balla, Steven J. and John R. Wright. 2001. "Interest Groups, Advisory Committees, and Congressional Control of the Bureaucracy." *American Journal of Political Science* 45(4): 799–812.

Barr, William P. 2019. "Attorney General William P. Barr Delivers the 19th Annual Barbara K. Olson Memorial Lecture at the Federalist Society's 2019 National Lawyers Convention." https://www.justice.gov/opa/speech/attorney-gener al-william-p-barr-delivers-19th-annual-barbara-k-olson-memorial-lecture. Accessed June 24, 2020.

Baumgartner, Frank and Bryan Jones. 1993. *Agendas and Instability in American Politics*. Chicago: University of Chicago Press.

Bawn, Kathleen. 1995. "Political Control versus Expertise: Congressional Choices about Administrative Procedures." *American Political Science Review* 89(1): 62–73.

Bawn, Kathleen. 1997. "Choosing Strategies to Control the Bureaucracy: Statutory Constraints, Oversight, and the Committee System." *Journal of Law, Economics, & Organization* 13(1): 101–126.

Belco, Michelle and Brandon Rottinghaus. 2014. "In Lieu of Legislation: Executive Unilateral Preemption or Support during the Legislative Process." *Political Research Quarterly* 67(2): 413–425.

Belco, Michelle and Brandon Rottinghaus. 2017. *The Dual Executive: Unilateral Orders in a Separated and Shared Power System*. Stanford, CA: Stanford University Press.

Bell, David E. 1982. "Regret in Decision Making under Uncertainty." *Operations Research* 30(5): 961–981.

Bell, David E. 1983. "Risk Premiums for Decision Regret." *Management Science* 29(10): 1156–1166.

Berry, Michael J. 2009. "Controversially Executing the Law: George W. Bush and the Constitutional Signing Statement." *Congress and the Presidency* 36(3): 244–271.

Bertelli, Anthony M. and Christian R. Grose. 2007. "Agreeable Administrators? Analyzing the Public Positions of Cabinet Secretaries and Presidents." *Presidential Studies Quarterly* 37(2): 228–247.

Bianco, William T. 1994. *Trust: Representatives and Constituents*. Ann Arbor: University of Michigan Press.

Bianco, William T., Ivan Jeliazkov, and Itai Sened. 2004. "The Uncovered Set and Limits of Legislative Action." *Political Analysis* 12(3): 256–276.

Biden, Joseph R. 2021. Executive Order 14000. https://www.federalregister.gov /documents/2021/01/26/2021–01864/supporting-the-reopening-and-continu ing-operation-of-schools-and-early-childhood-education-providers. Accessed July 20, 2022.

Biden v. Nebraska, 600 US ___ (2023).

Binder, C. 2014. "Plural Identities and Preference Formation." *Social Choice and Welfare* 42: 959–976.

Binder, Sarah A. 1997. *Majority Rights, Minority Rule: Partisanship and the Development of Congress*. New York: Cambridge University Press.

Binder, Sarah A. and Frances Lee 2015. "Making Deals in Congress." In Nathaniel

Persily, ed., *Solutions to Political Polarization in America*, 240–261. New York: Cambridge University Press.

Black, Duncan. 1958. *The Theory of Committees and Elections*. Cambridge: Cambridge University Press.

Black, Ryan C., Michael Lynch, Anthony J. Madonna, and Ryan J. Owens. 2011. "Assessing Congressional Responses to Growing Presidential Powers: The Case of Recess Appointments." *Presidential Studies Quarterly* 41(3): 570–589.

Black, Ryan C., Anthony J. Madonna, Ryan J. Owens, and Michael Lynch. 2007. "Adding Recess Appointments to the President's 'Tool Chest' of Unilateral Powers." *Political Research Quarterly* 60(4): 645–654.

Blackman, Josh and Shelby Baird. 2014. "The Shooting Cycle." *Connecticut Law Review* 46(4): 1513–1579.

Blechman, Barry M. 1992. *The Politics of National Security: Congress and U.S. Defense Policy*. New York: Oxford University Press.

Blizzard, Brittany and Jocelyn M. Johnston. 2021. "State Policy Control and Local Deviation: The Case of Immigration." *State and Local Government Review* 52(4): 309–320.

Boatright, Robert G. 2013. *Getting Primaried: The Changing Politics of Congressional Primary Challenges*. Ann Arbor: University of Michigan Press.

Bolter, Jessica, Emma Israel, and Sarah Pierce. 2022. "Four Years of Profound Change: Immigration Policy during the Trump Presidency." Migration Policy Institute. https://www.migrationpolicy.org/research/four-years-change-immigration-trump. Accessed April 1, 2022.

Bolton, Alexander and Sharice Thrower. 2016. "Legislative Capacity and Executive Unilateralism." *American Journal of Political Science* 60(3): 649–663.

Bond, Jon R. and Richard Fleisher. 1990. *The President in the Legislative Arena*. Chicago: University of Chicago Press.

Bonica, Adam, Jowei Chen, and Tim Johnson. 2015. "Senate Gate-Keeping, Presidential Staffing of 'Inferior Offices,' and the Ideological Composition of Appointments to the Public Bureaucracy." *Quarterly Journal of Political Science* 10(1): 5–40.

Bracey, John H., Jr. and August Meier. 1991. "Allies or Adversaries? The NAACP, A. Phillip Randolph, and the 1941 March on Washington." *Georgia Historical Quarterly* 75(1): 1–17.

Bush, George W. 2007. "President Bush's Plan for Comprehensive Immigration Reform." https://georgewbush-whitehouse.archives.gov/stateoftheunion/2007/initiatives/immigration.html. Accessed June 7, 2022.

Byrd, Robert C. 2005. *Losing America: Confronting a Reckless and Arrogant Presidency*. New York: W.W. Norton.

Calabresi, Steven G. and Christopher S. Yoo. 1997. "The Unitary Executive during the First Half Century." *Case Western Reserve Law Review* 47: 1451–1461.

Calabresi, Steven G. and Christopher S. Yoo. 2003. "The Unitary Executive during the Second Half Century." *Harvard Journal of Law and Public Policy* 26: 668–801.

Cameron, Charles M. 2000. *Veto Bargaining: Presidents and the Politics of Negative Power*. Cambridge: Cambridge University Press.

Canes-Wrone, Brandice. 2001. "A Theory of Presidents' Public Agenda Setting." *Journal of Theoretical Politics* 13(2): 183–208.

Canes-Wrone, Brandice. 2006. *Who Leads Whom? Presidents, Policy and the Public*. Chicago: University of Chicago Press.

Canes-Wrone, Brandice, William G. Howell, and David E. Lewis. 2008. "Toward a Broader Understanding of Presidential Power: A Reevaluation of the Two Presidencies Thesis." *Journal of Politics* 70(1): 1–16.

Carmines, Edward and James Stimson. 1989. *Issue Evolution: Race and the Transformation of American Politics*. Princeton, NJ: Princeton University Press.

Carsey, Thomas M. and Barry Rundquist. 1999. "Party and Committee in Distributive Politics: Evidence from Defense Spending." *Journal of Politics* 61(4): 1156–1169.

Carson, Jamie, Joel Seivert, and Ryan Williamson. 2023. Nationalized Politics: Evaluating Electoral Politics across Time. New York: Oxford University Press.

Caruson, Kiki and Victoria A. Farrar-Myers. 2007. "Promoting the President's Foreign Policy Agenda: Presidential Use of Executive Agreements as Policy Vehicles." *Political Research Quarterly* 60(4): 631–644.

Chafetz, Josh. 2020. *Congress' Constitution: Legislative Authority and the Separation of Powers*. New Haven, CT: Yale University Press.

Cheathem, Mark R. 2013. *Andrew Jackson, Southerner*. Baton Rouge: Louisiana State University Press.

Cherepanov, Vadim, Timothy Feddersen, and Alvaro Sandroni. 2013. "Rationalization." *Theoretical Economics* 8(3): 775–800.

Chiou, Fang-Yi and Lawrence S. Rothenberg. 2013. "The Elusive Search for Presidential Power." *American Journal of Political Science* 58(3): 653–668.

Chiou, Fang-Yi and Lawrence S. Rothenberg. 2017. *The Enigma of Presidential Power: Parties, Policies, and Strategic Uses of Unilateral Action*. New York: Cambridge University Press.

Christenson, Dino P. and Douglas L. Kriner. 2020a. "Beyond the Base: Presidents, Partisan Approval, and the Political Economy of Unilateral Action." *Journal of Political Institutions and Political Economy* 1: 79–103.

Christenson, Dino P. and Douglas L. Kriner. 2020b. *The Myth of the Imperial Presidency: How Public Opinion Checks the Unilateral Executive*. Chicago: University of Chicago Press.

Clinton, Hillary Rodham. 2016. "Immigration Reform." https://www.hillaryclinton.com/issues/immigration-reform/. Accessed June 7, 2022.

Clogg, Clifford, Eva Petkova, and Adammantios Haritou. 1995. "Statistical Methods for Comparing Regression Coefficients between Models." *American Journal of Sociology* 100(5): 1261–1293.

CNN. 2017. "Interview with Oklahoma Senator James Lankford; Trump's New Immigration Policy; Interview with Senate Minority Whip Dick Durbin, Democrat from Illinois." *CNN The Lead with Jake Tapper*. Aired August 2.

CNN. 2019. "Trump: Article II Gives Me the Right to Do Whatever I Want." July 23. https://www.cnn.com/videos/politics/2019/07/23/rep-sean-maloney-trump-not-above-the-law-sot-ebof-vpx.cnn. Accessed June 5, 2020.

Cohen, Tom 2012. "Obama Administration to Stop Deporting Some Young Illegal Immigrants." CNN. June 16. https://www.cnn.com/2012/06/15/politics/immigration. Accessed May 12, 2021.

Congressional Record. 2007. 110th Cong. 1st sess. Page S8744.

Converse, Philip E. 1964. "The Nature of Belief Systems in Mass Publics." In David Apter, ed., *Ideology and its Discontents*, 206–261. New York: Free Press of Glencoe.

Cooper, Phillip J. 2002. *By Order of the President: The Use and Abuse of Executive Direct Action*. Lawrence: University of Kansas Press.

Cooper, Phillip J. 2005. "George W. Bush, Edgar Allan Poe, and the Use and Abuse of Presidential Signing Statements." *Presidential Studies Quarterly* 35(3): 515–532.

Cortina, Jeronimo. 2020. "From a Distance: Geographic Proximity, Partisanship, and Public Attitudes toward the U.S.-Mexico Border Wall." *Political Research Quarterly* 73(3): 740–754.

Council on Foreign Relations. 2012. "The Candidates on Immigration." https://www.cfr.org/backgrounder/candidates-immigration. Accessed June 7, 2022.

Courser, Zachary and Kevin R. Kosar 2021. "Restoring the Power of the Purse: Earmarks and Re-empowering Legislators to Deliver Local Benefits." American Enterprise Institute. http://kevinrkosar.com/wordpress/wp-content/uploads/2021/02/Courser-Kosar-Restoring-the-Power-of-the-Purse-02-09-2021-1.pdf. Accessed April 12, 2021.

Cox, Gary W. and Mathew D. McCubbins. 1993. *Legislative Leviathan: Party Government in the House*. Berkeley: University of California Press.

Cox, Gary W. and Mathew D. McCubbins. 2005. *Setting the Agenda: Responsible Party Government in the U.S. House of Representatives*. New York: Cambridge University Press.

CQ Almanac. 2014. "Obama Wins Border War for Now." *CQ Almanac*. https://library.cqpress.com/cqalmanac/document.php?id=cqal14-1770-97588-2704368. Accessed April 1, 2022.

Crawford, Vincent P. 2013. "Boundedly Rational versus Optimization-Based Models of Strategic Thinking and Learning in Games." *Journal of Economic Literature* 51(2): 512–527.

Crenson, Matthew and Benjamin Ginsburg. 2007. *Presidential Power: Unchecked and Unbalanced*. New York City: W.W. Norton.

Crouch, Jeffrey. 2008. "Presidential Misuse of the Pardon Power." *Presidential Studies Quarterly* 38(4): 722–734.

Crouch, Jeffrey, Mark J. Rozell, and Mitchel A. Sollenberger. 2017. "The Unitary Executive and President Donald J. Trump." *Presidential Studies Quarterly* 47(3): 561–573.

Crouch, Jeffrey, Mark J. Rozell, and Mitchel A. Sollenberger. 2020. *The Unitary Executive: A Danger to Constitutional Government*. Lawrence: University Press of Kansas.

Curry, James M. and Frances E. Lee. 2020. *The Limits of Party: Congress and Lawmaking in a Polarized Era*. Chicago: University of Chicago Press.

D'Agostino, Ralph B. 1998. "Propensity Score Methods for Bias Reduction in the Comparison of a Treatment to a Non-randomized Control Group." *Statistics in Medicine* 17(9): 2265–2281.

De Boef, Suzanne and Luke Keele. 2008. "Taking Time Seriously: Dynamic Regression." *American Journal of Political Science* 52(1): 184–200.

de Figueiredo, Rui J. P., Jr., Tonja Jacobi, and Barry R. Weingast. 2008. "The New Separation of Powers Approach to American Politics." In Barry R. Weingast and D. Wittman, eds., *The Oxford Handbook of Political Economy*, 199–222. Oxford: Oxford University Press.

Deering, Christopher J. and Forrest Maltzman. 1999. "The Politics of Executive Orders: Legislative Constraints on Presidential Power." *Political Research Quarterly* 52(4): 767–783.

Denzau, Arthur, William H. Riker, and Kenneth A. Shepsle. 1985. "Farquharson and Fenno: Sophisticated Voting and Home Style." *American Political Science Review* 79: 1117–1134.

Department of Homeland Security 2019. "Yearbook of Immigration Statistics 2019." https://www.dhs.gov/immigration-statistics/yearbook/2019. Accessed June 7, 2022.

Department of Homeland Security et al. v. Regents of the University of California et al., 591 U.S. ___ (2020).

Diamond, Alexis and Jasjeet J. Sekhon. 2013. "Genetic Matching for Estimating Causal Effects: A General Multivariate Matching Method for Achieving Balance in Observational Studies." *Review of Economics and Statistics* 95(3): 932–945.

Diermeier, Daniel and Keith Krehbiel. 2003. "Institutionalism as a Methodology." *Journal of Theoretical Politics* 15(2): 123–144.

Dion, Douglas. 1997. *Turning the Legislative Thumbscrew: Minority Rights and Procedural Change in Legislative Politics*. Ann Arbor: University of Michigan Press.

Dodd, Lawrence C. and Richard L. Schott. 1979. *Congress and the Administrative State*. New York: John Wiley and Sons.

Dodds, Graham G. 2013. *Take Up Your Pen: Unilateral Directives in American Politics*. Philadelphia: University of Pennsylvania Press.

Doubek, James. 2017. "Thousands Protest at Airports Nationwide Against Trump's Immigration Order." NPR. January 29. https://www.npr.org/sections/thetwo-way/2017/01/29/512250469/photos-thousands-protest-at-airports-nationwide-against-trumps-immigration-order. Accessed October 10, 2020.

Duke, Elaine C. 2017. "Rescission of the June 15, 2012 Memorandum Entitled 'Exercising Prosecutorial Discretion with Respect to Individuals Who Came to the United States as Children.'" Department of Homeland Security. https://

www.dhs.gov/news/2017/09/05/memorandum-rescission-daca. Accessed April 1, 2022.

Edwards, George C., III. 1989. *At the Margins: Presidential Leadership of Congress.* New Haven, CT: Yale University Press.

Edwards, George C. III. 2006. *On Deaf Ears: The Limits of the Bully Pulpit.* New Haven, CT: Yale University Press.

Edwards, George C. III. 2009. *The Strategic President: Persuasion and Opportunity in Presidential Leadership.* Princeton, NJ: Princeton University Press.

Edwards, George C. III. 2020. *Changing Their Minds? Donald Trump and Presidential Leadership.* Chicago: University of Chicago Press.

Edwards, George C., III and Stephen J. Wayne. 1999. *Presidential Leadership.* New York: St. Martins Press.

Eggers, Andrew C. and Jens Hainmueller. 2009. "MPs for Sale? Returns to Office in Postwar British Politics." *American Political Science Review* 103(4): 513–533.

Enns, Peter K., Nathan J. Kelly, Takaaki Masaki, and Patrick C. Wohlfarth. 2016. "Don't Jettison the General Error Correction Model Just Yet: A Practical Guide to Avoiding Spurious Regression with the GECM." *Research and Politics* 3(2): 1–13.

Epstein, David and Sharyn O'Halloran. 1994. "Administrative Procedures, Information, and Agency Discretion." *American Journal of Political Science* 38(3): 697–722.

Epstein, David and Sharyn O'Halloran. 1999. *Delegating Powers: A Transaction Cost Politics Approach to Policy Making under Separate Powers.* New York: Columbia University Press.

Epstein, Lee and Thomas G. Walker. 2020. *Constitutional Law for a Changing America.* 10th ed. Thousand Oaks, CA: CQ Press.

Evans, Diana. 2004. *Greasing the Wheels: Using Pork Barrel Projects to Build Majority Coalitions in Congress.* New York: Cambridge University Press.

Ex Parte Milligan, 71 U.S. 2 (1866).

Farhang, Sean. 2010. *The Litigation State: Public Regulation and Private Lawsuits in the U.S.* Princeton, NJ: Princeton University Press.

Federal Register. 2022. Presidential Documents. https://www.federalregister.gov/presidential-documents. Accessed April 1, 2022.

Fenno, Richard. 1978. *Home Style: Members of Congress in their Districts.* New York: Little and Brown.

Fett, Patrick J. 1994. "Presidential Legislative Priorities and Legislators' Voting Decisions: An Exploratory Analysis." *Journal of Politics* 56(2): 502–512.

Fiorina, Morris P. 1982a. "Congressional Control of the Bureaucracy: A Mismatch of Incentives and Capabilities." In Lawrence C. Dodd and Bruce I. Oppenheimer, eds., *Congress Reconsidered*, 2nd ed., 332–348. Washington, DC: Congressional Quarterly Press.

Fiorina, Morris P. 1982b. "Legislative Choice of Regulatory Reforms: Legal Process or Administrative Process." *Public Choice* 39(1): 33–66.

Fisher, Louis. 1993. "The Legislative Veto: Invalidated, It Survives." *Law and Contemporary Problems* 56(4): 273–292.

Fisher, Louis. 1997. *Constitutional Conflicts between Congress and the President.* 4th ed. Lawrence: University Press of Kansas.

Fisher, Louis. 2001. *Constitutional Conflicts between Congress and the President.* Lawrence: University Press of Kansas.

Fisher, Louis. 2007–2008. "Signing Statements: Constitutional and Practical Limits" *William and Mary Bill of Rights Journal* 16(1): 183–210.

Fisher, Louis. 2012. "National Security Surveillance." In David P. Auerswald and Colton C. Campbell, eds., *Congress and the Politics of National Security,* 189–229. New York: Cambridge University Press.

Fitts, Michael A. 1996. "The Paradox of Power in the Modern State: Why a Unitary, Centralized Presidency May Not Exhibit Effective or Legitimate Leadership." *University of Pennsylvania Law Review* 144(3): 827–902.

Fowler, Linda L. 2015. *Watchdogs on the Hill: The Decline of Congressional Oversight of U.S. Foreign Policy.* Princeton, NJ: Princeton University Press.

Francis, Katherine and Tracy Sulkin. 2013. "Legislative Coalitions and Presidential Signing Statements." *Congress and the Presidency* 40: 230–254.

Fuller, Stephen S. 2012. "New Report Predicts Widespread American Job Losses." Aerospace Industries Association. https://spacenews.com/new-report-predicts -widespread-american-job-losses/ . Accessed August 13, 2024.

Garber, Marc and Kurt Wimmer. 1987. "Presidential Signing Statements as Interpretations of Legislative Intent: An Executive Aggrandizement of Power." *Harvard Journal on Legislation* 24: 363–366.

Gelman, Andrew and Jennifer Hill. 2007. *Data Analysis Using Regression and Multilevel /Hierarchical Models.* New York: Cambridge University Press.

Gilligan, Thomas W. and Keith Krehbiel. 1987. "Collective Decisionmaking and Standing Committees: An Informational Rationale for Restrictive Amendment Procedures." *Journal of Law, Economics, & Organization* 3(2): 287–335.

Good, Chris. 2011. "Bart Stupak, a Year after Health Care: Getting 'Bitched Out' in Airports, How the Deal Went Down, and More." *The Atlantic.* March 23. https://www.theatlantic.com/politics/archive/2011/03/bart-stupak-a-year-aft er-health-care-getting-bitched-out-in-airports-how-the-deal-went-down-and -more/72938/ Accessed October 12, 2020.

Gormley, William T. 1986. "Regulatory Issue Networks in a Federal System." *Polity* 18(4): 595–620.

Government Accountability Office. 2020. "Department of Homeland Security— Legality of Service of Acting Secretary of Homeland Security and Service of Senior Official Performing the Duties of Deputy Secretary of Homeland Security." August 14. https://www.gao.gov/assets/710/708830.pdf. Accessed December 2, 2020.

Graham, Lindsey. 2019. Twitter. https://twitter.com/LindseyGrahamSC. Accessed April 1, 2022.

Greene, William H. 2017. *Econometric Analysis*. 8th ed. New York: Pearson Longman.

Grose, Christian R., Neil Malhotra, and Robert Parks Van Houweling. 2014. "Explaining Explanations: How Legislators Explain Their Policy Positions and How Citizens React." *American Journal of Political Science* 59(3): 724–743.

Hainmueller, Jens and Dominik Hangartner. 2019. "Does Direct Democracy Hurt Immigrant Minorities? Evidence from Naturalization Decisions in Switzerland." *American Journal of Political Science* 63(3): 530–547.

Hall, Richard L. 1996. *Participation in Congress*. New Haven, CT: Yale University Press.

Hall, Thad. 2004. *Authorizing Policy*. Columbus: Ohio State University Press.

Halloran, Liz. 2013. "Gang of 8 Champion Plan, Declare 'Year Of Immigration Reform.'" NPR. April 18. https://www.npr.org/sections/itsallpolitics/2013/04/18/177780665/bipartisan-senate-gang-prepares-to-sell-immigration-plan. Accessed April 1, 2022.

Halstead, T. J. 2008. "Presidential Signing Statements: Executive Aggrandizement, Judicial Ambivalence and Congressional Vituperation." *Government Information Quarterly* 25(4): 563–591.

Harriger, Katy. 2020. "*The Law*: 'Witch Hunts' and the Rule of Law: Trump, the Special Counsel, and the Department of Justice." *Presidential Studies Quarterly* 50(1): 176–192.

Harstad, Ronald M. and Reinhard Selten. 2013. "Bounded-Rationality Models: Tasks to Become Intellectually Competitive." *Journal of Economic Literature* 51(2): 496–511.

Harward, Brian M. and Kenneth W. Moffett. 2010. "The Calculus of Cosponsorship in the U.S. Senate." *Legislative Studies Quarterly* 35(1): 117–143.

Head, Megan L., Luke Holman, Rob Lanfear, Andrew T. Kahn, and Michael D. Jennions. 2015. "The Extent and Consequences of P-Hacking in Science." *Plos Biology* 13(3): e1002106.

Heo, Uk. 2010. "The Relationship between Defense Spending and Economic Growth in the United States." *Political Research Quarterly* 63(4): 760–770.

Herzberg, Roberta. 1992. "An Analytic Choice Approach to Concurrent Majorities: The Relevance of John C. Calhoun's Theory for Institutional Design." *Journal of Politics* 54(1): 54–81.

Ho, Daniel E., Kozuke Imai, Gary King, and Elizabeth A. Stuart. 2007. "Matching as Nonparametric Preprocessing for Reducing Model Dependence in Parametric Causal Inference." *Political Analysis* 15(3): 199–236.

Howell, William G. 2003. *Power without Persuasion: The Politics of Direct Presidential Action*. Princeton, NJ: Princeton University Press.

Howell, William G. 2005. "Introduction: Unilateral Powers: A Brief Overview." *Presidential Studies Quarterly* 35(3): 417–439.

Howell, William G. 2011. "Presidential Power in War." *Annual Review of Political Science* 14: 89–105.

Howell, William G. and Faisal Z. Ahmed. 2014. "Voting for the President: The Supreme Court during War." *Journal of Law, Economics, and Organization* 30(1): 39–71.

Howell, William G. and Saul P. Jackman. 2013. "Interbranch Negotiations over Policies with Multiple Outcomes." *American Journal of Political Science* 57(4): 956–970.

Howell, William G., Saul P. Jackman, and Jon C. Rogowski. 2013. *The Wartime President: Executive Influence and the Nationalizing Politics of Threat.* Chicago: University of Chicago Press.

Howell, William G. and Douglas L. Kriner. 2007. "Bending So as Not to Break: What the Bush Presidency Reveals about the Politics of Unilateral Action." In George C. Edwards and Desmond S. King, eds., *The Polarized Presidency of George W. Bush*, 96–141. Oxford: Oxford University Press.

Howell, William G. and Terry Moe. 2016. *Relic: How our Constitution Undermines Effective Government—and Why We Need a More Powerful Presidency.* New York: Basic Books.

Howell, William G. and Terry Moe. 2020. *Presidents, Populism, and the Crisis of Democracy.* Chicago: University of Chicago Press.

Howell, William G. and Jon C. Pevehouse. 2011. *While Dangers Gather: Congressional Checks on Presidential Power.* Princeton, NJ: Princeton University Press.

Huber, John D. and Charles R. Shipan. 2000. "The Costs of Control: Legislators, Agencies, and Transaction Costs." *Legislative Studies Quarterly* 25(1): 25–52.

Huber, John D. and Charles R. Shipan. 2002. *Deliberate Discretion: The Institutional Foundations of Bureaucratic Autonomy.* New York: Cambridge University Press.

Huber, John D., Charles R. Shipan, and Madelaine Pfahler. 2001. "Legislatures and Statutory Control of Bureaucracies." *American Journal of Political Science* 45(2): 330–45.

Hudak, John. 2014. *Presidential Pork: White House Influence over the Distribution of Federal Grants.* Washington, DC: Brookings Institution Press.

Imbens, Guido and Donald B. Rubin. 2015. *Causal Inference for Statistics, Social, & Biomedical Sciences: An Introduction.* New York: Cambridge University Press.

Issa, Darrel E., Claire McCaskill, Elijah E. Cummings, and Charles E. Grassley. 2013. "Letter to President Obama." January 17, 2013. House of Representatives and United States Senate.

Jacobson, Gary C. 1987. "Running Scared: Elections and Congressional Politics in the 1980s." In Mathew D. McCubbins and Terry Sullivan, eds., *Congress: Structure and Policy*, 39–81. New York: Cambridge University Press.

Jacobson, Gary C. 2015. "It's Nothing Personal: The Decline of the Incumbency Advantage in U.S. House Elections." *Journal of Politics* 77(3): 861–873.

Jacobson, Cary C. and Jamie Carson. 2019. *The Politics of Congressional Elections.* 10th ed. Landham, MD: Rowman and Littlefield.

Jeong, Gyung-Ho, Gary J. Miller, and Itai Sened. 2009. "Closing the Deal: Negotiating Civil Rights Legislation." *American Political Science Review* 103(4): 588–606.

Jeong, Gyung-Ho, Gary J. Miller, Camilla Schofield, and Itai Sened. 2011. "Cracks in the Opposition: Immigration as a Wedge Issue for the Reagan Coalition." *American Journal of Political Science* 55(3): 511–525.

Johnson, Jeh. 2014. "Exercising Prosecutorial Discretion with Respect to Individuals Who Came to the United States as Children and with Respect to Certain Individuals Whose Parents are U.S. Citizens or Permanent Residents." Department of Homeland Security. https://www.aila.org/infonet/dhs-exercising-prosecutorial-discretion. Accessed April 1, 2022.

Jones, Charles O. 1994. *The Presidency in a Separated System*. Washington, DC: Brookings Institution Press.

Jones, Ernest, 1908. "Rationalisation in Every-Day Life." *The Journal of Abnormal Psychology* 3(3): 161–169.

J.W. Hampton, Jr. & Co. v. U.S., 276 U.S. 394 (1928).

Kagan, Elena. 2001. "Presidential Administration." *Harvard Law Review* 114(8): 2245–2385.

Kahneman, Daniel. 1994. "New Challenges to the Rationality Assumption." *Journal of Institutional and Theoretical Economics* 150(1): 18–36.

Kahneman, Daniel and Richard H. Thaler. 2006. "Utility Maximization and Experienced Utility." *Journal of Economic Perspectives* 20(1): 221–234.

Kamlet, Mark S. and David C. Mowery. 1983. "Budgetary Side Payments and Government Growth." *American Journal of Political Science* 27(4): 636–664.

Kane, Paul. 2014. "Boehner to Sue Obama over Executive Orders." *Washington Post*. June 25. https://www.washingtonpost.com/news/post-politics/wp/2014/06/25/boehner-to-sue-obama-over-executive-orders/. Accessed October 25, 2020.

Kapur, Sahil. 2020. "Republican Senators in Tough Races Obscure Their Position Pre-existing Conditions." NBC News. September 15. https://www.nbcnews.com/politics/2020-election/republican-senators-tough-races-obscure-their-position-pre-existing-conditions-n1240133. Accessed October 12, 2020.

Keith, Tamara. 2014. "Wielding a Pen and a Phone, Obama Goes It Alone." NPR. January 20. https://www.npr.org/2014/01/20/263766043/wielding-a-pen-and-a-phone-obama-goes-it-alone. Accessed April 1, 2022.

Kelley, Christopher. 2007. "A Matter of Direction: The Reagan Administration, the Signing Statement, and the 1986 Westlaw Decision." *William and Mary Bill of Rights Journal* 16: 283–306.

Kelley, Christopher and Bryan W. Marshall. 2008. "Assessing Presidential Power: Signing Statements and Veto Threats as Coordinated Strategies." *American Politics Research* 37(3): 508–533.

Kelley, Christopher and Bryan W. Marshall. 2010. "Going It Alone: The Politics of Signing Statements from Reagan to Bush II." *Social Science Quarterly* 91(1): 168–187.

Kernell, Samuel. 2005. *Presidential Veto Threats in Statements of Administration Policy*. Washington, DC: CQ Press.

Kernell, Samuel. 2006. *Going Public: New Strategies of Presidential Leadership*. Washington, DC: CQ Press.

Kernell, Samuel and Henry A. Kim. 2006. "Presidential Veto Threat as a Negotiating Instrument with the Bicameral Congress." Presented at the Annual Meeting of the American Political Science Association, Philadelphia, PA.

Kernell, Samuel and Laurie L. Rice. 2005. "Do Veto Threats Move Congress? Congressional Responses to Threats of Legislation in Conference." Presented at the Annual Meeting of the Southern Political Science Association, New Orleans, LA.

Kiewiet, D. Roderick and Mathew D. McCubbins. 1991. *The Logic of Delegation: Congressional Parties and the Appropriations Process*. Chicago: University of Chicago Press.

Kinane, Christina M. 2021. "Control without Confirmation: The Politics of Vacancies in Presidential Appointments." *American Political Science Review* 115(2): 599–614.

King, David C. 1997. *Turf Wars: How Congressional Committees Claim Jurisdiction*. Chicago: University of Chicago Press.

King, Gary, Christopher Lucas, and Richard A. Nielsen. 2017. "The Balance-Sample Size Frontier in Matching Methods for Causal Inference." *American Journal of Political Science* 61(2): 473–489.

King, Gary and Richard Nielsen. 2019. "Why Propensity Scores Should Not Be Used for Matching." *Political Analysis* 27(4): 435–454.

Kingdon, John W. 1984. *Agendas, Alternatives, and Public Policies*. Boston: Little, Brown.

Klein, Ezra. 2021. "100 Days of Big, Bold Partisan Change." *New York Times*. April 29. https://www.nytimes.com/2021/04/29/opinion/biden-schumer-manchin-bipartisanship.html. Accessed May 11, 2021.

Koopmans, Tjalling C. 1962. "On Flexibility of Future Preference." Cowles Foundation Discussion Papers no. 379.

Korematsu v. U.S., 323 U.S. 214 (1944).

Korzi, Michael J. 2011. "'A Legitimate Function': Reconsidering Presidential Signing Statements." *Congress and the Presidency* 38(2): 195–216.

Kousser, Thad. 2014. "How America's 'Devolution Revolution' Reshaped Its Federalism." *Revue française de science politique* 64(2): 265–287.

Krehbiel, Keith. 1991. *Information and Legislative Organization*. Ann Arbor: University of Michigan Press.

Krehbiel, Keith. 1998. *Pivotal Politics: A Theory of U.S. Lawmaking*. Chicago: University of Chicago Press.

Kriner, Douglas L. 2010. *After the Rubicon: Congress, Presidents, and the Politics of Waging War*. Chicago: University of Chicago Press.

Kriner, Douglas L. and Andrew Reeves. 2015a. "Presidential Particularism and Divide-the-Dollar Politics." *American Political Science Review* 109(1): 155–171.

Kriner, Douglas L. and Andrew Reeves. 2015b. "Presidential Particularism in

Disaster Declarations and Military Base Closures." *Presidential Studies Quarterly* 45(4): 679–702.

Kriner, Douglas L. and Eric Schickler. 2016. *Investigating the President: Congressional Checks on Presidential Power*. Princeton, NJ: Princeton University Press.

Kroft, Steve. 2011. "President Obama: The Economy, the Congress, the Future." *60 Minutes*, CBS. December 12. https://www.cbsnews.com/news/president-obama-the-economy-the-congress-the-future/. Accessed December 9, 2020.

Krutz, Glen S. 2000. "Getting Around Gridlock: The Effect of Omnibus Utilization Legislative Productivity." *Legislative Studies Quarterly* 25(4): 533–549.

Krutz, Glen S. and Jeffrey S. Peake. 2009. *Treaty Politics and the Rise of Executive Agreements*. Ann Arbor: University of Michigan Press.

Leahy, Patrick. 2006. "Opening Statement of Sen. Leahy on Presidential Signing Statements." https://fas.org/irp/congress/2006_hr/062706leahy.html. Accessed December 2, 2020.

Lebo, Matthew and Chris Weber. 2015. "An Effective Approach to the Repeated Cross-Sectional Design." *American Journal of Political Science* 59(1): 242–258.

Lee, Frances. 2009. *Beyond Ideology: Politics, Principles and Partisanship in the U.S. Senate*. Chicago: University of Chicago Press.

Lee, Frances. 2016. *Insecure Majorities: Congress and the Perpetual Campaign*. Chicago: University of Chicago Press.

Lee, Malinda. 2008. "Reorienting the Debate on Presidential Signing Statements: The Need for Transparency in the President's Constitutional Objections, Reservations, and Assertions of Power." *UCLA Law Review* 55: 705–744.

Legal Information Institute. 2022. "Illegal Immigration Reform and Immigration Responsibility Act." https://www.law.cornell.edu/wex/illegal_immigration_reform_and_immigration_responsibility_act. Accessed June 7, 2022.

Levinson, Daryl J. and Richard H. Pildes. 2006. "Separation of Parties, Not Powers." *Harvard Law Review* 119(8): 2311–2386.

Lewallen, Jonathan. 2020. *Committees and the Decline of Lawmaking in Congress*. Ann Arbor: University of Michigan Press.

Lewis, David E. 2003. *Presidents and the Politics of Agency Design: Political Insulation in the United States Government Bureaucracy*. Stanford, CA: Stanford University Press.

Lewis-Beck, Michael S. 1990. *Economics and Elections: The Major Western Democracies*. Ann Arbor: University of Michigan Press.

Library of Congress. 2022a. "Executive Order, Proclamation, or Executive Memorandum?" https://guides.loc.gov/executive-orders/order-proclamation-memorandum. Accessed April 1, 2022.

Library of Congress. 2022b. "A Latinx Resource Guide: Civil Rights Cases and Events in the United States." https://guides.loc.gov/latinx-civil-rights/irca. Accessed June 7, 2022.

Light, Paul. 1998. *The President's Agenda: Domestic Policy Choice from Kennedy to Clinton*. Baltimore, MD: Johns Hopkins University Press.

Lin, Elbert. 2017–2018. "States Suing the Federal Government: Protecting Liberty or Playing Politics?" *University of Richmond Law Review* 2018: 633–652.

Lindsay, James M. 1992–1993. "Congress and Foreign Policy: Why the Hill Matters." *Political Science Quarterly* 107(4): 607–628.

Lleras, Juan Sebastián, Yusufcan Masatlioglu, Daisuke Nakajima, and Erkut Y. Ozbay. 2017. "When More Is Less: Limited Consideration." *Journal of Economic Theory* 170: 70–85.

Locke, John. 1689. *Second Treatise of Government.* https://www.gutenberg.org/files /7370/7370-h/7370-h.htm. Accessed September 28, 2022.

Loper Bright Enterprises v. Raimondo, 603 U.S. ___ (2024).

Lowande, Kenneth S. 2014. "*The Contemporary Presidency* after the Orders: Presidential Memoranda and Unilateral Action." *Presidential Studies Quarterly* 44(4): 724–741.

Lowande, Kenneth S. and Thomas Gray. 2017. "Public Perception of the Presidential Toolkit." *Presidential Studies Quarterly* 47(3): 432–447.

Lowande, Kenneth S. and Rachel Augustine Potter. 2021. "Congressional Oversight Revisited: Politics and Procedure in Agency Rulemaking." *Journal of Politics* 83(1): 401–408.

Lowande, Kenneth S. and Jon C. Rogowski. 2021. "Executive Power in Crisis." *American Political Science Review* 115(4): 1406–1423.

MacDonald, Jason A. 2007. "Agency Design and Postlegislative Influence over the Bureaucracy." *Political Research Quarterly* 60(4): 683–695.

MacDonald, Jason A. 2010. "Limitation Riders and Congressional Influence over Bureaucratic Policy Decisions." *American Political Science Review* 104(4): 766–782.

MacDonald, Jason A. and Robert J. McGrath. 2016. "Retrospective Congressional Oversight and the Dynamics of Legislative Influence over the Bureaucracy." *Legislative Studies Quarterly* 41(4): 899–934.

Macias-Rojas, Patrisia. 2018. "Immigration and the War on Crime: Law and Order Politics and the Illegal Immigration Reform and Immigrant Responsibility Act of 1996." *Journal on Migration and Human Security* 6(1): 1–25.

Madison, James, Alexander Hamilton, and John Jay. [1788] 1966. *The Federalist Papers.* Ed. Roy P. Fairfield. Garden City, NY: Anchor Books.

Madonna, Anthony, Ian Ostrander, and Simon Williamson. 2021. "Managers or Unitary Actors? Investigating the Effects of Staff on Legislative Productivity." Working paper, Michigan State University.

Major, Mark. 2016. "Focus on Research: Unilateral Presidential Politics in an Age of Polarized Politics." *Centre Daily.* April 23. https://www.centredaily.com/liv ing/article73563307.html. Accessed April 12, 2021.

Mares, Dennis and Kenneth W. Moffett. 2019. "Climate Change and Crime Revisited: An Exploration of Monthly Temperature Anomalies and UCR Crime Data." *Environment and Behavior* 51(5): 502–529.

Matthews, Donald R. 1960. "U.S. Senators and their World." Chapel Hill: University of North Carolina Press.

Matthews, Steven A. 1989. "Veto Threats: Rhetoric in a Bargaining Game." *Quarterly Journal of Economics* 104(2): 347–369.

Mayer, Kenneth R. 2001. *With the Stroke of a Pen: Executive Orders and Presidential Power*. Princeton, NJ: Princeton University Press.

Mayhew, David R. 1974. *Congress: The Electoral Connection*. New Haven, CT: Yale University Press.

Mayhew, David R. 2005. *Divided We Govern: Party Control, Lawmaking, and Investigations, 1946–2002*. New Haven, CT: Yale University Press.

McCain, John. 2017. "Statement by SASC Chairman John McCain on President Trump Signing into Law Russia, Iran and North Korea Sanctions Bill." https://www.mccain.senate.gov/public/index.cfm/2017/8/statement-by-sasc-chairman-john-mccain-on-president-trump-signing-into-law-russia-iran-north-korea-sanctions-bill. Accessed April 16, 2018.

McCarty, Nolan, Keith T. Poole, and Howard Rosenthal. 2016. *Polarized America: The Dance of Ideology and Unequal Riches*. 2nd ed. Cambridge, MA: MIT Press.

McCubbins, Mathew D., Roger G. Noll, and Barry R. Weingast. 1987. "Administrative Procedures as Instruments of Political Control." *Journal of Law, Economics, & Organization* 3(2): 243–77.

McCubbins, Mathew D., Roger G. Noll, and Barry R. Weingast. 1989. "Structure and Process, Politics and Policy: Administrative Arrangements and the Political Control of Agencies." *Virginia Law Review* 75(2): 431–482.

McCubbins, Mathew D. and Thomas Schwartz. 1984. "Congressional Oversight Overlooked: Police Patrols versus Fire Alarms." *American Journal of Political Science* 28(1): 165–179.

McDonnell Nieto Del Rio, Giulia. 2021. "What Is DACA? And Where Does It Stand Now?" *New York Times*. May 6. https://www.nytimes.com/article/what-is-daca.html. Accessed May 12, 2021.

McGrath, Robert J. 2013. "Congressional Oversight Hearings and Policy Control." *Legislative Studies Quarterly* 38(3): 349–376.

McGrath, Robert J., Jon C. Rogowski, and Josh M. Ryan. 2016. "Veto Override Requirements and Executive Success." Forthcoming, *Political Science Research Methods*. https://doi.org/10.1017/psrm.2015.80

McKelvey, Richard D. 1976. "Intransitivities in Multidimensional Voting Models and Some Implications for Agenda Control." *Journal of Economic Theory* 12: 472–482.

McKelvey, Richard D. 1979. "General Conditions for Global Intransitivities in Formal Voting Models." *Econometrica* 47: 1085–1111.

Merriman, Ben. 2019. *Conservative Innovators: How States Are Challenging Federal Power*. Chicago: University of Chicago Press.

Mershon, Carol and Olga Shvetsova. 2019. *Formal Modeling in Social Science*. Ann Arbor: University of Michigan Press.

Migration Policy Institute. 2022. "Data and Analysis Related to Trump Administration Actions on Immigrant and Refugee Policy." https://www.migrationpoli
cy.org/programs/us-immigration-policy-program/data-and-analysis-related-tr
ump-administration-actions. Accessed June 7, 2022.

Minta, Michael D. 2011. *Oversight: Representing the Interests of Blacks and Latinos in
Congress*. Princeton, NJ: Princeton University Press.

Minta, Michael D. 2021. *No Longer Outsiders: Black and Latino Interest Group Advo-
cacy on Capitol Hill*. Chicago: University of Chicago Press.

Moe, Terry M. 1989. "The Politics of Bureaucratic Structure." In John Chubb and
Paul Peterson, eds., *Can the Government Govern?*, 269–327. Washington, DC:
Brookings Institution Press.

Moe, Terry M. 1993. "Presidents, Institutions, and Theory." In George Edwards
III, John H. Kessel, and Bert Rockman, eds., *Researching the Presidency*, 337–
385. Pittsburgh, PA: University of Pittsburgh Press.

Moe, Terry M. and Scott A. Wilson. 1994. "Presidents and the Politics of Structure." *Law and Contemporary Problems* 57(2): 1–44.

Moe, Terry M. and William G. Howell. 1999. "The Presidential Power of Unilateral Action." *Journal of Law, Economics, & Organization* 15(1): 132–179.

Moe, Terry M. and Scott A. Wilson. 1994. "Presidents and the Politics of Structure." *Law and Contemporary Problems* 57(2): 1–44.

Montoya-Galvez, Camilo. 2022. "Biden Administration Moves to Formalize
DACA and Shield It from Legal Challenges." CBS News. https://www.cbsne
ws.com/news/immigration-daca-biden-federal-regulation-dreamers. Accessed
August 25, 2022.

Moraguez, Ashley. 2020a. "Policy Making in the Shadow of Executive Action."
Presidential Studies Quarterly 50(1): 63–89.

Moraguez, Ashley. 2020b. "Does Bipartisanship Pay? Manipulation of Legislative
Coalitions During the George W. Bush Presidency." *Congress and the Presidency*
47(1): 62–91.

Morello, Carol. 2016. "U.S. Surpasses Syrian Refugee Goal Set by Obama, Expects
More Next Year." *Washington Post*. September 27. https://www.washingtonpost
.com/world/national-security/us-surpasses-syrian-refugee-goal-set-by-obama
-expects-more-next-year/2016/09/27/59cedeb8-84e7-11e6-ac72-a299793814
95_story.html. Accessed June 7, 2022.

Morgan, Ruth. 1970. *The President and Civil Rights*. New York: St. Martin's Press.

Morton, Rebecca B. 1999. *Methods and Models: A Guide to the Empirical Analysis of
Formal Models*. New York: Cambridge University Press.

Mueller, Michael J. and H. Sonmez Atesoglu. 1993. "Defense Spending, Technological Change, and Economic Growth in the United States." *Defence Economics*
4(3): 259–269.

Muller, Marcus and Florian Boller. 2023. "The Tug-of-War over Drone Strike
Oversight: Congress and the Politics of Drone Warfare during the Obama
Presidency." *Congress and the Presidency* 50(1): 1–28.

Napolitano, Janet. 2012. "Exercising Prosecutorial Discretion with Respect to Individuals Who Came to the United States as Children." Department of Homeland Security. https://www.dhs.gov/xlibrary/assets/s1-exercising-prosec utorial-discretion-individuals-who-came-to-us-as-children.pdf. Accessed April 1, 2022.

Nathan, Richard. 1969. *Jobs and Civil Rights: The Role of the Federal Government in Promoting Equal Opportunity in Employment and Training.* Washington, DC: Government Printing Office.

Neustadt, Richard E. 1990. *Presidential Power and the Modern Presidents: The Politics of Leadership from Roosevelt to Reagan.* New York: Free Press.

Nichols, Austin. 2007. "Causal Inference with Observational Data." *Stata Journal* 7(4): 507–541.

Nickell, Stephen. 1981. "Biases in Dynamic Models with Fixed Effects." *Econometrica* 49(6): 1417–1426.

Nincic, Miroslav and Thomas R. Cusack. 1979. "The Political Economy of U.S. Military Spending." *Journal of Peace Research* 16(2): 101–115.

Nixon v. Fitzgerald, 457 U.S. 731 (1982).

Nussbaum, Matthew and Elana Schor. 2017. "Trump Signs Russia Sanctions Bill but Blasts Congress." Politico. https://www.politico.com/story/2017/08/02/tr ump-signs-bipartisan-russia-sanctions-bill-241242. Accessed April 16, 2018.

Obama, Barack. 2009. Memorandum on Signing Statements, March 9, 2009, 74 *Federal Register* 10669–10670. Document number E9–5442

Obama, Barack. 2012. "Remarks by the President on Immigration." June 15. https://obamawhitehouse.archives.gov/the-press-office/2012/06/15/remarks -president-immigration. Accessed April 1, 2022.

Obama, Barack. 2013a. "Statement on Signing the National Defense Authorization Act for Fiscal Year." December 26, 2013. http://www.presidency.ucsb.edu /ws/index.php?pid=104530. Accessed January 10, 2017.

Obama, Barack. 2013b. "President Obama's Four Part Plan for Comprehensive Immigration Reform." January 29, 2013. https://obamawhitehouse.archives .gov/blog/2013/01/29/president-obamas-four-part-plan-comprehensive-immi gration-reform. Accessed June 7, 2022.

Obama, Barack. 2016. "Memorandum on Promoting Smart Gun Technology." January 4. https://www.presidency.ucsb.edu/documents/memorandum-promo ting-smart-gun-technology. Accessed May 11, 2021.

O'Connell, Anne Joseph. 2019. "Acting Leaders: Recent Practices, Consequences, and Reforms." Brookings Institution. https://www.brookings.edu/research/acti ng-leaders/. Accessed April 1, 2022.

Oleszek, Walter. 1995. *Congressional Procedures and the Policy Process.* Washington, DC: CQ Press.

Oleszek, Mark and Walter Oleszek. 2012. "Institutional Challenging Confronting Congress after 9/11: Partisan Polarization and Effective Oversight." In David P. Auerswald and Colton C. Campbell, eds., *Congress and the Politics of National Security*, 45–67. New York: Cambridge University Press.

Oosterbeek, Hessel, Mirjam van Praag, and Auke Ijsselstein. 2010. "The Impact of Entrepreneurship Education Entrepreneurship Skills and Motivation." *European Economic Review* 54(3): 442–454.

Ostrander, Ian. 2015. "The Contemporary Presidency: Powering Down the Presidency: The Rise and Fall of Recess Appointments." *Presidential Studies Quarterly* 45(3): 558–572.

Ostrander, Ian and Joel Sievert. 2013a. "The Logic of Presidential Signing Statements." *Political Research Quarterly* 66(1): 141–153.

Ostrander, Ian and Joel Sievert. 2013b. "What's So Sinister about Presidential Signing Statements?" *Presidential Studies Quarterly* 43(1): 58–80.

Ouyang, Yu and Richard W. Waterman. 2015. "How Legislative (In)Activity, Ideological Divergence and Divided Government Impact Executive Unilateralism: A Test of Three Theories." *Congress and the Presidency* 42(3): 317–341.

Owens, John E. 2009. "Congressional Acquiescence to Presidentialism in the US 'War on Terror.'" *Journal of Legislative Studies* 15(2–3): 147–190.

Patty, John W. and Elizabeth Maggie Penn. 2014. *Social Choice and Legitimacy: The Possibilities of Impossibility.* New York: Cambridge University Press.

Pelosi, Nancy. 2017. "Pelosi Statement after President Trump Signing Veto-Proof Russia Sanctions Law." https://pelosi.house.gov/news/press-releases/pelosi-statement-after-president-trump-signs-veto-proof-russia-sanctions-law . Accessed August 13, 2024.

Peterson, Mark A. 1990. *Legislating Together: The White House and Capitol Hill from Eisenhower to Reagan.* Cambridge, MA: Harvard University Press.

Pfiffner, James P. 2009. "Presidential Signing Statements and Their Implications for Public Administration." *Public Administration Review* 69(2): 249–255.

Pious, Richard M. 1979. *The American Presidency.* New York: Basic Books.

Pious, Richard M. 2009. "Prerogative Power and Presidential Politics." In George C. Edwards and William G. Howell, eds., *The American Presidency* 455–476. Oxford: Oxford University Press.

Ponder, Daniel E. 2017. *Presidential Leverage: Presidents, Approval, and the American State.* Stanford, CA: Stanford University Press.

Potter, Rachel Augustine. 2017. "Slow-Rolling, Fast-Tracking, and the Pace of Bureaucratic Decisions in Rulemaking." *Journal of Politics* 79(3): 841–855.

Potter, Rachel Augustine. 2019. *Bending the Rules: Procedural Politicking in the Bureaucracy.* Chicago: University of Chicago Press.

Potter, Rachel Augustine, Andrew Rudalevige, Sharice Thrower, and Adam L. Warber. 2019. "Continuity Trumps Change: The First Year of Trump's Administrative Presidency." *PS: Political Science and Politics* 52(4): 613–619.

Potter, Rachel Augustine, Andrew Rudalevige, Sharice Thrower, and Adam L. Warber. 2022. "Not by the Numbers: Evaluating Trump's Administrative Presidency." *Presidential Studies Quarterly* 52(3): 596–625.

Potter, Rachel Augustine and Charles R. Shipan. 2019. "Agency Rulemaking in a Separation of Powers System." *Journal of Public Policy* 39(1): 89–113.

The Prize Cases, 67 U.S. 635 (1863).

Rabin, Matthew. 1998. "Psychology and Economics." *Journal of Economic Literature* 36(1): 11–46.

Rabin, Matthew. 2013. "An Approach to Incorporating Psychology into Economics." *American Economic Review: Papers & Proceedings* 103(3): 617–622.

Rao, Neomi. 2015. "Administrative Collusion: How Delegation Diminishes the Collective Congress." *New York University Law Review* 90(5): 1463–1526.

Redekop, Benjamin W. 2012. "The Environmental Leadership of Theodore Roosevelt." In Deobrah Rigling Gallagher, ed., *Environmental Leadership: A Reference Handbook*, 95–104. Thousand Oaks, CA: Sage Publications.

Reeves, Andrew. 2011. "Political Disaster: Unilateral Powers, Electoral Incentives, and Presidential Disaster Declarations." *Journal of Politics* 73(4): 1142–1151.

Reeves, Andrew and Jon C. Rogowski. 2015. "Public Opinion toward Presidential Power." *Presidential Studies Quarterly* 45(4): 742–759.

Reeves, Andrew and Jon C. Rogowski. 2016. "Unilateral Powers, Public Opinion, and the Presidency." *Journal of Politics* 78(1): 137–151.

Reeves, Andrew, and Jon C. Rogowski. 2018. "The Public Cost of Unilateral Action." *American Journal of Political Science* 62(2): 424–440.

Reeves, Andrew, and Jon C. Rogowski. 2022. *No Blank Check: The Origins and Consequences of Public Antipathy towards Presidential Power*. New York: Cambridge University Press.

Reeves, Andrew, Jon C. Rogowski, Min Hee Seo, and Andrew R. Stone. 2016. "By All Means: How Issue Popularity Emboldens Presidential Power." Working paper, Washington University in St. Louis and Harvard University.

Reich, Gary. 2018. "Hitting a Wall? The Trump Administration Meets Immigration Federalism." *Publius: The Journal of Federalism* 48(3): 372–395.

Rice, Laurie L. 2010. "Statements of Power: Presidential Use of Statements of Administration Policy and Signing Statements in the Legislative Process." *Presidential Studies Quarterly* 40(4): 693–711.

Riker, William H. 1980. "Implications from the Disequilibrium of Majority Rule for the Study of Institutions." *American Political Science Review* 74(2): 432–446.

Riker, William H. 1982. *Liberalism against Populism: A Confrontation between the Theory of Democracy and the Theory of Social Choice*. San Francisco, CA: W.H. Freeman.

Ritchie, Melinda N. 2023. *Backdoor Lawmaking: Evading Obstacles in the US Congress*. New York: Oxford University Press.

Rohde, David. 1991. *Parties and Leaders in the Postreform House*. Chicago: University of Chicago Press.

Romero, Dennis 2020. "Federal Judge Rules Acting DHS Head Chad Wolf Unlawfully Appointed, Invalidates DACA Suspension." NBC News. November 14. https://www.nbcnews.com/politics/immigration/federal-judge-rules-acting-dhs-head-chad-wolf-unlawfully-appointed-n1247848. Accessed December 2, 2020.

Roosevelt, Theodore. 1913. *The Rough Riders: An Autobiography*. New York: Macmillan.

Rothenberg, Stuart. 2021. "Politicians Rarely Regret Voting 'No.'" *Roll Call*. March 16.

Rubio, Marco. 2014. Letter about Immigration to President Obama. https://www.rubio.senate.gov/public/_cache/files/d76fde58-6703-4e70-a5cc-e934679fab2d/EACF5AD1D3B9E432882479BC1FD675F8.lettertopresidentobamafromsenrubioconcerningimmigration.pdf. Accessed April 1, 2022.

Rudalevige, Andrew. 2005. *The New Imperial Presidency: Renewing Presidential Power after Watergate*. Ann Arbor: University of Michigan Press.

Rudalevige, Andrew. 2012. "Executive Orders and Presidential Unilateralism." *Presidential Studies Quarterly* 42(1): 138–160.

Rudalevige, Andrew. 2021. *By Executive Order: Bureaucratic Management and the Limits of Executive Power*. Princeton, NJ: Princeton University Press.

Rutledge, Paul E. and Heather A. Larsen Price. 2014. "The President as Agenda Setter-in-Chief: The Dynamics of Congressional and Presidential Agenda Setting." *Policy Studies Journal* 42(3): 443–464.

Samuelson, William and Richard Zeckhauser. 1988. "Status Quo Bias in Decision Making." *Journal of Risk and Uncertainty* 1: 7–59.

Savage, Charlie. 2006a. "Bush Could Bypass New Torture Ban." *Boston Globe*. January 4, A1.

Savage, Charlie. 2006b. "Bush Challenges Hundreds of Laws: President Cites Powers of His Office." *Boston Globe*. April 30, A1.

Savage, David. 2006c. "Memo Draws Alito into Presidential Powers Debate." *Chicago Tribune*. January 8. https://www.chicagotribune.com/news/ct-xpm-2006-01-08-0601080204-story.html. Accessed June 3, 2021.

Schickler, Eric. 2001. *Disjointed Pluralism: Institutional Innovation and the Development of the U.S. Congress*. Princeton, NJ: Princeton University Press.

Schlesinger, Arthur V., Jr. 1973. *The Imperial Presidency*. New York: Houghton Mifflin.

Schofield, Norman. 1978. "Instability of Simple Dynamic Games." *Review of Economic Studies* 45: 575–594.

Schorpp, Susanne and Charles J. Finocchiaro. 2017. "Congress and the President in Times of War." *American Politics Research* 45(5): 840–865.

Schraufnagel, Scot and Steven M. Shellman. 2001. "The Two Presidencies, 1984–1998: A Replication and Extension." *Presidential Studies Quarterly* 31(4): 699–707.

Schumer, Charles. 2017. "Schumer Statement on President Trump Signing Russia Sanctions Bill." https://www.facebook.com/senschumer/posts/10155697350154407. Accessed April 16, 2018.

Sekhon, Jasjeet J. 2011. "Multivariate and Propensity Score Matching Software with Automated Balance Optimization: The Matching Package for R." *Journal of Statistical Software* 42(7): 1–52.

Sen, A. K. 1970. *Collective Choice and Social Welfare*. San Francisco, CA: Holden-Day.

Sen, A. K. 1973. *On Economic Inequality*. Oxford: Clarendon Press.

Sen, A. K. 2004. "Incompleteness and Reasoned Choice." *Synthese* 140: 43–59.

Sessions, Jefferson. 2017. "Letter to Acting Secretary Duke." Office of the Attorney General. https://www.dhs.gov/sites/default/files/publications/17_0904_DOJ_AG-letter-DACA.pdf. Accessed April 1, 2022.

Shepsle, Kenneth A. 1979. "Institutional Arrangements and Equilibrium in Multidimensional Voting Models." *American Journal of Political Science* 23: 27–59.

Shepsle, Kenneth A. 1986. "Institutional Equilibrium and Equilibrium Institutions." In *Political Science: The Science of Politics*, ed. Herbert F. Weisberg, 51–81. New York: Agathon.

Shepsle, Kenneth A. 2010. *Analyzing Politics: Rationality, Behavior, and Institutions*. New York: W.W. Norton.

Shepsle, Kenneth A. and Barry R. Weingast. 1981. "Structure-Induced Equilibrium and Legislative Choice." *Public Choice* 37: 503–519.

Sievert, Joel and Ian Ostrander. 2017. "Constraining Presidential Ambition: Controversy and the Decline of Signing Statements." *Presidential Studies Quarterly* 47(4): 752–776.

Sinclair, Barbara. 2016. *Unorthodox Lawmaking: New Legislative Processes in the U.S. Congress*. Thousand Oaks, CA: CQ Press.

Sinclair, Harriet. 2019. "Who Is Chad Wolf? Donald Trump Names New Acting Secretary of Homeland Security." *Newsweek*. https://www.newsweek.com/donald-trump-acting-secretary-homeland-security-chad-wolf-kevin-mcaleenan-1469358. Accessed April 1, 2022.

Skidmore v Swift & Co., 323 U.S. 134 (1944).Skowronek, Stephen. 1997. *The Politics Presidents Make: Leadership from John Adams to Bill Clinton*. 2nd ed. Cambridge, MA: Harvard University Press.

Skowronek, Stephen. 1997. *The Politics Presidents Make: Leadership from John Adams to Bill Clinton*. Cambridge, MA: Harvard University Press.

Smith, Donna. 2007. "Senate Kills Bush Immigration Reform Bill." *Reuters*. https://www.reuters.com/article/us-usa-immigration/senate-kills-bush-immigration-reform-bill-idUSN2742643820070629. Accessed June 7, 2022.

Smith, Keith. 2003. "The Growth of Congressional Oversight." Presented at the Annual Meeting of the American Political Science Association, Philadelphia, PA.

Smith, Laura Ellyn. 2021. "Trump and Congress." *Policy Studies* 42(5–6): 528–543.

Smith, Steven and Christopher J. Deering. 1997. *Committees in Congress*. Washington, DC: CQ Press.

Sollenberger, Mitchel A. and Mark J. Rozell. 2012. *The President's Czars: Undermining Congress and the Constitution*. Lawrence: University Press of Kansas.

Stanley-Becker, Isaac. 2023. "Jeffrey Clark Is GOP Star after Trying to Use DOJ to Overturn Election." https://www.washingtonpost.com/national-security/2023/08/03/jeffrey-clark-trump-coconspirator-doj-indictment/. Accessed August 4, 2023.

Stanton, John. 2007. "Specter Pushes Bill to Rein in Presidential Signing Statements." https://www.rollcall.com/2007/07/03/specter-pushes-bill-to-rein-in-presidential-signing-statements/. Accessed September 30, 2020.

Stein, Jeff. 2024. "As GOP Rivals Collapse, Wall Street Warms to Second Trump Term." https://www.washingtonpost.com/business/2024/01/24/trump-wall-street-donors/. Accessed January 24, 2024.

Stuart, Elizabeth A. 2010. "Matching Methods for Causal Inference: A Review and a Look Forward." *Statistical Science* 25(1): 1–21.

Sulkin, Tracy. 2005. *Issue Politics in Congress*. Cambridge: Cambridge University Press.

Swers, Michele L. 2002. *The Difference Women Make: The Policy Impact of Women in Congress*. Chicago: University of Chicago Press.

Swers, Michele L. 2013. *Women in the Club: Gender and Policy Making in the Senate*. Chicago: University of Chicago Press.

Taft, William Howard. 1916. *Our Chief Magistrate and his Powers*. New York: Columbia University Press.

Texas v. United States, 328 F. Supp. 3d 662 (2018).

Thiessen, Marc A. 2020. "Trump's Unilateral Actions Were a Brilliant Political Move. And He's Just Getting Started." *Washington Post*. August 11. https://www.washingtonpost.com/opinions/2020/08/11/obstinate-democrats-handed-trump-big-political-win-coronavirus-relief/. Accessed April 12, 2021.

Thrower, Sharece. 2013. "Presidential Power and Judicial Constraint." PhD dissertation. Department of Politics, Princeton University.

Thrower, Sharece. 2019. "Presidential Action and the Supreme Court: The Case of Signing Statements." *Journal of Theoretical Politics* 31(4): 677–698.

Tichenor, Daniel J. 2013. "Historical Set Points and the Development of US Presidential Emergency Power." *Perspectives* 11(3): 769–788.

Trump, Donald J. 2015. "Donald Trump's Presidential Announcement Speech." C-Span. https://www.youtube.com/watch?v=apjNfkysjbM. Accessed April 1, 2022.

Trump, Donald J. 2016. "Remarks on the Affordable Care Act." November 1. CBS News. https://www.youtube.com/watch?v=0kuLxPEhz_g. Accessed July 20, 2022.

Trump, Donald J. 2017a. "Statement by President Donald J. Trump on Signing the Countering America's Adversaries Through Sanctions Act." https://www.presidency.ucsb.edu/documents/statement-signing-the-countering-americas-adversaries-through-sanctions-act. Accessed October 7, 2020.

Trump, Donald J. 2017b. "Statement by President Donald J. Trump on Signing the 'Countering America's Adversaries Through Sanctions Act.'" https://www.presidency.ucsb.edu/documents/statement-signing-the-countering-americas-adversaries-through-sanctions-act-0. Accessed August 13, 2024.

Trump, Donald J. 2017c. "Statement by President Donald J. Trump on Signing H.R. 244 into Law." https://www.presidency.ucsb.edu/documents/statement-signing-the-consolidated-appropriations-act-2017/. Accessed August 13, 2024.

Trump, Donald J. 2020a. "Proclamation Suspension of Entry as Immigrants and Nonimmigrants of Persons Who Pose a Risk of Transmitting 2019 Novel Coronavirus." https://www.presidency.ucsb.edu/documents/proclamation-99

84-suspension-entry-immigrants-and-nonimmigrants-persons-who-pose-risk. Accessed August 13, 2024.

Trump, Donald J. 2020b. Signing Statement on the CARES Act. https://www.pres idency.ucsb.edu/documents/statement-signing-the-coronavirus-aid-relief-and -economic-security-act. Accessed August 13, 2024.

Trump v United States. (Docket 23-939) Oral arguments, April 25, 2024.

Touby v. U.S., 500 U.S. 160 (1991).

Trump v. U.S., 603 U.S. ___(2024).

Tsebelis, George. 2002. *Veto Players: How Institutions Work.* Princeton, NJ: Princeton University Press.

Tsebelis, George and Jeannette Money. 1997. *Bicameralism.* Cambridge: Cambridge University Press.

Turner, Ian R. 2020. "Policy Durability, Agency Capacity, and Executive Unilateralism." *Presidential Studies Quarterly* 50(1): 40–62.

Tversky, Amos and Eldar Shafir. 1992. "Choice under Conflict: The Dynamics of Deferred Decision." *Psychological Science* 3: 358–361.

US Congress. House of Representatives. Committee on Armed Services. Oversight and Investigations Subcommittee. 2008. "The Impact of the Presidential Signing Statement on the Department of Defense's Implementation of the Fiscal Year 2008 National Defense Authorization Act." https://www.congress.gov /110/chrg/CHRG-110hhrg42902/CHRG-110hhrg42902.pdf. Accessed July 12, 2023.

US Congress. House of Representatives. Office of the Clerk. 2009. "Historical Information about the United States House of Representatives." http://clerk .house.gov. Accessed various dates.

US Congress. Senate. 2006a. Hearings on Signing Statements. http://www.judicia ry.senate.gov. Accessed December 5, 2013.

US Congress. Senate. 2006b. Judiciary Committee. *Signing Statements.* 109th Cong. 2nd sess., June 26.

US Congress. Senate. 2016. Appropriations Subcommittee on Commerce, Justice, Science, and Related Agencies. Hearings on President Obama's Executive Actions on Gun Control. https://www.c-span.org/video/?403241-1/hearing-pr esident-obamas-executive-actions-gun-control. Accessed May 11, 2021.

Vande Kamp, Garrett. 2022. "Severability Doctrine and the Exercise of Judicial Review." *Political Research Quarterly* 76(2): 593–606.

Vaughn, Justin S. and Jose D. Villalobos. 2015. *Czars in the White House: The Rise of Policy Czars as Presidential Management Tools.* Ann Arbor: University of Michigan Press.

Vidal, et al., v. Wolf, et al., 16-CV-475617 (2020).

Waterman, Richard W. 2009a. "The Administrative Presidency, Unilateral Power, and the Unitary Executive Theory." *Presidential Studies Quarterly* 39(1): 5–9.

Waterman, Richard W. 2009b. "Assessing the Unilateral Presidency." In George C. Edwards and William G. Howell, eds., *The American Presidency*, 477-498. Oxford: Oxford University Press.

Weaver, R. Kent. 1986. "The Politics of Blame Avoidance." *Journal of Public Policy* 6(4): 371–398.

West Virginia v. Environmental Protection Agency, 597 U.S. 697 (2022).

White House. 2016. "Fact Sheet: New Executive Actions to Reduce Gun Violence and Make Our Communities Safer." January 4. https://obamawhitehouse.arch ives.gov/the-press-office/2016/01/04/fact-sheet-new-executive-actions-reduce -gun-violence-and-make-our. Accessed May 11, 2021.

Whittington, Dale and W. Norton Grubb. 1984. "Economic Analysis in Regulatory Decisions: The Implications of Executive Order 12291." *Science, Technology and Human Values* 9(1): 63–71.

Whittington, Keith E. 2009. "Constitutional Constraints in Politics." In Steven Kautz, Arthur Melzer, Jerry Weinberger, and M. Richard Zinman, eds., *The Supreme Court and the Idea of Constitutionalism*, 221–227. Philadelphia: University of Pennsylvania Press.

Wildavsky, Aaron. 1966. "The Two Presidencies." *Trans-Action* 4(December): 7–14.

Wilentz, Sean. 2007. *Andrew Jackson: The American Presidents Series: The 7th President, 1829–1837*. New York: Times Books.

Wolf, Chad F. 2020. "Reconsideration of the June 15, 2012 Memorandum Entitled 'Exercising Prosecutorial Discretion with Respect to Individuals Who Came to the United States as Children.'" Department of Homeland Security. https://www.dhs.gov/sites/default/files/publications/20_0728_s1_daca-reconsiderati on-memo.pdf. Accessed April 1, 2022.

Wooldridge, Jeffery M. 2016. *Introductory Econometrics: A Modern Approach*. 5th ed. New York: Cengage Learning.

Youngstown Sheet & Tube Co. v. Sawyer, 343 U.S. 579 (1952).

Index